OFF THE BEATEN PATH®
KANSAS →

Praise for previous editions

"[This book] uses detailed maps, lists the top ten attractions in each region, gives an extensive list of more conventional places to stay and eat (along with the more colorful, highlighted ones in the text), and points out spots worth a visit. The fresh look, level of detail, and helpful organization make the guide a must for any Kansas traveler."
—*The Wichita Eagle*

"This little handbook offers a varied menu of historic sites . . . and natural attractions for the visitor to Kansas. . . . The book is an intriguing guide to many of the state's unique points of interest. . . . For those who choose to stop and smell some roses, this little gem should serve them well."
—Western Library

"Whether your trip into Kansas is for a weekend or a week, it is sure to be more enjoyable with this guidebook along. Covering a range of sights, the volume always includes a touch of the flavor and history of each region."
—*St. Joseph* (Mo.) *News-Press*

Help Us Keep This Guide Up to Date

We would love to hear from you concerning your experiences with this guide and how you feel it could be improved and kept up to date. Please send your comments and suggestions to:

editorial@GlobePequot.com

Thanks for your input, and happy travels!

OFF THE BEATEN PATH® SERIES

NINTH EDITION

OFF THE BEATEN PATH®
KANSAS

A GUIDE TO UNIQUE PLACES

PATTI DELANO

Revised and Updated by Sarah Smarsh

gpp®
travel

Guilford, Connecticut

All the information in this guidebook is subject to change. We recommend that you call ahead to obtain current information before traveling.

To buy books in quantity for corporate use or incentives, call **(800) 962-0973** or e-mail **premiums@GlobePequot.com.**

Editor: Amy Lyons
Project Editor: Heather M. Santiago
Layout: Joanna Beyer
Text Design: Linda R. Loiewski
Maps: Equator Graphics © Morris Book Publishing LLC

Library of Conress Cataloging-in-Publication Data is available on file.

ISBN 978-0-7627-5043-6

Printed in the United States of America
10 9 8 7 6 5 4 3 2 1

About the Authors

Heartland native **Patti DeLano** has been traveling the globe since she was twenty. A flight attendant for Trans World Airlines for ten years, she gave up flying to raise a family. She and her late husband, Bob, a pilot for TWA, traveled extensively and, after his retirement, took to the roads in a motor home to see the small towns of America.

Now she is spending time on the Gulf of Mexico—off the coast of Venice, Florida—on sailing vessel *Serafina de Mare* (*Angel of the Sea*), a 38-foot Islander Freeport, as she and her new husband, Tom, sail in search of off-the-beaten-path places along the coast of Florida and in the islands of the Caribbean.

Kansas native **Sarah Smarsh** is an assistant professor of English at Washburn University in Topeka, where she teaches creative nonfiction writing. Smarsh, who holds an MFA in nonfiction writing from Columbia University, has written for *The Huffington Post* and Village Voice Media.

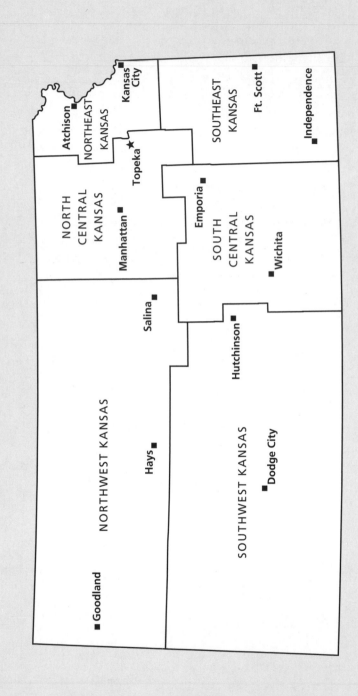

Goodland ■

NORTHWEST KANSAS

Hays ■

■ Dodge City

SOUTHWEST KANSAS

Salina ■

Hutchinson ■

Manhattan ■

NORTH
CENTRAL
KANSAS

Wichita ■

SOUTH
CENTRAL
KANSAS

Emporia ■

Topeka ★

Atchison

NORTHEAST
KANSAS

Kansas
City ■

SOUTHEAST
KANSAS

Ft. Scott ■

Independence ■

Contents

Introduction

The Kansas landscape may prove a surprise if you were weaned on *The Wizard of Oz*. The real Heartland in Kansas, the state Dorothy and Toto couldn't wait to come home to, has tall limestone monoliths, red buttes that mimic the Southwest, and flint outcroppings forming long, bony escarpments. There are rich, mixed forests, rolling hills, fast-flowing rivers, and bottomless springs.

Once, prairie grasses blew like the ocean in billowing waves, with few natural landmarks; courses were set by the sun and stars. One woman, forced to move to Colorado, complained bitterly that her view of the sky was blocked by the Rocky Mountains. William Inge, Kansas playwright, echoed her sentiments when he said that in other places the "heavens are trimmed down like a painting to fit a smaller frame." Here, "as far as the eye can see" is a long way; you sense the meaning of infinity.

The endless skies can be an innocent blue, and then, like an unruly child, they can send havoc to a peaceful scene. Blizzards, tornadoes, hail, and relentlessly burning sun ride in on the Kansas winds, destroying crops as quickly as an Old Testament curse.

But when it's right, it's right. Solid gold sunsets reflected in the summer wheat fields melt into the horizon. Acres of sunflowers and the sweet smell of prairie grass after a spring rain delight each of the senses. The ever-changing prairie is covered with the colors of its wildflowers: the sunflower, of course, and the buttercup, primrose, wild daisy, gayfeather, and wild onion—each a different color and each lasting only a few days.

Wheat fields stretch mile after golden mile across the state. There are no crowds here. It takes the combined population of all seven Plains states to equal the population of New York City.

The waves of prairie grasses reflect the prehistoric inland sea that once covered the state; the bedrock is salted with fossils of sharks and oysters with 3-foot shells. Kansas is a great place to hunt fossils, arrowheads, and—because of the openness of the terrain—meteorites. The largest Pleistocene meteorite ever found is here.

This is a state known for its sunshine; western Kansas has been known to have as many as 300 clear days in a year. The mountains in nearby Colorado block the rain, making this part of the state sunny and dry. Temperatures may be warm (or even hot), but a low relative humidity in the western part of the state makes summer days more comfortable than you would expect and the nights cool and pleasant.

Gentle sun, pleasant warm days, and cool nights make the spring and fall weather almost perfect. The many bed-and-breakfast inns get you out of the motel rut and onto working farms (some of them in Amish communities) or into elegant Victorian homes across the state, where a country breakfast means fresh eggs from the barn and bread made with wheat ground from the field next door. Kansas is the breadbasket of the world. Sheltered by the mountains, the Heartland beats a slow, steady rhythm year after year.

Interstate 70 is more than a fast way to Colorado. It is a path rich with history. From 1830 to 1854 the region was Indian Territory. It was inhabited by Native Americans displaced from other parts of North America; by indigenous tribes, among them the village builders—the Pawnee, Osage, Kansa, and Wichita; and by nomadic hunters—the Cheyenne, Comanche, and Arapaho.

Then, the Kansas-Nebraska Act gave the people of the territory the right to choose whether slavery would be permitted in the future state of Kansas. Many people came to try to influence the decision, among them abolitionist John Brown and the infamous Southern sympathizer William Quantrill and his band of marauders.

The 1870s brought settlers. Both the Oregon Trail and the Santa Fe Trail cut through this state. The Santa Fe Trail was called "The Big Lonely," and Kansas was the jumping-off place. It was where the railroads broke ground heading west and cattle drives from Texas ended. The Wild West was wildest in Cimarron and Dodge City, where you can relive the legend on Front Street, filled with the ghosts of buffalo hunters, railroad workers, cowboys, and drifters, the "baddest" of the bad guys laid to uneasy rest at Boot Hill Cemetery. Wild Bill Hickok, Bat Masterson, and Buffalo Bill Cody called Kansas home.

Temperance leader Carry Nation swung her bar-busting hatchet here, too. But then, the women of Kansas have always been ahead of their time. The first female mayor in the country—in the world, they say—was elected here. The first woman to be elected to the Senate, the first black woman to be admitted to the American Bar Association, the first female dentist in the world, and Amelia Earhart, that brave lady of the skies, were from the state of Kansas.

When Joan Finney served as governor (1991–1995), Kansas became the first state in U.S. history to have a female governor, a female senator (Nancy Landon Kassebaum), and a female congressperson (Jan Meyers) all at once. Dorothy would be proud to come home to today's Kansas.

There are canoe trails and hiking trails, bike trips and trail rides, and even a covered-wagon jaunt for real history buffs tough enough to measure themselves against our forebears as they journeyed west to claim the land.

What can we say about Kansas? Plenty. Spend some time here, and you will understand why Dorothy and Toto wanted to leave the Land of Oz and return to the state that is called the Heartland.

Welcome to Kansas!

NORTHEAST KANSAS →

Sure, Kansas has the reputation of being flat, but Northeast Kansas's Smoky Hills, where the Kansas and Missouri Rivers meet, are anything but. From the bustle of Kansas City to the quiet of farmlands, these rolling hills offer a variety of lifestyles.

Some of the suburban communities of Kansas City are stylish and sophisticated; others are small-town friendly. The city of Overland Park, for example, is a shopper's paradise, with unusual shops offering designer clothes and upscale merchandise.

But as you leave Kansas City and head west into Kansas, you will experience the dramatic change from big-city life to the quiltwork of fields and fences of the Kansas countryside. This is the most agriculturally productive section of the state, the soils thick and fertile.

Greater rainfall in the eastern part of the state makes it favorable for a wider variety of crops than can be grown in the west. Northeast Kansas is an ideal location for growing fruit. In a good year, orchard-graced Doniphan County can produce more than four million pounds of apples.

Northeast Kansas is also home to several Native American tribes: The Sac, Fox, Kickapoo, and Potawatomi have

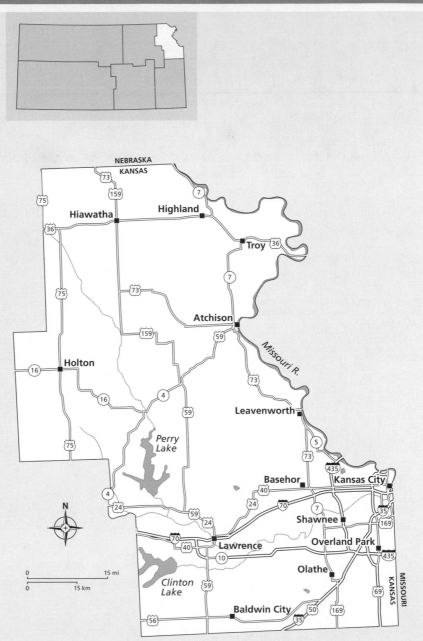

reservations in this area. From 1830 to 1854 the region was designated as Indian Territory. The Native Americans who inhabited the area were displaced from other parts of the country as relentless waves of settlers moved west. Kansas began to attract white settlers in the 1870s. Many of them were Mennonites from Russia, who brought the seeds of Turkey Red wheat. The seeds took well to the prairie soil, turning a wild and unsettled land into America's breadbasket.

The river heritage here is strong. The Kansas (called the Kaw) and Missouri Rivers join here to rush together to the Mississippi. Meriwether Lewis and William Clark camped on the Kansas side of the Missouri River several times in June and July of 1804 while exploring the Louisiana Purchase.

This region was crossed by settlers on the California, Oregon, and Santa Fe Trails. Businessmen and railroad tycoons made fortunes here in those early days and left grand homes to mark their journey through life in Kansas.

Kansas City Metro Area

Kansas City suffers from a split identity. Most of the metropolitan area is actually in Missouri, although a lot of people across the country think otherwise. Kansas City, Kansas, is a good-size city in its own right, with its own downtown and the **Kansas Speedway,** west of Kansas City near the junction of Interstates 70 and 435. Fans can watch NASCAR racing at the 1.5-mile trioval track as well as Indy cars. For information, check the Web site at www .kansasspeedway.com. For tickets, call (866) 460-RACE toll free.

If the scent of cinnamon rolls, brownies, apple and cherry strudel, and cookies of all kinds calls you, look for **MeMa's Old-Fashioned Bakery** at

AUTHOR'S FAVORITES

Davis Memorial
Hiawatha

Deanna Rose Children's Farmstead
Overland Park

Downtown Lawrence

Frontier Army Museum
Fort Leavenworth

Gates Bar-B-Q
Kansas City

Jalisco Restaurant
Kansas City

Perry State Park

Ruchi Indian Cuisine
Overland Park

Sylas and Maddy's Homemade Ice Cream
Olathe and Lawrence

1829 Village West Parkway, Suite T131. MeMa's has—of course—povitica bread, too. If you have never tasted this Croatian delicacy, be sure to try it. Call (913) 299-9121 or (866) GET-MEMA.

kawriver

The Kansas River is known as the Kaw River around here. The tribe the state was named for, the Kansa, is known as the Kaw Native American Tribe.

The city is actually a consolidation of eight towns, so the streets are not in a grid pattern. There are many main streets and residential neighborhoods as well as several ethnic communities worth a visit, such as the Strawberry Hill neighborhood, a Slavic settlement. You can learn the history of these people at the **Strawberry Hill Museum** (913-371-3264) at 720 North Fourth St. A completely restored, high-Victorian–style home built in 1872, the museum houses ever-changing exhibits of Croatian artifacts from the peoples of Eastern Europe. The gift shop offers a variety of unique ethnic items. It is open on Sat and Sun from noon to 5 p.m. Admission is $7 for adults, $3 for children ages six to twelve, and free for those under six.

Another part of the city's melting pot is the Argentine District, a Mexican-American neighborhood. You can't miss the Anthology of Argentina mural, painted on a wall more than 200 yards long, at Thirty-first Street and Metropolitan Avenue. Nearby, you'll find the **Jalisco Restaurant,** which serves soft, handmade tortillas, homemade tamales, real Mexican chili with pieces of tender pork (no hamburger in this stuff), chicken mole, Mexican beer, and sopapillas for dessert. The 1411 South Twenty-sixth St. location is tricky to find, but worth the effort. The 5000 State Avenue site (913-287-9268) is more on the beaten path (and more crowded). The tortillas are made at the State Avenue restaurant. You can watch them being made one day a week. Call (913) 831-9001 for more information. Jalisco restaurants are open seven days a week.

what'sinaname?

The term *Huron* is not really the name of a Native American tribe but a somewhat derisive nickname bestowed by the French. The Wyandot people wore a traditional headdress that reminded the French of the bristly hairs on the back of a wild boar, or a *huron* in French.

Hours at the State Avenue site are from 11 a.m. to 9 p.m. Sun through Thurs and until. 10 p.m. on Fri and Sat. Hours at the Twenty-sixth Street location are from 11 a.m. to 9 p.m. Mon through Thurs, until 10 p.m. Fri and Sat, and 1 to 4 p.m. on Sun.

Because this region was Indian Territory for years, there are several places to do research on Native American genealogies. The **Huron Indian Cemetery** was established by the Wyandot

Indians in 1843, after they were moved west from Sandusky, Ohio. The burial ground is in downtown Kansas City at Ann and Seventh Streets. Call (913) 321-5800.

The historic **White Church** (913-299-4056), at 2200 North Eighty-fifth St., is the oldest established church in the state and includes an exhibit of Native American relics. A Delaware Indian cemetery is on the grounds. It is open weekdays from 7:30 a.m. to 2 p.m. Church services are still held here on Sun.

Settlers came and began to push the Native Americans west. The **Grinter Place State Historic Site** (913-299-0373), at 1420 South Seventy-eighth St., was built around 1857 by Moses R. Grinter and his wife, Annie, a member of the Delaware tribe. Their family included ten children. Grinter is credited with being the first permanent white settler in what is now Wyandotte County, and one of the earliest settlers in Kansas.

The house is modeled after a Kentucky farmhouse built in 1800 by Grinter's uncle. Structural timbers are made

trivia

Kansas City, Kansas, is the hometown of Olympic track and field champion Maurice Greene.

of native walnut. The woodwork inside is walnut and white pine hauled from Leavenworth with an ox team. Hours are 9:30 a.m. to 5 p.m., Wed through Sat. Admission is $3 for adults, $1 for students. For more information, check the Web site at www.kshs.org.

Kansas City is famous for its barbecue, and the Kansas side has its share of great places in both the city and the suburbs. **Gates Bar-B-Q** at 1026 State Ave. (913-621-1134) is one of the top choices in Kansas City; Ollie Gates has served some of the finest meat in the area for more than fifty years. Featuring 100 percent hickory-smoked meats to eat there or carry out, the restaurant also serves all the usual trimmings. Another Gates can be found at 103rd and State Line (913-383-1752). Hours are 10 a.m. to midnight Mon through Sat and until 10 p.m. Sun. Visit www.gatesbbq.com.

You and the children will enjoy **Fritz's Union Station Railroad Restaurant** at 250 North Eighteenth St., where food is delivered to each table by model train. Railroad paraphernalia is everywhere—on shelves, for sale behind the counter, and hanging on the walls. Each employee wears a ticking-striped engineer's uniform, complete with cap. Children wear a paper engineer hat. Call (913) 281-2777 for more information. Hours are Mon through Sat 6 a.m. to 8:30 p.m., with train service beginning at 11 a.m.

Chateau Avalon, 701 Village West Parkway in Kansas City, Kansas, is fairy-tale romantic. Sneak your honey off to this retreat and choose the dream you want to play out. The Camelot suite is kingly, to say the least.

It has a bathtub fashioned to resemble Arthur's ship and a round bedroom with a knight in armor and a 180-degree view. If you feel more like Cleopatra than Guinevere, the Egyptian palace is for you. Looking for something more manly? Ask for the Tahitian tree house or the Mayan rain forest, sure to impress her. Is a Venetian palace on your vacation list, or is a New York penthouse more your thing? The sixty-two-room hotel features other fanciful environments. Call (877) 522-8256 for more information. Weekends start around $169 per night.

Leaving metro Kansas City, the drive south along State Line Road will take you to *Fairway.* The *Shawnee Indian Methodist Mission* (913-262-0867), at 3403 West Fifty-third St., Fairway, was established in 1830 by the Reverend Thomas Johnson and became a school for Native American children. The first territorial legislature met in these stately redbrick buildings in 1855. The Oregon and Santa Fe Trails passed through the mission complex, and it served as a camp for Union soldiers during the Civil War. There is a small admission charge for the recently renovated mission. Visit the state historical society's Web page for hours and more information (www.kshs.org, click on Historic Properties) or e-mail shawneemission@kshs.org.

TOP ANNUAL EVENTS

MAY
Riverbend Art Fair and Antique
Airplane Fly-In
Atchison
(800) 234-1854

JUNE
Great Lenexa Barbeque Battle
Lenexa
(913) 888-1414

JULY
Amelia Earhart Festival
Atchison
(800) 234-1854

AUGUST
Civil War on the Western Frontier
Lawrence
(888) 529-5267

Lawrence Busker Festival
(785) 842-3883

SEPTEMBER
Grinter Applefest
Kansas City
(913) 299-0373

SEPTEMBER–OCTOBER
Lawrence Indian Arts Show
(785) 864-2675

DECEMBER
Festival of Poinsettias
Lawrence
(785) 865-4499

State Line Road also crosses the suburb of *Mission Hills,* filled with show-place mansions on acres of grounds. At about Forty-fifth Street and State Line Road is a cluster of very fine antiques shops on both the Kansas and Missouri sides of the street. You can spend an entire day browsing this area. *Show-Me Antiques and Consignments* (913-236-8444) is at 4500 State Line Rd. and is open Tues through Sat 11:30 a.m. to 4:30 p.m., as are most of the shops in the area. Many shops are located in buildings dating from the 1920s and 1930s and carry eighteenth- and nineteenth-century European and American furniture and accessories.

If you leave Kansas City on U.S. Highway 69 toward the south, you'll go through the city of *Mission,* a very upscale suburban community. There is no shortage of places to shop or eat.

A nightspot you might want to visit is *The Roxy* at 7230 West Seventy-fifth St. There's live music every night, a mix of classic rock 'n roll and blues. The Roxy is open seven days a week from 11 a.m. to 2 a.m. You can grab a quick burger here and enjoy the music. Call (913) 236-6211.

If you're leaving Kansas City toward the southwest on Interstate 35, you'll pass through *Merriam,* Lenexa, and Olathe. At the turn of the twentieth century, Merriam was known as the playground of Kansas because of its amusement park. President Ulysses S. Grant dedicated Merriam Park in 1880, and for two decades, rail travelers came by the thousands to enjoy boating, baseball, tennis, a merry-go-round, and a zoo. The Hocker Grove area still has some of the beautiful summer homes of the wealthy families who visited from Chicago and Denver. Kansas City built its own amusement parks in the early 1900s, drawing away the tourists, but trolley service extended to the Hocker Grove neighborhood soon attracted many permanent residents.

If you have a sweet tooth, Merriam today will be dear to your heart because of the gooey sweets produced by *Sifers Candy Company,* founded in 1903. Owner Russell Sifers and his son have become the fifth generation to use the original copper pots and recipe. One day in 1931, an employee (who, they say, sampled too much of the bourbon vanilla) botched a batch of marshmallow filling. The marvelous result was the Valomilk, known to Midwesterners as the favorite thing to find in their "dinner bucket" at school. These shells of blended light and Brazilian dark chocolate

didyouknow?

The state's first newspaper was the *Shawnee Sun,* a monthly paper published in 1835 at the Shawnee Indian Methodist Mission. It was printed in the Shawnee language by the missionary Jotham Meeker. The first weekly newspaper was the *Kansas Weekly Herald,* published in Leavenworth in 1854.

Brown v. Topeka Board of Education

The city of Merriam has an interesting bit of history attached to it: Brown Park is named for Esther Brown, a local Jewish woman who led a court fight in 1946 at the Walker Grade School, now the Philadelphia Missionary Baptist Church (9430 West Fiftieth Terrace) to demand integration. This was one of nineteen known cases that preceded the *Brown v. Topeka Board of Education* case, decided in 1954 by the U.S. Supreme Court, making segregated schools illegal across the country. Although Esther Brown was not one of the Browns named in that landmark case, she is honored for her extensive work and fundraising for the NAACP.

filled with super-sweet marshmallow goo are sold only in the Midwest and through a few specialty catalogs. There are no factory tours because there are only six employees (and even the boss gets in the way sometimes), and there is no outlet store. But once you're hooked, you can order them by the box (in cool weather). Visit their Web site, www.valomilk.com.

The spicy food of India is yours to sample at **Korma Sutra,** 7217 W. 110th St. in **Overland Park.** The lunch buffet, from 11 a.m. to 2:30 p.m., has every kind of dish on it. Dinner is served from 5 to 9 p.m., and the menu is full of fascinating foods. The sauces are creamy; the food is spicy. You can try everything from tender boneless goat to a large selection of vegetarian specialties. Try lamb vindaloo (a mango cream smoothie is served to help with the burn) or simply butter chicken with saffron rice. All are served with fresh warm naan (bread). Save room for exotic desserts such as rasma lai—cheese with rose water—and pistachio or mango kulfi (ice cream), and end your meal with chai tea and a silver finger bowl with fresh lemons. Call (913) 34-kurri (345-8774).

Shopping is the sport of choice in Overland Park, especially on 119th Street and 135th Street between Metcalf and Roe. The neighborhood is filled with designer shops, gourmet foods, huge health-food stores, and choices upon choices of places to spend money on anything you can imagine.

Ice cream aficionados have disagreed forever on where to find the best ice cream. **Sylas and Maddy's Homemade Ice Cream** in **Olathe,** at 11925 South Strang Line Rd., (913-393-3500) is one of the contenders. Owner Cindy England has a couple of favorites in the running: Maddy's Mud (coffee, brownie pieces, and Oreos) and da Bomb (Oreos, cookie dough, and chocolate flakes). Named for the owners' two pets, Sylas and Maddy's has over a hundred varieties on rotation, available in a cup or a giant waffle cone. Hours are 12:30 to 9:30 p.m. during the week and noon to 10:30 p.m. on weekends.

Another location—the original, actually—can be found in downtown Lawrence (785-832-8323).

When you are ready to slip away from the shops for lunch, and if you have never had slow-cooked goat or have a craving for a hot and spicy chicken dish served with homemade flat bread, try the lunch buffet from 11 a.m. to 2:30 p.m. seven days a week at *Ruchi Indian Cuisine.* This restaurant, at 11168 Antioch Rd. (College and Antioch) in Overland Park, offers authentic, unusual, and delicious dishes from both north and south India. Dinner is served from 5 to 10 p.m. every day. Call Reddy at (913) 661-9088.

In Overland Park, the *Deanna Rose Children's Farmstead* (913-897-2360; www.opkansas.org), at 13800 Switzer, is a tribute to a local policewoman. Rose, who loved animals, was killed while making a routine traffic stop. This minifarm has every kind of farm animal you can think of. When members of the Epsilon Iota chapter of Beta Sigma Phi opened the park in 1977, they didn't know how popular it would become. It soon grew beyond petting animals and looking at flowers.

The City of Overland Park now operates the replica of an 1850 Kansas farmstead, complete with a dairy barn. The farmstead also has a nature trail through a wooded area with many native Kansas birds, including the great horned owl, red-tailed hawk, and grouse. A working windmill recirculates water through a tank, and vegetables and perennial flowers grow in a community garden. A chicken coop and farm equipment are on display. There's even a fishing pond and pony rides. Horse-drawn wagon rides run 10 a.m. to 3 p.m. weekdays, 10 a.m. to 4 p.m. Sat, and 11 a.m. to 4 p.m. Sun. Rides are $2. The children's farmstead is open daily from 9 a.m. to 5 p.m. Apr 1 through Oct 31 and until 8 p.m. Tues and Thurs, Memorial Day to Labor Day. Admission to the facility is free.

Eight times a week, fifty-two weeks a year, the *New Theatre Restaurant,* 9229 Foster, Overland Park, treats an audience of about 600 to Broadway

ALSO WORTH SEEING

Constitution Hall State Historic Site Lecompton	**Ottawa Antique Mall & Restaurant** Ottawa
Great Mall of the Great Plains Olathe	**Prairie Center** Olathe
Linn County Park at La Cygne Lake—near La Cygne	

comedies and musicals and five-star cuisine. Nationally known stars including Don Knotts, Loretta Swit, Bonnie Franklin, Jamie Farr, and Tom Poston have performed here. Five different shows are produced each year. Make reservations by calling (913) 649–SHOW seven days a week. For other information, check the Web site at www.newtheatre.com.

Visit the ***Overland Park Arboretum and Botanical Gardens,*** 300 acres on the edge of Overland Park's residential neighborhood. The seven ecosystems in the park can be enjoyed from asphalt walks and chip-and-bark trails. Walk past water gardens and through dense forests along Wolf Creek, which runs past 30-foot bluffs. A family of pileated woodpeckers draws a lot of visitors. A meadow features waterfalls, pools, a butterfly garden, and a wildflower collection. Less than ⅓ of the total acreage has been touched. The arboretum, 8909 West 179th St., is just west of Antioch Road, about ½ mile west of US 69, which is a continuation of Metcalf Avenue. The park is open daily from 8 a.m. to 7:30 p.m. Apr 10 through Sept 30 and until 5 p.m. the rest of the year. For more information call (913) 685-3604, or check the Web site at www.opkansas.org.

Boulevard Drive-In Theatre at 1051 Merriam Lane (near I-35) is not only a very nice and well-maintained drive-in movie with Fri and Sat night triple features for one price, but—and this is the best part—a giant swap-and-shop flea market is open on the grounds on weekend days, year-round. The theater is open from Apr until Oct. Call (913) 262-0392.

Old Shawnee Town, at 11501 West Fifty-seventh St. in ***Shawnee,*** has seventeen original and replica buildings from the nineteenth and twentieth centuries, as well as period gardens. See the first jailhouse in Kansas, dating from 1843, the 1878 Hart House, Amos Undertakers, All Faiths Chapel, Franke Barber Shop, and the Shawnee Fire Barn. Old Shawnee Town is open Tues through Sat from 10 a.m. to 4:30 p.m. Mar through Oct. Admission is $1 for adults, 50 cents for children ages six through twelve. For information call (913) 248-2360 or visit www.shawneetown.org.

The ***Legler Barn Museum,*** at 14907 West Eighty-seventh St. Pkwy.,

alongthe oregontrail

Between the 1840s and the 1870s, about 300,000 hardy souls walked the Oregon Trail to the northwest in the greatest peacetime migration in world history. The 1,172-mile journey still makes an exciting tour. In Kansas the trail passes through the towns of Olathe, Lenexa, Lawrence, Topeka, St. Marys, Manhattan, Wamego, Westmoreland, Blue Rapids, and Marysville. The towns have historic sites that date from that great migration, and wagon ruts are still visible in several places.

Lenexa, was originally located on the old Santa Fe Trail. Using stone from the original barn, it was rebuilt and restored in the fifty-three-acre Sar-Ko-Par Trails Park. On the grounds of the barn is more history, including the old Frisco Railroad depot. The museum also contains a gift shop. Hours are Tues through Fri 10 a.m. to 4 p.m. and Sat and Sun 1 to 4 p.m. Call (913) 492-0038 for information. There's no admission fee, but donations are welcome.

If you're traveling with kids, be sure to stop at the **Wonderscope Children's Museum,** at 5700 King in Shawnee. Kids can paint their faces, create an indoor sand castle, conduct water experiments or take in a puppet show. There also is a Small Wonders Play Space for kids age six months to two years. Hours are Tues through Sat from 10 a.m. to 5 p.m., Sun from noon to 5 p.m.; Mar through Aug the museum is open seven days a week 10 a.m. to 5 p.m. Admission is $7 for ages three to sixty-three, $6 for seniors, $4 for ages one to two and free for those under one. Call (913) 287-8888 or log on to www .wonderscope.org for more information.

Olathe is home to the **Prairie Center,** where the rich natural history of Kansas has been preserved with 300 acres of native tallgrass prairie. Six miles of hiking trails wander through woodlands and across creeks and are open for cross-country skiing. A five-acre lake provides fishing, and the park is open daily from dawn to dusk at 26325 W. 135th St. (Note: There are no public buildings open here.) For more information contact the Kansas Department of Wildlife and Parks at (913) 856-7669.

Neon beer signs glimmer in the windows of **Side Pockets,** at 13320 West Eighty-seventh St., in Lenexa, but this is not your neighborhood bar and pool hall. It is a billiards parlor, and even though the players perhaps are drinking a beer, they are there for a serious game. Many players carry their own cues in cases as they come through the door. After 5 p.m. on weekdays, they pay $8 per hour for professional-size tables (only $1 per game for regular bar-size tables). You can hold the table for the evening, or if you are competitive, you can play at the challenge tables, where a better player can come after you. Prices are lower during the day and on weekends.

There are twenty-four tables in the 10,000-square-foot hall, and it is filled with groups of women, men, and couples. You can have a sandwich or a steak dinner and watch the action while listening to the classic rock 'n' roll from the jukebox. Hours are from 10 a.m. to 2 a.m. every day. Call Keith Robinson and Rich Hawkins at (913) 888-7665.

Looking for some povitica? Find the Croatian bread at **Strawberry Hill Povitica** (913-631-1002, or 800-634-1002 toll free), at 8609 Quivira Rd., Lenexa. Hours are 9 a.m. to 5 p.m. Mon through Fri, 9 a.m. to 2 p.m. Sat. Visit the Web site at www.povitica.com.

Everywhere in the state are reminders of the area's history, and Olathe is no different, despite its nearness to metropolitan Kansas City. Just off Highway 7, about 3 miles north of town, is the lonely grave of a baby boy who died a century and a half ago on the Santa Fe Trail. Several years ago a Boy Scout troop cleaned the grave site and surrounded it with a small pipe fence. Sometimes fresh flowers can be seen on the grave of nine-month-old Asa Smith, born Nov 15, 1856, died Aug 30, 1857.

Olathe has a fine collection of charming old homes within just a few blocks of each other on West Park Street (the city's first street) and South Pine Street. West Park was part of the Santa Fe Trail and boasts some of the oldest homes in the county. For more information on the town, stop at the Olathe Convention and Visitors Bureau at 12051 S. Renner Blvd.

Mahaffie Stagecoach Stop and Farm (913-971-5111), 1100 Kansas City Rd., Olathe, was the first "home station" (stop providing meals for travelers) on the Santa Fe Trail. It's also the only remaining stop preserved and open to the public. Still standing on the fifteen-acre farmplace, which dates from 1865 and is on the National Register of Historic Places, are the original farmhouse, a wood-peg barn, and a stone icehouse. A stagecoach and prairie schooner are there, too. Open 10 a.m. to 4 p.m. Wed through Sat, 1 to 4 p.m. Sun. Closed Jan, Feb, and all major holidays. Admission $5.25, children five through eleven $3. Log on to www.olatheks.org/mahaffie/about.

Serendipity Accents, 233 South Cherry, Olathe, is in a historic 1870s home. You will find a unique array of home-decor boutique items, custom-painted furniture, and one-of-a-kind items from local artists, hand-painted glasses, baby clothes and christening gowns, and unusual jewelry made of pebbles and odds and ends from around the house. Serendipity is open Tues through Sat from 10 a.m. until 5 p.m. Call (913) 768-1818 or visit the Web site at www.serendipityaccents.com.

The Dolphin Song in *Gardner* makes its home in a building at 102 South Elm, at the corner of Main and Elm Streets. It is an "environmentally conscious" shop, with hand-carved toys, pottery, jewelry, and crafts. Owner Linda Meisinger purchases many items through international programs dedicated to promoting cultural understanding with Eastern Europe and Asia. All merchandise is fair traded. Wander in and spend hours browsing from noon to 5 p.m. Wed through Fri and 10 a.m. to 4 p.m. Sat. Call (913) 856-7513, or visit www.thedolphinsong.com.

Experience old-time country education at *Lanesfield School Historic Site* (913-893-6645), 18745 South Dillie Rd. in *Edgerton* on U.S. Highway 56, a one-room stone schoolhouse built in 1869. It is the only structure left on the town site of Lanesfield, a mail stop on the Santa Fe Trail, and it has been restored to serve as a living-history classroom for Johnson County children. Hours are Tues through Sun from 1 to 5 p.m. Admission is free. See www.joco museum.org/visit.shtml.

Tonganoxie wins the prize for the best town name in Kansas; it has a catchy sound to it that stays in your brain for days. *Tonganoxie, Tonganoxie,* your brain whispers to you over and over. So, of course, you have to stop in the heart of Tonganoxie for lunch at **Bichelmeyer's Steakhouse** or you won't be able to sleep tonight. It's in the old Zoeller Mercantile building (circa 1907) at 427 East Fourth St. Matt and Vicki Bichelmeyer have been in the food business for a long time. Try the chicken-fried steak—or the chicken-fried chicken, for that matter—and enjoy

> ## trivia
>
> Several colleges were chartered in the 1800s when Kansas was a territory. Only three of these are still in existence. They are Baker University in Baldwin City, Highland Community College in Highland, and Benedictine College in Atchison.

the mashed potatoes and country gravy with it. Steaks, pork chops, and seafood are also on the menu. Hours are Mon through Thurs from 11 a.m. to 9 p.m. and Fri, Sat until 10 p.m., and Sun noon until 8 p.m. Call (913) 369-2337 or visit www.bichelmeyes.com.

Kaw River Road

Around **Baldwin City** are places that are worth the short drive. Douglas County State Fishing Lake has excellent fishing, sailing, canoeing, and boating 2 miles northeast of Baldwin City; the Ivan Boyd Prairie Preserve, 3 miles east of Baldwin City, is a good place to see virgin tallgrass prairie as well as the ruts carved by the thousands of wagons that traveled the Santa Fe Trail. The ruts are easier to see in early spring when the grass is short. Park at the roadside lot and walk.

Another interesting stop in Baldwin City is Baker University. The **Clarice L. Osborne Memorial Chapel** on the campus was constructed in 1864 in Sproxton (pronounced *prose-ton*), England, and had fallen into disrepair. The university discovered the chapel was for sale, and with the help of a $1 million donation from R. R. Osborne, the chapel was disassembled, moved, and reconstructed. Named in memory of Osborne's wife, it now stands as the spiritual heart of the campus.

Interesting facts about the move: A time capsule was found in the cornerstone. The original pump organ and stained glass have been restored. New to the chapel is the English garden, which brightens the surrounding landscape. It is, as you would guess, very popular for weddings. Open to the public 6 a.m. to midnight on weekdays and 8 a.m. to 8 p.m. weekends if there are no functions.

The former British prime minister Margaret Thatcher visited the campus in 1996 to dedicate the chapel. Thatcher's father had served as a lay minister at the English chapel in the 1930s. Call (785) 594-4553 for more information.

Also at Baker University is the *Old Castle Complex,* a three-story native limestone edifice built as a college in 1858. It could be seen for miles over the treeless prairie by the pioneers traveling the historic Santa Fe Trail. Noting Kansas's prevailing southern winds, the nineteenth-century builders designed a concave south wall to withstand them. The Old Castle houses an outstanding museum.

Other buildings of note on the campus include Case Hall, built of native blue limestone, and Parmenter Hall, a sandstone structure that is famous locally for the grasshoppers that stacked themselves as high as the building's foundation—18 inches—during an 1870s plague of the insects. The Old Castle, Case Hall, and Parmenter Hall are all on the National Register of Historic Places.

Both you and the children will enjoy the famous "train to nowhere," which leaves Baldwin City, rain or shine, Apr through Oct. This excursion train runs on a line constructed in 1867 and travels to Norwood, crossing a 200-foot trestle 24 feet above a stream. The *Midland Railway Depot,* on the National Register of Historic Places, is next to the grain elevator at 1515 West High St. (8 blocks west of downtown Baldwin City).

October is the busiest time for the railway; trains run hourly during the city's Maple Leaf Festival and at special hours on Halloween (on which day arrival times are "spook-dependent"). Call (800) 651-0388 for fare information, or visit www.midland-ry.org.

If you're a history buff, ask at the chamber of commerce for a guided tour of Baldwin City. You will be put in touch with local experts on the Santa Fe Trail, on abolitionist John Brown, and on the Civil War. You can even find the site of the Battle of Black Jack, where Captain Pate and his Westport Sharpshooters tried but failed to capture John Brown.

The *Three Sisters Inn* at 1035 Ames was built in 1905. It has been restored with elegance, charm, and antiques. There are four rooms with private baths; rates range from $99 to $149, including full breakfast. The innkeepers offer packages including gourmet picnic baskets to be enjoyed in the privacy of the gazebo, Victorian high tea, and massage. Check the Web site at www.3sistersinn.com for details, or call (785) 594-3244.

The city of *Lawrence* on I-70 is more than just the home of the fierce University of Kansas Jayhawks. It is also a very livable city, nestled between the valleys of the Kansas and Wakarusa Rivers.

Tax Night at the Lawrence Post Office

Lawrence's downtown post office, 645 Vermont St., has become the go-to place on April 15—not just because that tax deadline is looming, but also because the Tax Night festivities, a tradition for more than seventeen years, have gained national attention. What once was the impromptu idea of Steve Mason and his Alferd Packer Memorial String Band has become an annual event that draws quite a crowd. The bluegrass band, dressed in strange cowboy/Civil War costumes, plays contra dance numbers, waltzes, and bluegrass numbers laced with corny jokes. Outside, Mike Coffman simmers a pot of "Roadkill Stew" for hungry latecomers. There has even been a wedding to beat the deadline for a joint return. At 11:45 p.m. a balloon gauntlet forms at the door to cheer in the very, very latecomers and the hand clapping matches the foot stamping as midnight approaches. At 11:55 the band plays the *William Tell Overture*—the *Lone Ranger* theme, for you youngsters—for the last holdouts, and at the stroke of midnight, Postmaster Judy Raney locks the doors.

See, paying income tax *can* be kinda fun.

Drop by the **_Lawrence Visitor Information Center,_** 402 North Second St., located in a renovated Union Pacific depot dating from 1888. The center is at North Second and Locust Streets, just north of downtown along the Kansas River or about a mile south of exit 204 off I-70/Kansas Turnpike. Summer hours are Mon to Sat from 8:30 a.m. to 5:30 p.m. and Sun from 1 to 5 p.m.; hours are slightly shorter in winter but still daily. Call (785) 865-4499 for information. At www.visitlawrence.com, you will find a current calendar of events as well as information on accommodations, dining, attractions, and the city's history.

An entire neighborhood, bounded by Tennessee and Indiana Streets on the east and west and Sixth and Ninth Streets on the north and south, all within walking distance of downtown, is designated as a historic district. Old West Lawrence contains some of the finest nineteenth- and early-twentieth-century houses around. The architectural styles range from Italianate and Queen Anne to Gothic revival and neoclassical. The gentle slopes of the hills have an atmosphere of nineteenth-century New England, with broad lawns and brick and stone mansions. A map is available from the visitor center.

The settling of Kansas was different from that of any other state because of the Kansas-Nebraska Act, which allowed settlers to vote and choose between being a free or slave state. Many came to Kansas Territory to make it free, and the result was violent border wars with neighboring (pro–slavery) Missouri. The number of pro–slavery proponents who crossed the border to Kansas resulted in a pro–slavery territorial government, but the anti–slavery people

William Quantrill: Schoolteacher?

At the age of only twenty-six, William Quantrill was the leader of the violent pro–slavery guerrillas called Quantrill's Raiders. Before conducting his infamous assault, Quantrill was a schoolteacher in the Lawrence system. He spent the school year of 1859-1860 living in the city to learn the local geography necessary to plan a successful assault on Lawrence. In August 1863 he assembled 450 men in Missouri and launched a perfect attack. The order was to burn every house and kill every man. Women and children were robbed but not harmed. Four hours of looting, burning, and murdering made Quantrill's raid what many historians call the greatest atrocity of the Civil War. It left 85 women as widows and 250 children fatherless. Damage was estimated at $2.5 million.

refused to obey the new legislature. A new constitution was written, and Kansas entered the Union as a free state in 1861. When the Civil War erupted, Kansas had the largest proportion of fighting men in the Union army.

The sacking of Lawrence by the pro-South William Quantrill's Raiders in August 1863 was one of many skirmishes along the Kansas-Missouri border. His band of marauders, including "Bloody" Bill Anderson, Dick Yeager, and the James Boys, laid Lawrence to ashes. More than 200 men and boys died, and the town was devastated. The bloodshed is remembered each August with living-history events during Lawrence's Civil War on the Western Frontier.

Set aside time to stroll historic downtown Lawrence, where shops, galleries, and eateries line Massachusetts Street (referred to as "Mass" here) from Sixth to Eleventh Streets. Lawrence is much more than a college town; it is a honeycomb of activity ranging from the familiar to the bizarre. You can have it all—from a massage at Salon di Marco and Day Spa to a tattoo at Big Daddy Cadillac's. You can enjoy a bubble tea at House of Chá or a double martini at Teller's. Or if you want more action than that, you can do a swan dive into a mosh pit at the Bottleneck. It's all here: farmers and professors, wine-sipping artists, and beer-drinking sports fans.

What's more, almost everything is locally owned with a blue-million small shops carrying unique items. At **Waxman Candles,** 609 Massachusetts (785-843-8593), Bob Werts has been pouring candles for thirty years (his wares can be seen at www.waxmancandles.com, as well as at a Chicago location). Open Mon through Sat 9:30 a.m. to 7 p.m. and Sun noon to 5 p.m. Sarah Fayman at **Sarah's Fabrics,** 925–927 Massachusetts St. (785-842-6198, www.sarahs fabrics.com), has offered quilting classes for nearly as long. Hours are Mon through Fri 10 a.m. to 6 p.m., Sat 10 a.m. to 5:30 p.m., Sun 12:30 to 4 p.m. **Au Marché,** 931 Massachusetts St. (785-865-0876 or 877-386-5551) is the place to find European goods, from French soap to Belgian chocolates. Their hard-to-find products can be purchased at www.aumarche.com or during store hours, 10 a.m. to 6 p.m. Mon through Sat, until 8 p.m. Thurs, and Sun noon to 5 p.m. While at the *Lawrence Antique Mall,* 830 Massachusetts St. (785-842-1328), you might find something reminiscent of Grandma's attic. Hours are Mon through Sat 10 a.m. to 6 p.m. and Sun 1 to 5 p.m. *The Bay Leaf,* at 717 Massachusetts St. (785-842-4544 or 800-894-8717), is a favorite for kitchenware and table settings. Hours are Mon through Sat 9:30 a.m. to 5:30 p.m., but owner Geri Reikhof keeps the place open on Thurs night until 8:30 p.m. and on Sun from noon to 5 p.m. Colorful murals are painted in the breezeways between the buildings in the 700 and 800 blocks. Nearby, you can shop for fine jewelry and crafts at *Goldmakers,* 723 Massachusetts St. (785-842-2770), open 10 a.m. to 5:30 p.m. Tues through Sat,Thurs until 8 p.m.,and Sun 1 to 5 p.m. Then walk to 919 Massachusetts St. to visit the *Phoenix Gallery* (785-843-0080), where local artists show ceramics, wood, jewelry, textiles, glass, prints, and much more. This colorful gallery specializes in custom stained glass; its Web site is www.phoenixgallery.biz.

If you happen to be in town between the second weekend of April and the weekend before Thanksgiving, be sure to sample one of Lawrence's greatest community treasures: the oldest, most booming *farmers market* in the state. Nearly a hundred vendors share their locally grown produce, grass-fed beef, baked goods, flowers and much, much more. The Saturday market, 7 to 11 a.m. in the public parking lot between 8th and 9th Streets and New Hampshire and Rhode Island Streets, is something of a social event for locals who greet one another with smiles, steaming coffee in hand. Smaller markets take place 4 to 6 p.m., Tues and Thurs from May to Oct, in the lot between 10th and 11th Streets on the east side of Vermont Street. Call Downtown Lawrence Inc. (785-842-3883) for information on the farmers markets, as well as store hours the businesses listed here.

If you can't make the open-air market, the next best place to sample local meats and veggies is *Local Burger* (714 Vermont), a unique take on a burger joint. Owner Hilary Brown made national news for her novel idea: fast-food staples like burgers and fries, made from fresh, local ingredients. Dozens of farmers within a hundred miles or so supply the beef, elk, buffalo, pork, turkey, tofu and fixin's for this ethically

tributetodole

The Robert J. Dole Institute of Politics in Lawrence honors Kansas's World War II veterans and the career of this native son. It's located on the western edge of the KU campus, at Fifteenth and Iowa Streets. Call (787) 864-4900 or visit www.doleinstitute.org.

minded restaurant with funky, '50s-ish decor. Plenty of vegetarian, vegan and even gluten-free options line the menu, as well. Favorite sides include the Progressive Potatoes—organic taters fried in organic palm kernel oil—and the Master Cleanse Brown Rice with apple cider vinegar and garlic. Hours are 11 a.m. to 9 p.m. Mon through Sat and until 8 p.m. Sun. Call (785) 856-7827 or go to www.localburger.com.

Around Twelfth Street and Massachusetts is South Park, where you can catch an outdoor band concert on a summer evening. The last concert of the summer always includes the 1812 Overture with real cannon fire and the ringing of church bells. On the other side of South Park is *Footprints,* 1339 Massachusetts St. (800-488-8316, www.footprints.com), known for its Birkenstocks and its murals by local artist Missy McCoy in a style inspired by regionalist painter and Kansas native John Steuart Curry.

The *Eldridge Hotel* at Seventh and Massachusetts Streets, built in 1855, first was called the Free State Hotel and housed abolitionists who were building homes in Lawrence. It was a symbol of defiance of the laws passed by the pro–slavery territorial legislature. Pro–slavery forces burned it in 1856 and again in 1863 as raiders tore "Bloody Kansas" asunder.

This die-hard hotel has been restored to its 1925 grandeur, including a molded plaster ceiling and a splashing fountain and goldfish pond in the lobby piano bar. The all-suite hotel contains forty-eight units with such luxuries as wet bars and coffeemakers. Call (785) 749-5011 or (800) 527-0909 or visit www .eldridgehotel.com for details.

Now that you have worked up a thirst, you'll need something cold. The *Free State Brewing Company* (785-843-4555), at 636 Massachusetts St. (in a converted trolley barn just north of the Liberty Hall Opera House), founded in 1989, is the oldest brewery in the state because in 1880 Kansas became the first state to pass a constitutional prohibition against alcohol. (Kansas had 113 breweries in the days before Prohibition, due to the large population of German and Slavic immigrants.)

The beer is brewed on the premises in huge, stainless-steel tanks behind a glass wall, and great foods are served. All ages are welcome in the bright glass, cedar, and brick building. Brewmaster Steve Bradt and owner Chuck Magerl offer five types of house beer on tap or in carry-out kegs. Wheat State Golden, Ad Astra Ale, and Hefe-Weizen are standard beers available most times, with

trivia

The term Jayhawk was first used to describe territorial soldiers fighting to defend the territory from bushwhackers from the neighboring slave state of Missouri. Later a regiment of Kansas soldiers fighting in the Civil War made the legendary Jayhawk their mascot.

special brews introduced from time to time to keep it interesting. In the fall there is an Oktoberfest beer and in the winter a holiday stout.

The brewery is open Mon through Sat from 11 a.m. to midnight and on Sun from noon to 11 p.m. Visit the Web site at www.freestatebrewing.com.

If you're not in the mood for beer, perhaps an exotic Latin drink will do the trick. Local favorite *La Parilla* (814 Massachusetts St.), has aguas frescas, Horchata and all order of margaritas (melon, anyone?). Authentic tacos (no crunchy shells here), enchiladas and tamales are the backbone of the unique menu, which includes a bevy of top-notch vegetarian options (try the Salvadoran enchiladas, stuffed with yucca, potatoes and peas and covered in cheese).

For fine dining at lunch or dinner, head to *Teller's Restaurant* in a beautiful 1877 bank building at 746 Massachusetts St. (The restrooms are in the old bank vault, so you will feel very safe while washing your hands.)

The seasonal menu leans toward Italian dishes, and the wood-fired brick ovens are enclosed in glass so patrons can watch the chef at work. This is an eating experience to remember. Lunch is served from 11:30 a.m. to 2 p.m. Mon through Sat. Dinner runs from 5 to 10 p.m. Fri and Sat and until 9 p.m. Sun. Sunday brunch, 10 a.m. to 2 p.m., is among the best you'll find; the buffet is a gorgeous spread of egg dishes, meats, fruits and their signature bread pudding. The mimosas are top-notch.Call (785) 843-4111 or visit www.746mass.com.

Although the city was sacked twice and burned in the first ten years of its life, Lawrence has risen like the fabled phoenix to become the educational center of the state. "Rock Chalk Jayhawk!" is the cry heard in Lawrence, where the red-roofed limestone buildings of the *University of Kansas* can be seen on the summit of Mount Oread, as the hill is known locally.

What to do at KU? Start at the *Museum of Natural History* in Dyche Hall on Jayhawk Boulevard. Here's why:

Almost everyone knows about Lt. Col. George Armstrong Custer's last stand on June 25, 1876, at the Little Bighorn River in what is now Montana. Well, there was one lone survivor of that bloody clash of the Seventh Cavalry and the Sioux and other Native Americans—a cavalry horse named Comanche. Several days after the battle, the men of the Seventh Cavalry found the horse, severely wounded, standing over the body of her master. They took the horse back to the fort in north central Kansas and nursed her back to health.

When Comanche died at Fort Riley in 1891, the men of the Seventh Cavalry employed a taxidermist to prepare the horse for permanent display. Today Comanche stands proudly in this museum, along with one of the country's largest collections of fossils and mounted animals in natural habitats. The museum is open year-round Tues through Sat from 9 a.m. to 5 p.m. and Sun from noon

to 5 p.m. Call (785) 864-4450, or visit the museum's Web site at www.nhm.ku
.edu. Suggested contribution is $5 for adults, $3 for children and seniors.

The *Helen F. Spencer Museum of Art,* at 1301 Mississippi St., also on
the KU campus in Lawrence, is one of the finest university museums in the
country. Its collection ranges from medieval to modern art. Hours are 10 a.m.
to 4 p.m. Tues through Sat and Sun from noon to 4 p.m. Admission is free.
Call (785) 864-4710 or visit www.spencerart.ku.edu.

The unique *Vormehr & Youngquist Gallery,* at 2859 Four Wheel Dr.
(784-749-0744), features KU-inspired jewelry and Harley Davidson–style art.

Not far from KU is *Haskell Indian Nations University,* at Haskell Avenue and Twenty-third Street. It opened in 1884 as an elementary school and
has evolved into an intertribal university that attracts Native American students
from 150 tribes and 35 states. The 320-acre campus includes twelve National
Historic Landmarks as well as the American Indian Athletic Hall of Fame and a
24-foot-tall medicine wheel totem pole. For more information, call (785) 749-
8404, or check the Web site at www.haskell.edu.

At the *Halcyon House,* 1000 Ohio St., Lawrence (785-841-0314 or 888-
441-0314, www.thehalcyonhouse.com), Esther Wolfe and her daughter, Con-
stance, offer an elegantly renovated, century-old bed-and-breakfast close to the
University of Kansas campus and downtown. This light-blue, European-style
hotel is only 3 blocks west of the "Mass" Street shopping area.

Nine guest rooms featuring walnut woodwork, some with a private bath,
some with a king-size bed, are on three floors. Coming down to the big

Sailing a Hobie Cat

Visitors are often surprised to learn that sailing is a popular summer pastime in Kansas. Though natural lakes are few, the state boasts numerous reservoirs and plenty
of wind.

At Perry State Park, Hobie Cats are a common sight. The twin-hulled catamaran sailboats have a trampoline between the hulls, nothing more. On windy days, the boat
reaches very high speeds and heels, or tilts, to the point where the sail touches the
water and the hull you sit on can be 5 to 8 feet above the water. That's called "flying
a hull" and can result in the boat tipping over. Fortunately, the boat is easily turned
right side up again.

Fleet 149, a group of local Hobie Cat sailors with a passion for sailing and racing,
holds annual regattas open to other Hobie Cat enthusiasts. Any member of the Fleet
would be happy to tell you about the Hobie Cat lifestyle if you drop by. The sport is a
great way to cool off in Kansas's summer heat.

kitchen, with its brick floor and window-lined wall, for the house specialties (Morning Glory Pie and homemade biscuits) will get your day off to a good start. Prices are from $55 for the rooms with semiprivate bath to $139 for the rooms with private bath and king-size bed.

Just outside town, 4 miles south and 0.7 mile east of Twenty-third and Iowa Streets, is **Wells Overlook County Park,** which features a 27-foot-tall wooden tower with a spectacular view of the countryside. Hike the trails or enjoy this perfect spot for a quiet picnic.

If you would like to surround yourself with open space on a grand scale, try the **Circle S Ranch and Country Inn,** which covers endless acres of rolling hills waiting to be explored. There's biking, bird-watching, and fishing on the property of this elegant country inn, where romantic fires burn in cool weather. Mary Beth Cronemeyer will welcome you to the 1,200-acre ranch, home to the cattle and bison that wander over the tallgrass prairie. More than twenty ponds dot the ranch, and heavy timber surrounds it. Exploring the ranch reveals signs of early settlement, including several old stone walls. You can even bring your own horse for a trail ride through the countryside.

The inn is built to resemble a Kansas barn and has twelve guest rooms, each with a private bath and beautiful view. Some have claw-foot tubs or fireplaces. Complimentary breakfast is served; dinner is available at additional cost by reservation. The ranch is at 3325 Circle S Lane, in Lawrence. Call (800) 625-2839 or (785) 843-4124 or visit www.circlesranch.com. The ranch is located east of Wellman Road (County Road 1045) 2 miles along a county road. Barbed-wire fencing with wooden fence posts will guide you to the old-fashioned archway entrance. Rooms are from $150 to $250.

Clinton Lake has high bluffs and a wooded shoreline. The roads follow the contour of the land, and everything is planned to have as little impact on the natural landscape as possible.

This lake is unique in the number of recreational opportunities available. There are more than 400 campsites, and the Rockhaven area is the trailhead to 30-plus miles of bridle paths and hiking trails. The Woodridge area has 450 acres for backpackers who enjoy roughing it. A total of 9,000 acres of public hunting lands feature mourning doves, quail, and small game, as well as waterfowl, and plenty of fishing coves. There is also a full-service marina. The lake is just 4 miles west of Lawrence on U.S. Highway 40 and 2 miles south on Highway 10. For information, call Clinton State Park at (785) 842-8562.

Tony and Kay Kugler's **Kugler Vineyard** is a family-owned vineyard and winery. The vineyard, at 1235 North 1100 Rd. near Lawrence, was planted in 1996 and is a you-pick-'em grape source in Aug and Sept. Several varieties of grapes are available—Concord, Niagara, Seyval, Vidal, and Cynthiana—most of which are good for winemaking. So if you want to make your own wine, go pick a few bushels, or—better idea—buy some wine there. Wines are sold by appointment year-round (most Saturdays or weekday evenings). Call (785) 843-8516 or go to www.kuglersvineyard.com.

The Kaw River bottom land is great for growing wheat, soybeans, and a variety of other grains, but who would have thought to plant grapes here in Kansas? C. W. and Mary Davenport did back in 1960, and now grandson Greg and his wife Charlee have a fine vineyard and orchard 4 miles east of Lawrence on Highway 10. *Davenport Orchards and Winery* at 1394 East 1900 Rd., in *Eudora,* began its commercial operation in 1997 and has been turning out good wine ever since. The winery is open on a limited schedule. Please phone ahead to check wine availability and sales hours, (785) 542-2278. Take Highway 10 east from Lawrence to County Road 1057 (Church Street), then north ½ mile.

Did you want to take your granddaughter to tea? It's fun to drop into *Madame Hatter's* at 228 Oak St. in Bonner Springs. You can put on old hats and boas as you dine. Bonnie Freeland has fifty kinds of tea and a special every day, and everything is homemade fresh. Choose the quiche or the famous chicken salad on croissant, or the hot salmon Swiss sandwich. Save room for Death by Chocolate or one of the other heavenly desserts. Hours are Mon through Sat from 11 a.m. until 3 p.m. Call (913) 422-8800.

trivia

Many Native Americans in Kansas were moved here from eastern states, but other tribes were native to the area. The original Kansas tribes included the village build- ers—the Kansa, Osage, Pawnee, and Wichita—and the nomadic hunters—the Cheyenne, Coman- che, and Arapaho.

Take U.S. Highway 59/159 north from Lawrence to *Old Jefferson Town,* on US 59 at *Oskaloosa.* A collection of vintage buildings moved from other locations throughout the county, the town is a replica of early Jefferson County settlements. Old Jefferson Town includes a two-story Victorian home, an 1887 schoolhouse, a 1909 jail, a blacksmith shop, a general store, and the Edmonds Church, built in 1891 and still used for Easter sunrise services and weddings. The 125-year-old iron *Bow String Bridge* is also here. The free site is open May through Sept on week- end afternoons. For more information call (785) 863-2070.

In the hills of northeast Kansas, a century-plus-old barn that once put up Buffalo Bill and his horse waits for you. The *Barn Bed and Breakfast* at 14910 Bluemound Rd. in Valley Falls is owned by Tom and Marcella Ryan, who, along with their daughter and son Patricia and Thomas, offer you a chance to get away for some peace and quiet while still near the big cities and Lake Perry.

The Barn has twenty-one guest rooms and will sleep fifty-three people, so groups are welcome. Breakfast is served in the all-glass east dining room, where you can watch the sun come up and enjoy a good old-fashioned country breakfast with homemade bread. But that's not all. Guests also get supper in the evening—country cooking done by the whole family. The bedrooms in the hayloft have king-size beds and private baths. You'll also find fitness equipment, an indoor 20-by-40-foot heated pool, and a conference room—not to mention massage therapy services. It is open year-round. To find the Barn, turn north at milepost 354 on Highway 4. Call (800) 869-7717 or (785) 945-3225. The cost is under $150 per room, double occupancy. Additional charges apply for extra people in the room. For more information check www.thebarn bb.com.

Nearby **Perry State Park** and **Slough Creek Park,** a recreational area administered by the Army Corps of Engineers, offers all kinds of outdoor fun. Perry Lake is great for sailboats (always plenty of wind on the prairie). There are miles of trails designated for specific uses, including a 25-mile-long equestrian trail, hiking trails, and all-terrain-vehicle trails. On the east side of the lake, hikers can connect with a National Hiking Trail. A state park pass is required for admittance to the park. Visit www.kdwp .state.ks.us.

Reservation Country

North and west of Atchison are the reservations of several Native American tribes. The Prairie Band of the Potawatomi nation is located in Jackson County. A casino (785-966-7777) is a popular attraction here. Three more reservations, the Kickapoo, Sac and Fox, and Iowa, are in Brown County. Inquire locally for a schedule of powwows and other events open to the public.

Holton, north of Topeka on US 75 and Highway 16, is a Victorian town with original brick sidewalks, historic lighting, and a lovely courtyard square. There are several antiques and gift shops, an old-fashioned five-and-dime store, and a number of accommodations to choose from. **The Hotel Josephine** has been in operation at Fifth and Ohio Streets since 1890 and retains its early charm but with modern comforts (it's air-conditioned but filled with antiques). It is 1 block off the square. Rooms are $50 to $70; call (785) 364-3151 or (888) 610-6990 (toll free), or visit www.hoteljosephine.com. The hotel is a good starting point for a stroll around the square to visit the antiques shops and eating places there.

Called the "City of Beautiful Maples," **Hiawatha** has streets lined with hard maples planted and cultivated by the residents through the years. Visitors from throughout the Midwest travel here to enjoy the fall splendor. But the lovely maples are not the real reason for coming to Hiawatha. The Mount Hope Cemetery in Hiawatha, 3 blocks north of the U.S. Highway 36/73 junction, contains the **Davis Memorial,** eleven life-size statues showing Mr. and Mrs. John M. Davis at various stages of their lives.

The first pair of statues shows the couple newly married; the next four show them as the years passed. The last pair, done before Mrs. Davis's death, reveals the aged couple sitting in overstuffed parlor armchairs. The final statue shows Mr. Davis, with a long white beard, sitting alone in his great armchair, beside which stands an empty chair.

The ten Italian marble statues were carved from photographs sent to an artist in Rome; the final granite statue was done by a Vermont sculptor. The memorial was built in the early 1900s by Mr. Davis, a wealthy farmer, who is said to have spent more than $100,000 on this tomb. Mr. and Mrs. Davis had no children. To some, the memorials are an enduring record of the couple's love, although some locals have a different story. Mrs. Davis's will, they say, stipulated that her husband build a fitting memorial and return the remaining funds to the estate to be distributed to other relatives; Mr. Davis was careful to spend it all. It is open year-round in daylight hours.

trivia

The first library in the state was established in 1859.

At the **Brown County Agricultural Museum,** at 301 East Iowa St., is an unusual tribute to area farmers. More than forty full-size windmills, each erected by family or friends of local farmers in their memory, turn briskly in the wind. Each windmill is a little different; the tallest reaches 65 feet. Admission is $5 for adults and $2.50 for kids ages five to twelve; hours are 10 a.m. to 4 p.m., Tues through Fri and 10 a.m. to 2 p.m. Sat. Call the museum at (785) 742-3702 for more information.

On Highway 136 just off US 36, 2 miles east of **Highland,** is the Highland Presbyterian Mission, built for the Iowa, Sac, and Fox Indians in 1845. It was the first white settlement in Doniphan County, 2 miles west of Wolf River. The mission followed the removal of Native Americans from lands as distant as north of the Great Lakes, as well as from northwestern Missouri. A portion of the original mission still stands at the **Iowa and Sac & Fox Mission State Historic Site.** This drive-through attraction is open daily, dawn to dusk.

Missouri River Valley

The town of **Troy,** on US 36 southeast of Highland, is in the fertile hills of the Missouri River valley. Thousands of acres here are planted in apple orchards. On the lawn of the Doniphan County courthouse is the wooden sculpture of an Indian with an interesting story to tell. Hungarian-born sculptor and writer Peter Wolf Toth's statue Tall Oak is part of the **Trail of the Whispering Giants.** Toth has produced one for each of the fifty states; this was his twenty-ninth. (He also is in *Ripley's Believe It or Not;* Kansas is a pretty incredible place.) The burr oak sculpture stands 35 feet high and weighs about ten tons. Toth now has erected a total of sixty-seven such carvings throughout the United States and Canada.

Go south on Highway 7 to the city of **Atchison,** where the Lewis and Clark Expedition camped in 1804. The town lies on the west bank of the Missouri River in an area scooped out during the glacial epoch and surrounded by low hills. In 1958 two flash floods in two weeks wiped out downtown Atchison but earned it the reputation of "the town that refused to die." A 10-foot wall of water swept through the city's downtown after torrential rainfall saturated the hills surrounding it.

But plans for rebuilding the town were begun even before the mud had dried. Now Atchison has twenty-five watershed dams on the city perimeter, with recreational facilities and one of the first downtown pedestrian shopping malls, turning the destruction into 2½ blocks of tree-lined walks and a mall shaded by concrete canopies with benches, fountains, and old-fashioned streetlights.

The 120-year-old limestone **Atchison, Topeka & Santa Fe Depot** at 200 South Tenth St. has been renovated and now houses the visitor center, Historical Museum (its exhibits include firearms dating from the Revolutionary and Civil Wars), and gift shop. There is a walking and driving tour to see the city's magnificent mansions, historic buildings, and churches. The depot also is the starting point of the **Atchison Trolley.** The fully enclosed trolley is wheelchair accessible and operates Apr through Oct. Trolley fare is $6 for adults, $2 for children ages four to twelve; kids age three and younger are free. The center is open daily. The trolley operates Apr through

trivia

Fort Leavenworth was established in 1827 on the bluffs of the Missouri River as a frontier post to protect trade on the Santa Fe Trail. Today it is the oldest U.S. Army fort west of the Mississippi and the home of the U.S. Army Command and General Staff College, considered the finest senior tactical school in the world for advanced military education.`

Oct, the latter featuring wildly popular "Haunted Atchison" tours through this town that claims to be the most haunted place in Kansas. Call the visitor center (913-367-2427 or 800-234-1854) for information about the trolley and other attractions, or visit the city's Web site at www.atchisonkansas.net.

Amelia Earhart was born in Atchison in 1897, and people have not forgotten "Lady Lindy," America's First Lady of Flying, the lost lady of the sky. The *Amelia Earhart Birthplace Museum* at 223 North Terrace St. overlooks the Missouri River; the house was constructed in 1861. It's been renovated and is open to the public year-round. The house is owned by the 99s, an international organization of women pilots. Earhart was its first president in 1929. The house is restored to the era in which she lived. Tour hours are 10 a.m. to 4 p.m. Wed through Sat, and Sun hours are 1 to 4 p.m. Admission is $4 for adults and $1 for kids. Call (913) 367-4217, or visit www.ameliaearhartmuseum.org.

The *International Forest of Friendship* at 925 Main was founded and maintained by the 99s and the city of Atchison. The quiet forest overlooks Warnock Lake and is made up of trees from fifty states and forty-one foreign countries. It is dedicated to a special dream of Earhart's—peace on earth and the fellowship of humanity—embodied in the poem "Let There Be Peace on Earth, and Let It Begin with Me." A tree grown from a seed that traveled to the moon on *Apollo 14* is in the center of a memorial to the American astronauts who lost their lives in space exploration. Call (913) 367-1419 or (800) 234-1854 or go to www.ifof.org.

The *Evah C. Cray Historical Home Museum,* at 805 North Fifth St., a three-story Victorian mansion and carriage house built in 1882, contains nineteenth-century period rooms, special children's displays, and a country store. This castlelike home designed by Alfred Meier contains a bracketed cornice above the second floor, mansarded third level, and lantern tower of late-Victorian origin. The round tower on the northeast side has a battlement-topped crown and was added after the owner became fascinated with Scottish castles. All this and a magnificent porte cochere on the north side make it an astonishing sight. Tours are conducted daily May through Oct, and Fri through Mon in Apr. For current information on winter hours call (913) 367-3046.

The *Muchnic Gallery* (pronounced *mush-nik*), at 704 North Fourth St., a striking fourteen-room Victorian brick structure, was built in 1885 and features parquet floors of walnut, mahogany, and oak, intricately carved woodwork, and huge, ornate newel posts. The doors have bronze hardware with windows of leaded glass, and there are many unusual fireplaces. The gallery is filled with works of art and is a project of the Atchison Art Association. It's open Wed from 10 a.m. to 5 p.m. and Sat and Sun from 1 to 5 p.m. Call (913) 367-4278 or log on to www.atchison-art.org.

Consider staying at a former governor's mansion while you're visiting Atchison. *The Tuck U Inn at Glick Mansion,* at 503 North Second St., was built in 1873 by Governor George Glick. The mansion underwent renovations that transformed it from a Victorian-style home to a Tudor Revival manor. Innkeeper Chris Wildy has created a warm atmosphere of a past era with the modern conveniences of today. The four rooms each have a private bath and the comfortable mansion gleams with 110 windows. The rooms range from $50 to $130 a night, including a candlelight breakfast in the formal dining room or sun room. Visit www.glickmansion.com.

Stan Herd is a well-known artist who creates magnificent works in the fields of Kansas. His "paintings" are made with plow and plantings and usually last just one season. *Stan Herd's Amelia Earhart Earthwork* near Warnock Lake, about 3 miles southwest of Atchison, is the first permanent one he created. You don't have to fly over this one to see it, as you do his other incredible displays in wheatfields, because a viewing stand has been built so that you can look down and see the one-acre portrait of Amelia Earhart.

> ## trivia
>
> Mother Xaviar Ross was founder of St. Mary College, St. John's Hospital, and the Sisters of Charity of Leavenworth. She was born Ann Ross, the daughter of a Methodist minister. When she converted to the Catholic faith as a teenager, her brothers used to lock her in the closet to prevent her from attending Mass.

If you're hungry, the *Marigold* (913-367-3858) at 715 Commercial St. is a fine bakery and cafe, serving not just bakery goodies such as homemade pies, but soup and sandwiches, too. It is open Mon through Sat from 7:30 a.m. to 4 p.m. For something more substantial, try the *River House,* at 101 Commercial, offering fine dining and a view of the Missouri River. The River House Veggie Sandwich is a favorite at lunch time. You can enjoy a glass of wine or a cocktail with dinner. Call (913) 367-1010 for hours.

About 8 miles east of Holton, *Larkenburg* is on Highway 116, but you have to look quickly to see it—it is just two streets, at right angles to the highway (162 Hwy. 116). But here is the kind of place many folks, for some reason, love to spend hours in: a hardware store. *Wheeler's Hardware* is a "farmer's hardware store," the owners say. They carry farm implements, feed, lumber, 3-inch roofing nails, and specialty tools designed for everything. You can walk up and down the aisles and see most any size bolts and all kinds of twine and wire. When Jerry Wheeler's dad, Winston, ran the store, he used to restock by buying out old hardware stores, which accounts for some of the unusual items in the inventory. Hours are 7:30 a.m. to 5 p.m. Mon through Fri. Call (785) 872-3515.

A Pop Counterculture Quiz

What do Kansas City boss Tom Pendergast, George "Machine Gun" Kelly, "Bugs" Moran, Manuel Noriega, and Leonard Peltier have in common? Okay, here's a hint: Throw in Robert Stroud, the "Bird Man of Alcatraz." You guessed it. The prisons in Leavenworth and Lansing (south of Leavenworth on Highway 45) have been home to many infamous criminals. Stroud worked with his birds for twenty-eight years here before being transferred to Alcatraz. "Rocky" Graziano got his start in boxing while incarcerated here. The Kansas State Penitentiary was also home to Richard Hickock and Perry Smith, whose tale was chillingly recounted in Truman Capote's *In Cold Blood.*

Take Highway 7/US 73, the tree-lined scenic route from Atchison to Leavenworth, once the center for steamboat and river traffic on the west bank of the Big Muddy. Three Mile Creek flows through the town, which in 1883 spread out over the high bluffs and rolling hills.

This land was inhabited by the Kansa, Osage, and Delaware Indians, and many streets are named after these and other Native Americans. The fort on the bluffs of the Missouri played an important role in keeping the peace between the various tribes and the increasing number of settlers headed west.

In 1854 *Leavenworth* became the first city in Kansas. One of the more famous residents was Buffalo Bill Cody, who spent part of his youth here as a Pony Express rider and army scout. Pick up a brochure for a self-guided walking or driving tour at the city's Welcome Center off US 73.

Fort Leavenworth and the federal penitentiary are the two best-known places in Leavenworth. The prison, known as "The Big House," was built in 1906 and is still in use. There are no tours of this towering city of gray stone and redbrick buildings, of course, but you can take photos from across the street (just keep off prison property). A small buffalo herd west of the main building can be seen from a pull-off on Metropolitan Avenue and Santa Fe Trail Road.

Leavenworth has been called "the mother-in-law of the army" because of the number of locals who have married officers stationed at the fort. Fort Leavenworth was built to protect covered wagons and prairie schooners headed west; it was established in 1827. The Main Parade has been beautifully preserved, and the *Frontier Army Museum* at 20 Reynolds Ave. (913-684-3767) houses an exhibit on the fort's history from the 1800s to the present and a collection of horse-drawn vehicles covering everything from Conestoga wagons to Abraham Lincoln's black buggy.

There are self-guided tours of the post, the oldest in continuous operation west of the Mississippi. The museum is open Mon through Fri from 9 a.m. to 4 p.m. and Sat from 10 a.m. to 4 p.m.

Leavenworth is full of things to see. The ***Buffalo Soldier Monument*** on Grand Avenue has brought national attention to the Ninth and Tenth Cavalries, made up of black soldiers when the army was segregated.

The grand old Harvey Residence, circa 1883, is being restored and is home to the ***National Fred Harvey Museum*** at 620 Olive St. It was put on the National Register in 1972. The home is filled with the finest arts and comforts of the era when the family observed the custom of English afternoon tea and evening high tea. Who in the world was Fred Harvey? He was a man who emigrated from England in 1850 and began as a dishwasher in a New York City restaurant. He had vision, though, and in 1876 he opened a small restaurant of his own. Later he contracted to supply food along the Santa Fe rail lines. Eventually the restaurants opened in depots and then airports across the country, staffed by the well-recognized Harvey Girls. His policy of "maintenance of standard regardless of costs" helped him create the first restaurant chain in the country. Call (913) 682-7947 to arrange for a tour of this work in progress, or go to the Web site at www.firstcitymuseums.org.

trivia

When Bishop John Baptist Miege was appointed bishop to the West, he sent the appointment back and asked the pope to reconsider, writing that he would be a thousand times more willing to go back to Europe than take on this task. The pope insisted, and the new bishop eventually built a cathedral in Leavenworth that was the largest house of worship in the United States up to that time.

The Towne Pub (1001 Ottawa St.) is a favorite for grabbing a bite. This traditional bar and grill has a major following, perhaps due in part to the fried zucchini. Lunch is on from 11 a.m. to 2 p.m. Tues through Sat, followed by dinner from 4 to 9 p.m. Mon is supper-only, and the place is closed Sun. Call (913) 682-5456.

Not far from Leavenworth is the town of ***Basehor,*** near US 24/40, where you can stop in for wine tasting, or bring a picnic lunch and purchase a bottle to enjoy with it at the ***Holy-Field Vineyard and Winery,*** 18807 158th St. (158th Street and State Avenue). Holy-Field makes sixteen wines and has won dozens of international awards. The winery uses grapes from the twelve-acre vineyard of Les Meyer and his daughter Michelle. Free walking tours of the vineyards are available on summer weekends by appointment. The popular Jazz Night on some summer Fridays continues; attendance is $5 per person over twelve years of age. Food is available and wine is sold by the bottle from the tasting room, but no outside alcohol is allowed. You might want to pack some lawn chairs. The interactive Murder Mystery Dinners also draw a crowd. Mystery performance and catered dinner are $40, and all shows begin promptly at 7 p.m.

Except for a few special events, the Wine Deck is always open and you may bring a picnic basket and enjoy the fantastic view of 12,000 vines located on fourteen acres adjacent to the winery. The wines begin in this vineyard with carefully tended grapes, all harvested by hand and pressed immediately. The wines are then fermented, aged, and bottled in the cellars beneath the tasting room.

The gift shop is home to the Meyers' custom-made wine-filled chocolates. Choose between the heartbreakingly sinful raspberry wine-filled milk chocolates and the St. Francis dessert-wine-filled dark chocolates available Thanksgiving through Christmas. They are popular and sell out in a few days, so plan your trip accordingly. You can order custom-made holiday gift baskets, too. The winery is open from 11 a.m. to 6 p.m. Mon through Fri, 9:30 a.m. to 6 p.m. Sat, and noon to 6 p.m. Sun. It's open later in the summertime. Call (913) 724-9463 or visit www.holyfieldwinery.com.

Bonner Springs, just west of Kansas City on I-70, is the home of the annual *Renaissance Festival,* held each fall for seven weekends beginning Labor Day weekend. It is a huge festival covering acres of wooded land, with roving troubadours and lots of food. You become part of the action as you watch craftspeople at work and meet wandering characters such as the Rat Lady, Mad Tom from Bedlam, and various storytellers and ladies-in-waiting. Royalty abounds—handsome knights in full armor, princesses, and a king who will greet ladies with a kiss upon the hand (guaranteed to make you blush). Misbehave and find yourself pilloried and wearing a sign around your neck accusing you of a crime too unmentionable to speak of—lying, stealing, adultery—while strolling jesters taunt you and more blameless citizens eat turkey drumsticks as they discuss your obviously guilty face. If you and your family have never experienced a Renaissance Festival, this is a must. Admission is $17.95 for adults, $8.95 for children ages five through twelve, under five free. Call (800) 373-0357 or log on to www.kcrenfest.com for more information.

Visit a museum dedicated entirely to American farmers, the *National Agricultural Center and Hall of Fame,* 630 Hall of Fame Dr. (North 126th St.), Bonner Springs. Along with antique farm implements and a gallery of rural art is a re-created early-twentieth-century farm town, including a farmstead, general store, one-room school, blacksmith shop, poultry hatchery, and railroad depot. The Agricultural Hall of Fame honors Luther Burbank, George Washington Carver, John Deere, Cyrus McCormick, Eli Whitney, and thirty other individuals for their contributions to agriculture. Open Tues through Sat from 9 a.m. to 5 p.m., Sun 1 to 5 p.m. mid-spring through Nov. Admission is $7 for adults, $6 for senior citizens, $5 for students and active military, and $3 for children ages five through sixteen. Call (913) 721-1075, or visit the Web site at www.aghalloffame.com.

There are two bed-and-breakfasts in Bonner Springs. ***Back in Thyme*** at 1100 South 130th St. is a Queen Anne with a wraparound veranda on ten acres of parklike grounds. As you can guess by the name, the B&B has herb gardens and an herb shop; also a fishing pond and a hiking trail, where you might spot deer, wild turkey, or fox. Inside, a parlor with a fireplace and a sun room with a tin ceiling are just a couple of the interesting features of this home. Hosts Clinton and Judy Vickers serve appetizers, dessert, and a full breakfast to their guests. There are three rooms with private baths. They range from $85 to $160. Call (913) 422-5207.

Lost your marbles in northern Kansas? Here comes the spot to replace them and find many more. ***Moon Marble,*** 600 East Front St. (on Highway 32 west of Highway 7) in Bonner Springs, has a gift shop full of any marble-related merchandise you can suggest, and of course, marbles galore. You can actually watch marbles being made if you come on the right day.

Bruce Breslow is a marble maker by trade and does demonstrations in this retail shop, especially around holiday time. There are also all sorts of marble-related games and toys, unusual gifts, and collectibles. (What is more collectible than marbles? you might ask. Well, there are Pez dispensers, nostalgic and retro toys, and tin toys—the list goes on.) Collectors come from all over the Midwest to see antique marble toys, thousands upon thousands of machine-made marbles, and a fine collection of artists' hand-made marbles, although people who live in Bonner Springs might not even know this little shop exists.

Call (913) 441-1432 to see when there are marble-making demos or look at the Web site at www.moonmarble.com. The shop is open Tues through Sat from 10 a.m. to 5 p.m. There are extended holiday hours for gift shoppers and for children to watch the marble-making demos.

Places to Stay in Northeast Kansas

ATCHISON

Comfort Inn
509 South Ninth St.
(913) 367-7666

BONNER SPRINGS

Holiday Inn Express
13031 Ridge
(913) 721-5300

HIAWATHA

Gateway Inn Express
207 Lodge Rd.
(785) 742-7450

KANSAS CITY

Best Western
501 Southwest Blvd.
(913) 677-3060

Days Inn South
7221 Elizabeth Ave.
(913) 334-3028 or
(800) 329-7466

LAWRENCE

Baymont Inn & Suites
740 Iowa St.
(785) 838-4242

Quality Inn
801 Iowa St.
(785) 842-5100

Eldridge Hotel
701 Massachusetts St.
(785) 749-5011

LEAVENWORTH

Days Inn
3211 South Fourth
(913) 651-6000

Super 8 Motel
303 Montana Court
(913) 682-0744

SELECTED CHAMBERS OF COMMERCE AND VISITOR BUREAUS

Call (800) 2–KANSAS
for a free travel guide to the entire state.

Atchison Chamber of Commerce
200 South Tenth St.
P.O. Box 126
Atchison 66002
(913) 367-2427 or (800) 234-1854
fax: (913) 367-2485
www.atchisonkansas.net

Hiawatha Chamber of Commerce
1711 Oregon St.
Hiawatha 66434
(785) 742-7136
www.hiawathachamber.com

**Kansas City Convention
& Visitors Bureau**
727 Minnesota Ave.
Kansas City 66101
(913) 321-5800 or (800) 264-1563
www.visitthedot.com

**Lawrence Convention
& Visitors Bureau**
734 Vermont St., Suite 101
P.O. Box 586
Lawrence 66044-0586
(785) 865-4411 or (800) 529-5267
fax: (785) 865-4400
www.visitlawrence.com

Lenexa Convention & Visitors Bureau
11180 Lackman Rd.
Lenexa 66219
(913) 888-1414 or (800) 950-7867
www.lenexa.org

**Overland Park Convention
& Visitors Bureau**
9001 West 110th St., Suite 100
Overland Park 66210
(913) 491-3600 or (800) 262-7275
www.opcvb.org

LENEXA

Days Inn
9630 Rosehill Rd.
(913) 492-7200 or
(800) 329-7466

La Quinta Inn
9461 Lenexa Dr.
(913) 492-5500

Wellesley Inn & Suites
8115 Lenexa Dr.
(913) 894-5550

LOUISBURG

Rutlader Outpost RV Park
Hwy. 69, 335th St. exit
(866) 888-6779

OLATHE

Days Inn
211 North Rawhide Dr.
(913) 782-4343

Econo Lodge
209 East Fleming Rd.
(913) 829-1312

Fairfield Inn by Marriott
12245 Strang Line Rd.
(913) 768-7000

OVERLAND PARK

Doubletree Hotel
10100 College Blvd.
(913) 451-6100

La Quinta and Suites
10610 Marty St.
(913) 648-5555

Places to Eat in Northeast Kansas

ATCHISON

Marigold Bakery
715 Commercial St.
(913) 367-3853

Paolucci Restaurant
113 South Third St.
(913) 367-6105

River House Restaurant
101 Commercial St.
(913) 367-1010

KANSAS CITY

Fritz's Union Station Railroad Restaurant
250 North Eighteenth St.
(913) 281-2777

Gates-Bar-B-Q
1026 State Ave.
(913) 621-1134
103rd and State Line
(913) 383-1752

LAWRENCE

Local Burger
714 Vermont St.
(785) 856-7827

Muncher's Bakery
925 Iowa St.
(785) 749-4324

LEAVENWORTH

High Noon Saloon
206 Choctaw St.
(913) 682-4876

LEAWOOD

Bristol Seafood & Grill
5400 West 119th St.
(913) 663-5777

LENEXA

Callahan's
12843 West Eighty-seventh St.
(913) 894-1717

OLATHE

Santa Fe Café
9946 West Eighty-seventh St.
(913) 648-5402

Zio's Italian Kitchen
11981 South Strang Line Rd.
(913) 782-2225

SOUTHEAST KANSAS →

When the tallgrass prairie was as high as a bison's eye and dry as tinder by autumn, wildfires raged across this region, traveling as fast as a horse could run. Black smoke darkened the sky; crackling tongues of fire devoured everything, leaving only charred desolation. Wild animals and birds fled before the wall of flame. Often crazed coyotes and rabbits would turn suddenly and run into the flames to die. But after the fire the prairie bloomed with new life.

Settlers fought fire with fire by burning out sections of land around their homes. (If you ever have wondered why Americans have an almost instinctive need for mowed lawns, the answer might be hidden here.) But most of the prairie is gone now, and most of the area is rocky and hilly and covered with trees.

Kansas depends on man-made lakes. Aside from the oxbows of the rivers and the occasional prairie sink, there are few natural lakes. In the southeast, many lakes are the result of strip mining for coal that supported the area for many years. They have been reclaimed into beautiful state parks, wildlife refuges, and hunting areas. There are some really fine fishing lakes all around here, and fishermen come from miles around to enjoy them. Nearby tree-covered wildlife areas are a mecca for hunters.

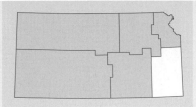

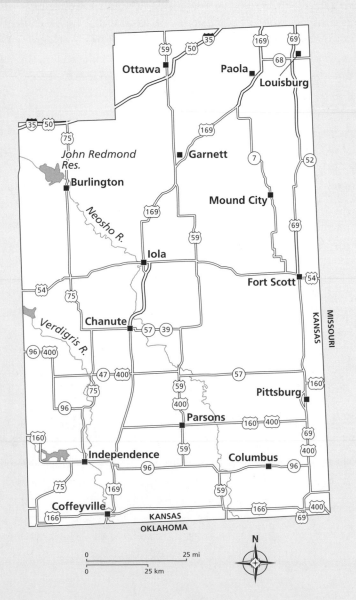

Ottawa

Paola

Louisburg

John Redmond Res.

Burlington

Garnett

Neosho R.

Mound City

Iola

Fort Scott

KANSAS

MISSOURI

Verdigris R.

Chanute

Pittsburg

Parsons

Independence

Columbus

Coffeyville

KANSAS

OKLAHOMA

0   25 mi

0   25 km

N

You can leave the Kansas City area on U.S. Highway 69, an old military road that runs along the Missouri border through the Ozarks of Kansas. It is a great road now with very little traffic.

Military Road

Louisburg originally was called Little St. Louis; the post office asked that the name be changed to avoid confusion. The *Louisburg Cider Mill* (913-837–5202 or (800) 748-7765, www.louisburgcidermill.com) is on Highway 68 about 3.5 miles west of town. You can watch the entire cider-milling operation in the shed. Cider and some tasty cider donuts are served Mon through Sat from 8 a.m. to 6 p.m. and Sun from 9 a.m. to 6 p.m.

There is a retail shop at the mill, too, selling products made there. Come apple season, the annual Ciderfest is held the last weekend of Sept and the first weekend of Oct. This bash draws some 15,000 to 20,000 people for barbecue, crafts booths, skydiving, and other festivities.

Powell Observatory is in Louis-Young Park. Take the Louisburg exit from US 69 to Highway 68. After about a mile, follow the maroon signs to Louis-Young Park. The 30-inch, f/4.5 Newtonian telescope was placed here by the Astronomical Society of Kansas City, a 300-member club, because it was the first town in Kansas where the Kansas City lights did not obscure the night sky. The telescope drive is computer-controlled to make it easy to find any object in the sky, and an ultra-low-light video camera is used to show images of the night sky on a monitor. The scope has a 20-foot dome that rotates and opens every Saturday evening May through Oct, plus special observations twelve times a year. There is seating for thirty people, with three or four programs in an evening. Gates open at dusk. Call (913) 837-5305 for a recording

AUTHOR'S FAVORITES

Arnold's Greenhouse
LeRoy

Fort Scott

Guy & Mae's
Williamsburg

Louisburg Cider Mill
Louisburg

Martin and Osa Johnson Safari Museum
Chanute

Powell Observatory
Louisburg

Prairie Spirit Rail Trail
Ottawa

Life in Kansas for Early Settlers

Life was bountiful for the Native Americans indigenous to Kansas. They enjoyed a varied diet (including corn, pumpkin, and tomatoes) not known in other cultures, but for the settlers the going was rough. Crossing the fords with wagons and oxen was hazardous because everything could suddenly sink into the muck. Cholera and malaria were constant threats, and plagues of grasshoppers swarmed the land, mowing down all vegetation in their path. During droughts the ferocity and speed of prairie fires could wipe out vegetation and wildlife for hundreds of miles.

of programs for the month; for reservations call (913) 438-3825. Donations of $5 for adults and $3 for children is suggested. For more information visit www .askconline.org/powell.htm.

Dennis and Cindy Reynolds operate **Somerset Ridge Winery** at 29725 Somerset Rd. in the town of **Somerset,** west of Louisburg on Highway 68. This is a family-owned vineyard and winery located in the rolling hills of south-eastern Kansas. They make handcrafted premium wines from locally grown grapes. You can sample and buy the award-winning wines at the winery. Hours are 11 a.m. to 5 p.m. Wed through Sat and noon to 5 p.m. Sun. Call (913) 491-0038 or visit the Web site, www.somersetridge.com.

The **Marais des Cygnes Wildlife Area** (pronounced *mare deseen* here) near Pleasanton, south of Louisburg on US 69, attracts birders from four states. French explorers came here about the same time as the establishment of the Province of Louisiana. The Marais des Cygnes was a route for trappers going west. The name probably comes from the Osage word *Maxackautsi,* which means "the spot abounding in wild swans" and translated into French as marais des cygnes or "swans' marsh." During fall and spring migrations, you may see thousands of ducks and geese, plus herons, pelicans, shorebirds, and warblers. Bring your binoculars and a thermos of coffee. The waterfowl are most active at sunrise and sunset. Also, be aware that some hunting is allowed here in season.

About 4 miles east of Pleasanton on 25939 East 1000 Rd. is the bed-and-breakfast **Cedar Crest Lodge.** Owners Matt and Laura Cunningham have redone the B&B in a rustic lodge style. It's surrounded by 113 acres of secluded countryside with trees, ponds, and beautiful views. They offer walking trails, fishing, a pool, and (this is the luxury) spa treatments and massages. Breakfast is a pleasure with special treats such as pumpkin pancakes and tasty frittatas. Eight of the eleven rooms, some with Jacuzzi and private bath, are $99 a night, while the luxury rooms are $139 to $225. For more information call (913) 352-6533 or visit www.cedarcrestlodge.com.

Nearby, on US 69, is the little town of Trading Post, an early Kansas settlement built on the Military Road, which connected a long line of frontier outposts. Because of its proximity to the Missouri border, it was the site of several skirmishes between pro– and anti–slavery groups, including the Marais des Cygnes Massacre, and is near a battle between Union and Confederate soldiers. The *Trading Post Museum Complex* features a restored 1857 cabin, an 1887 schoolhouse, and artifacts from the "Bleeding Kansas" days. Next to the museum is a monument honoring victims of the Marais des Cygnes Massacre and a cemetery where four of the slain are buried. The museum is open Apr through Oct from 9 a.m. to 4:30 p.m. Thurs through Sat and from 1 to 5 p.m. Sun. Admission is free; donations welcome. For other information, call (913) 352-6441.

Take a side trip off US 69 to little *Mound City,* birthplace of jazz saxophonist Harris "Sleepy" Johnson. It's nestled among the hills that give it its name, as though caught in a time warp. Sights include a beautiful old bandstand, old-style storefronts, the Linn County courthouse, the 1868 City Hall, and a cemetery where nearly one hundred Civil War veterans are buried. Mine Creek Battlefield, now a state historic site, is just outside town. In a city park on Highway 52, local volunteers are reconstructing the cabin of Col. James Montgomery, a conductor on the Underground Railroad. It's believed that several hundred former slaves hid under his cabin floor on their way to freedom. The cabin is an unusual vertical log style. Prize-winning author/filmmaker Gordon Parks, who grew up in nearby Fort Scott, filmed part of his autobiographical movie in Mound City. Call the Mound City Chamber of Commerce at (913) 795-2074 for more information on the area.

The Victorian showplace of the Midwest is on the banks of the Marmaton River. *Fort Scott's* brick streets and outstanding architecture can be seen from

The Battle of Mine Creek

On Oct 23, 1864, Union and Confederate forces clashed at Westport, 100 miles from the present-day Pleasanton–Mound City area. About 6,500 Confederates retreated, with 2,500 Union soldiers in pursuit. Weighted down by wagonloads of loot plundered during their raids, the Confederates were unable to outrun the Union troops and employed only rear-guard action to keep their pursuers at bay. On October 25 the wagons became lodged in Mine Creek and the Union forces prevailed. The battlefield is a state historic site, with a new visitor center located on Highway 52, a mile west of the junction of US 69 and Highway 52, or about 3 miles east of Mound City. You can visit from the first Wed of Apr to the last Sat of Oct, Wed through Sat from 10 a.m. to 5 p.m. Call (913) 352-8890 or visit www.kshs.org/places/minecreek.

Dolly the Trolley, a fifty-five-minute tour of the town and National Cemetery. The trolley runs Mar through Dec, Thurs through Sat, on the hour from 10 a.m. to 2 p.m. Tickets are $5 for adults, $4 for children thirteen and younger. The tour begins at the Tourist Information Station, 231 East Wall, and meanders down the main street and by the many restored homes and the fort; call (800) 245–FORT or visit www.fortscott.com. The shaded streets are filled with architectural styles popular from 1865 to 1919. One of the most impressive is the Queen Anne at Sixth and Judson Streets. Nearby on Crawford Street are Eastlake-style homes, one with a window in the brick chimney. Many homes, both mansions and smaller houses, feature ornate woodwork, gingerbread, stained-glass windows, turrets, and eyebrow windows, as well as hitching posts and stepping-stones for carriages. Wealthy old Marblecrest Street has a panoramic view of the Marmaton River valley that is vivid with color in the fall.

Fort Scott has many celebrations drawing visitors from all over the four-state area: The Good Ol' Days, the first full weekend in June, is a street fair featuring arts and specialty foods with street dancing. It is a celebration of life from the 1840s through today. The Bourbon County Fair takes place in July, and the Pioneer Harvest Fiesta in Oct. Homes for the Holidays offers visits to Victorian homes and other historic buildings, all decorated for Christmas.

The ***Fort Scott National Historic Site*** on Old Fort Boulevard is an 1840s military post built for peacekeeping efforts on the frontier. The restored military fort includes a hospital, officers' quarters, guardhouse, powder magazine, and museum. Living-history programs are offered Memorial Day, Independence Day, and Labor Day weekends. Call for dates and times of guided tours and interpretive talks. The fort also hosts four special events each year: Civil War Encampment, Good Ol' Days, American Indian Heritage Weekend, and Candlelight Tour. Contact the National Park Service at Fort Scott National Historic Site, Fort Scott, 66701; (620) 223-0310; Web site, www.nps.gov/fosc. Admission is $3 for adults; children fifteen and younger are free.

trivia

The *Shrine of St. Rose Philipine Duchesne* is located 7 miles north and 5 miles west of Mound City on Keokuk Road. In 1838 about 900 Potawatomi people were forced from their homes in Indiana and marched 681 miles in 61 days to resettle at the Sugar Creek Mission. Thirty-nine people, mostly children, died on this "trail of death." In 1841 a nun of the Sacred Heart order, seventy-two-year-old Sister Rose Philipine Duchesne, was one of several nuns who came to teach the children. She was canonized by Pope John Paul II in 1988.

The site also contains a five-acre preserve of tallgrass prairie. An available brochure offers descriptions to help identify the most prominent grasses and wildflowers in a mixed-prairie area.

The ***Fort Scott National Cemetery,*** at the end of East National Street, is one of the original fourteen national cemeteries chartered by President Lincoln. It contains the graves of eighteen Native American scouts of the Indian Home Guard. Thirteen Confederate soldiers lie alone in a row to themselves. Mass graves honor bomber and tank crews from later conflicts who could not be identified individually. White headstones in row after row pay moving tribute to those who gave their lives for their country.

The ***Lyons' Victorian Mansion*** at 742 South National in the city of Fort Scott is one of the Twin Mansions on the Prairie (a pair of side-by-side houses built for two sisters a century ago). It carries on a prairie tradition as a light in every window greets guests.

The brick Italianate mansion sits next to its twin on one of the highest spots on the prairie. Larry and Pat Lyons are famous in the area for the fine meals served in the large dining room, which seats thirty-six easily. Dinner is available for guests by reservation. The mansion is popular for weddings and business meetings as well. Pat is a southern lady, and her breakfasts are legendary in Fort Scott. There is enough to feed a dozen, even if only two guests are spending the night, although her eight guest rooms are usually full. Ask about booking a "Mystery in the Parlor" party—they're great fun.

Pat loves peacock feathers, and they appear everywhere. In fact, she has a stuffed peacock, about 8 feet long from head to tail, in the house. It took four years to build this house, and when you look around, you will see why: native black walnut woodwork in the north and south parlors, oak in the dining room, and six fireplaces. And now there is even more waiting for you.

The U.S. Army at Fort Scott

The U.S. Army established Fort Scott in 1842 to protect what was supposed to be the Permanent Indian Frontier. Army troops stationed here fought in the Mexican War (1846-1848) and patrolled the Santa Fe and Oregon Trails. The fort was abandoned by the army in 1853, and two years later the buildings were sold at auction and the fort became the town of Fort Scott. Violence plagued the area during the Bleeding Kansas years, prompting the periodic return of troops to restore order. The Civil War brought the military back in full force; the town served as an important supply base and training ground for Union troops. The final period of military occupation came between 1869 and 1873, when soldiers camped south of town during the construction of a railroad to protect it from attacks by squatters.

The **Paradise Day Spa** is part of the Lyons' Mansion, and here a massage therapist will make you feel like a new man, or woman, or even couple—they offer a couple's massage for those on first or second honeymoons. Check the Web site at www.lyonstwinmansions.com for more details and a peek at the mansion. The local number for day spa reservations is (620) 223-3644, and you can make bed-and-breakfast reservations, too. Call for reservations early (800–78–GUEST). Rooms start at $89.95 Sun through Thurs, $160 Fri and Sat.

Another lovely, historic lodging, the **Courtland Hotel and Day Spa** at 121 East First St., is a beautifully restored 1906 railroad hotel with sixteen guest rooms and four suites. Visit the Web site at www.courtlandhotel.com. Rooms are modest in size and in price ($59 to $99), as befits a hotel with a history of serving the men riding the rails. Each room has a private bath and cable TV. King-size, queen-size, double, and twin beds are available. In addition, the spa's four "therapy rooms" provide space for facials, waxing, body wraps and massage.Call (620) 223-0098 for reservations.

Fort Scott's North Main Street is a covered walkway chock-full of nice little shops. **Country Cupboard** (620-223-5980) at 12 North Main is the biggest country store in the area, with an old-fashioned flavor and a large selection of crafts, fabrics, cards, candy, dolls, and gifts—many made by local hands. It is open Mon through Sat from 9 a.m. to 6 p.m., Sun from noon to 5 p.m.

Hollister Wildlife Area, 8 miles southwest of Fort Scott on US 69, is open for hiking, bird-watching, and backpacking. Hunters, trappers, and fishermen are welcome, too. Call (620) 449-2539 for information.

The town of **Erie** has the wonderful metal sculptures of **Dinosaur Not So National Park,** located on a farm just a few miles southwest of town. The beasts were created entirely by retired Air Force engineer Robert Dorris.

Greenbush, on Highway 57 between Girard and St. Paul, was just a quiet prairie town until recently. Now it is home to the **Pittsburg State University–Greenbush Astrophysical Observatory** (620-235-4391), which has a 24-inch Cassegrain telescope more than 150 feet high. Skyviewing programs are held one Friday night each month. And there is more.

Dozens of school buses wend their way to the **Southeast Kansas Education Service Center.** In its instructional buildings is the nerve center for interactive classes, a kind of educational co-op, where students can communicate with NASA astronauts in Houston or students in Japan. The center has its own Web site—www.greenbush.org. Unique in the nation, the resources of many school districts have been pooled so the center can offer what the individual small-town schools cannot afford alone. Schools pay an annual membership and in return receive unlimited student access to the William L. Abernathy Science Education Center. There students can watch lizards skittering through a

TOP ANNUAL EVENTS

APRIL

William Inge Festival
Independence
(316) 331-7768

JUNE

Good Ol' Days
Fort Scott
(800) 245–FORT

Cowtown Days
Baxter Springs
(316) 856-3131

SEPTEMBER

Little Balkans Days
Pittsburg; Labor Day weekend
(800) 879-1112

Buster Keaton Celebration
Iola
(316) 365-4765

OCTOBER

Dalton Defender Days
Coffeyville
(316) 251-1194

humid rain forest with ninety species of plants from the Amazon, or visit the adjacent greenhouse. They can root around in the archaeological dig, which is "planted" with bones and pottery chucks from whatever civilization they are studying. The science center is open to the public weekdays from 8 a.m. to 4 p.m. Admission is free, but donations are welcome; instructional tours $5. Call (620) 724-6281 for information.

The *Frontenac Bakery,* 211 North Crawford in *Frontenac,* just off US 69 south of Fort Scott, is unusual because the company still produces Italian bread in the same manner as when it opened in 1900. George Vacca, a native of Valparga, Italy, started the bakery when he gave up coal mining in the area. Until recently the brick ovens were heated by wood but now have been converted to natural gas. The Duchess oven reaches 500 degrees Fahrenheit, then the fire is turned off, and the bread is baked with the heat retained in the bricks at about 400 degrees. The ovens are loaded with a custom-made "peel," the long paddle that is used to slide the loaves in and out. The floor of the oven is brick, and the bread is baked directly on it to give it a crisp crust. French bread is made from the same recipe but baked on pans for a softer crust. Most of the work is done by hand; visitors are welcome. The bakery is open Wed through Sun from 6 to around 10 a.m., with extra special hot cinnamon rolls and breads available Sunday morning. Call (620) 231-7980.

trivia

There are many small towns in Crawford County because of all the small campsites surrounding the mines. Most camps had one school and one church. Some also had a theater and a bank.

For a place to stay in the region, try the **Madison House B&B** at 211 North Summit in **Girard,** west of Arma on Highway 47. The three-story Victorian, built in 1907, has four guest rooms with private baths and is filled with antiques; a room includes a private bath, along with a full breakfast. Call (620) 724-4679 for rates.

Two of the best chicken places in the state (and there are quite a few really, really good ones) are in Pittsburg—**Chicken Annie's,** 1143 East 600th Ave., (620) 231-9460, and **Chicken Mary's,** 1133 East 600th Ave., (620) 231-9510. They are about a block from each other and a zillion signs will direct you to them (north on US 69, then about 3.5 miles east on a rural road). Both have super onion rings and the choice of mashed potatoes, French fries, or German potato salad. The competition is fierce and the opinions just as strong, so you will just have to eat at both places and decide for yourself which you prefer. Both restaurants are open Tues through Fri 4 to 8:30 p.m., Sat 4 to 9 p.m., and Sun 11 a.m. to 8 p.m.

At 400 North Main St. in **Scammon, Josie's Ristorante** (620-479-8202) is a family-owned and -operated restaurant named for Mike Saporito's grandmother. Mike and his wife, Sally, have been cooking dishes such as ravioli and linguini for years. Some of the recipes are Josie's, some Sally's. The bread is baked fresh daily. The restaurant is open Wed through Sat from 5 to 9 p.m. Scammon is 7 miles north of Columbus on Highway 7.

At US 69 and Highway 96, **Columbus** has a clock tower on the courthouse square with 4-by-8-foot windows so that passersby can see the works inside. An electric motor lifts the seventy-five-pound weights every twelve hours. The matching weights, which control the striker chimes, weigh 200 pounds each. Originally built in 1919, the clock was later dismantled and the parts stored. In 1983 Starr Smith found the rusted parts and rebuilt the old clock. A buff-brick tower with brown trim and mansard roof was erected by the town, and

The Union Wins One

The Pittsburg Public Library, built in 1910, is listed on the National Register of Historic Landmarks as an example of the Prairie School of architecture. But there is another reason for its landmark status. It is the only library built by Andrew Carnegie that does not bear his name on the exterior. Here's why: Carnegie was anti-Union, and Pittsburg was a Union stronghold. The Union supporters protested Carnegie's donation for the library. "You might as well put a skull and crossbones in the stained-glass windows," one Pittsburg woman was quoted as saying. Carnegie acceded to the city's wishes and built the library without his name.

now the 1,200-pound bell again rings out each half hour. Come to town on Columbus Day and see the hot-air balloon regatta that has become an annual tradition. The motto here is "Help America discover Columbus."

Mary Holt and her daughter Marva hated to see the circa 1938 barn collapsing. It was sagging and had become home to raccoons and other critters. So they decided to save it for the next generation. Now the barn is filled with bed-and-breakfast guests who enjoy biscuits, sausage, and the works each morning. *The Country Loft,* 2193 Northeast Center Star Rd., Columbus, has four bedrooms; the main floor is open, with a fireplace anchoring one end. There are four bedrooms at the top of the spiral staircase on the second floor. All are furnished with country antiques, handmade quilts, and knickknacks, and ferns and ivy thrive under skylights. Some guests come to shoot skeet at Shawnee Creek Preserve on the adjoining acreage owned by Marva's brother, Jon Holt. Room rates are from $30 to $55, or you can have the whole barn for $180. Call (620) 674-3348 for more information.

Maple UnCommon, at 120 East Maple, is designed with business travelers in mind. A former downtown department store, it also housed a bar at one time. The dance floor is now the lobby. Suites with big living areas and luxurious bathrooms are $58 to $125; breakfast is not included. Ask for Laura or Mel at (620) 429-3130 or visit www.mapleuncommon.com for more details. The *Gallery at Maple UnCommon* displays fine crafts, one-of-a-kind dolls, and other works by Kansas artists with prices ranging from $5 to $2,000.

For some pheasant hunting or sporting clays, try *Claythorne Lodge* at 1329 Northwest 100th St. in Columbus. (Drive 10 miles west of Columbus on U.S. Highway 160 and 1.5 miles north on 100th Street.) Sam and Frieda Lancaster offer sporting-clay courses as well as skeet, trap, and Fitasc. Hunt for quail, pheasant, and chukar (a bird somewhere between a pheasant and quail in size) in field and driven hunts. A standard hunt includes your choice of quail or pheasant, breakfast and lunch, a guide, dogs, and birds cleaned for $325. A deluxe hunt is also available. Lodging is available, and there is a pro shop, too. Rooms are $99 inside the lodge and $89 in the bunkhouse. Seasonal hunting from Sept 1 to Mar 31. Call (620) 597-2568 for more details or visit www.claythorne.com.

Thirteen miles from Columbus (that's 7 miles north of Columbus on Highway 7, 6 miles west on Highway 102) is *West Mineral,* the home of *Big Brutus,* who looms over the countryside in his vivid orange-and-black colors. At a height taller than a fifteen-story office building, Big Brutus was the world's second-largest electric mining shovel when he was built—he is a one-of-a-kind fellow. He weighs 11 million pounds and could scoop up 150 tons of rock and soil in a single bite of his giant bucket, enough to fill three railroad cars. He didn't dig coal but removed the "overburden" (dirt and rock covering the coal seams); men using huge coal strippers and 120-ton trucks then moved in on the exposed seams.

Brutus cost $6.5 million and worked twenty-four hours a day. But he was a workhorse, not a racehorse, moving at 0.22 miles per hour. When the coal supply was exhausted, he was too big to move to another mining site and too expensive to dismantle, so, his motors silenced, Brutus looked for another line of work. None was found. His usable parts were removed, and rust ate at his shell. Birds nested in his cavernous interior. The pits he had dug filled with water.

But as Brutus watched, the stripped land became picnic areas and the pits became lakes. Boats appeared, children swam, and soon the Kansas Senate passed a resolution proclaiming Brutus a historical museum dedicated to the mining history of the state. Brutus was reborn and has been attracting visitors

The Legend of the Bloody Benders

Back when this region was sparsely settled, an old man, his wife, and their grown son and daughter lived just outside the little village of Galesburg. There they kept an inn. One of them would stop a traveler and tell him that he could not reach his destination by nightfall and invite him to stay at their house. In the course of the evening, Miss Kate Bender would deal the traveler a blow to the back of the head with a large hammer, then another blow to the temple with a small hammer. Then the men would drag the victim to a trapdoor, where Kate would cut his throat. After taking his valuables, they would allow the unfortunate's corpse to drop through to the cellar. This went on for many years.

They were found out when a man left his wife in eastern Kansas to go to make arrangements for settling farther west. When he did not return, his wife set out to overtake him. She, too, stopped with the Benders. While there, she picked up a locket that was lying on a table. When she opened it, she was surprised to see her own picture in it and that of her little girl opposite. The locket belonged to her husband and was worn as a charm on his watch chain. That night she looked out the window and saw the light of a lantern in the orchard. She stole softly out of the house and drew near the light, where she found a newly dug grave. She hid on the prairie all night and in the morning went to a neighbor's home and told her story. The alarm spread, and soon a crowd gathered at the Benders' but the family had vanished. The mob set off in search of them, but when they returned, none would say if he or she had found the Benders.

There was a large reward offered for each member of the family who might be brought back dead or alive. Why the neighbors remained silent is a mystery to this day.

If this story seems too incredible to be true, track down the historical marker to this episode in Kansas history. It's west of Parsons; call the city at (620) 421-6500 for directions.

to West Mineral ever since. What a guy! You can climb steps 160 feet to the top of the Brute, if you are age thirteen or older and weather permits, and get a good look at the land for miles around. In 1987 the American Society of Mechanical Engineers designated Big Brutus a Regional Historic Mechanical Engineering Landmark. He wears the honor with pride. Admission is $8 for adults, $7.50 seniors, $5 children six to twelve. Brutus is open daily from 10 a.m. to 4 p.m. Jan through Mar, from 9 a.m. to 5 p.m. Apr through Memorial Day and from 9 a.m. to 7 p.m. from Memorial Day through Dec. Hours vary the rest of the year. Call (620) 827-6177, or check www.bigbrutus.org.

U.S. Highway 166 runs to *Baxter Springs,* the first cow town in the West, according to locals. Whether they mean the first one you come to—it's just north of the Oklahoma border—or the first one established is up for discussion. If you would like to discuss this premise with locals, *Café on the Route* on Military Avenue (620-856-5646), the main street, is the place to do it. Cafe on the Route—the "route" being 66, of course–is in a former bank building that was robbed by the notorious Jesse James in the 1870s, and hungry travelers have been refueling their bodies in the converted space for half a century. Chefs Richard and Amy Sanell offer a menu that includes seafood, steak, and ribs. The most infamous menu item is the Fried Potato Salad and huge Cowboy Steak. It's open for lunch and dinner daily and for breakfast on Sat, and it's closed between meals. Lunch is served 11 a.m. to 2:30 p.m. Mon through Sat; dinner is offered 4 to 8 p.m. Mon, Tues and Thurs, 4 to 6 p.m. Wed and 4 to 8:30 p.m. Fri and Sat. The Sunday lunch buffet, 11 a.m. to 2 p.m., is a steal—all you can eat, a drink, dessert and even the sales tax are covered with nine bucks. Visit www.cafeontheroute.com.

trivia

Nine miles east of Baxter Springs just off the access road that connects US 166 with Interstate 44, a marker indicates the spot where Oklahoma, Missouri, and Kansas meet. You can be in three states at one time if you are very agile.

Another popular eating place in Baxter Springs is *Red Ball Bar and Grill* at 539 West Fifth St. (620-856-2020). Stop in for breakfast or wait until the hour is right for a chili cheese dog, fried okra and a cold beer. Breakfast is served 6 to 10 a.m. Thurs through Sat and until 11 a.m. Sun. The rest of the fixin's can be had 11 a.m. to 2 p.m. Mon, 11 a.m. to 10 p.m. Tues through Thurs and 11 a.m. to midnight Fri and Sat.

In the same building is the only bed-and-breakfast in Kansas on the Mother Road. *The Little Brick Inn* has three suites with king-size beds, and four parlor rooms with full-size beds. All the rooms have private baths, and a full breakfast is included each morning. Rates range from $60 to $80 per night.

In 1863 Quantrill's Raiders attacked an army garrison in Baxter Springs. Eighty-seven men were killed; some of them are buried at Baxter Springs National Cemetery, where a granite monument stands.

Jim Bilke spends many of his days riding and roping in rodeos. But he made a real name for himself as one of the few remaining hatmakers in the country at **Bilke's,** 1041 Military Ave. Jim has been quoted as saying that a man's best friends are closer than his dog—they are his hat and boots. In front of his shop, a life-size sculpted horse will catch your eye first; then you will notice the mural of a cattle drive painted on the street-side wall. Inside, custom hatmaking is no longer offered, but Jim will refresh your favorite old Stetson for about $25 ("Men get attached to their hats"). Upstairs the **Bilke Western Museum** is open when Jim is in the building, typically Mondays. Call (620) 856-5707. Shop hours are from 9 a.m. to 6 p.m. Mon through Fri and until 4 p.m. Sat.

Baxter Springs is an avid baseball town. The **Little League Baseball Museum** is located on the grounds of Little League Park at Fourteenth Street

trivia

The Military Road, built in the early 1800s, connected all the forts from Fort Snelling in Minnesota to Fort Wachita on the Red River in Texas. Baxter Springs's main street, called Military Avenue, is on the old Military Road. Baxter Springs is one of three sites in Kansas where Civil War military engagements took place. During the war, when the town was known as Fort Blair, it was attacked by the Confederate guerrillas under William Quantrill and 400 men who rode with him. The fort was successfully defended, but Quantrill then attacked a large contingent of men from Fort Scott as they approached Fort Blair, which resulted in a total massacre of the Fort Scott troops.

and Grant Avenue. This is reputed to be one of the best Little League parks in the country and has been the site of many state and regional Little League playoffs. The museum is filled with baseball memorabilia dating from when wealthy paving contractor Harold Youngman and a friend named Harry Wells first knew Mickey Mantle, who worked for Youngman in the summertime. The museum is opened about an hour before Little League games so visitors and players can visit, or when an appointment is made with Wayne Metcalf (620-856-3903). The museum was built by a local industrialist who was a close friend and mentor of Mickey Mantle when Mantle was just beginning his baseball career. As a teenager, Mantle played ball for the Baxter Springs Whiz Kids (he was born and reared in nearby Commerce, Oklahoma).

Eight blocks east of Military Avenue on Twelfth Street is Kiwanis Park, where a granite home plate has been installed as a tribute to Mickey Mantle.

It sits on the spot where Mantle reputedly hit balls into the Spring River while he played for the Whiz Kids in the early 1950s. It was while playing ball here that he was noticed by a Yankee scout. Mantle signed his first baseball contract (in a rainstorm) immediately following the game.

The Baxter Springs Heritage Center, 740 East Ave. (620-856-2385), has a full-scale replica of a lead and zinc mine, 1800s and 1900s boardwalks, a circa 1910 farmhouse, and Civil War history. This outstanding museum has 13,000 square feet of climate-controlled displays on two floors. The History Room tells the interesting history of the town. Summer hours are 10 a.m. to 4:30 p.m. Mon through Staurday and 1 to 4:30 p.m. Sun; Nov through Mar, the hours are the same except that the place is closed Mon through Wed. Go to www.baxterspringsmuseum.org.

There is a sculpted frieze on the south side of the American Bank that can be seen from Thirteenth and Military. (The bank is at Twelfth and Military.) Artist Paula Collins created the frieze depicting the city's history. She used terra-cotta clay and sculpted the scenes in individual blocks that were fired and then fitted together. It is a very impressive work.

US 166 crosses the Spring River on the eastern boundary of Baxter Springs, at the western edge of the Ozark Plateau. The soil here is thin and rocky. Hardwood forests cover most of the hillsides. Sassafras and mistletoe grow in this part of Kansas, although they are not found anywhere else in the state.

Here the climate and vegetation are very different from the rest of the state; there are animals unique to this region. Caves and springs provide a wet habitat for unusual breeds of salamanders and frogs, some of which are endangered species. The area receives more than 40 inches of rain a year. Caverns fill and water percolates through the joints and fractures of rocks, creating caves and feeding springs. The springs, in turn, drain into clear streams that flow over gravel beds in steep-walled valleys, creating small waterfalls.

Lake Country

Coffeyville lies just north of the Oklahoma line on US 166. Low hills surround this sandy basin on the west and south; the Verdigris River borders it on the east and north. Once this was a cow town, with teams of oxen loaded with supplies to sell to the cattlemen, cowboys, Native Americans, and soldiers who came to trade.

Coming into Coffeyville from US 166, in town turn north and stop to see a vision of the past. The vision is part of a mural on the Center for the Arts at Ninth and Walnut Streets. It features the Condon Bank's triangular building in 1892, the year the Dalton Gang was admiring bank buildings, too. Coffeyville artist Don Sprague has transformed the sides of the buildings in town into reflections of the past, known as the ***Coffeyville Murals.***

The Dalton Gang lasted less than a year and a half but became part of western legend on Oct 5, 1892, when its members tried to hold up two banks at once in Coffeyville. Bob, Emmet, and Grat Dalton, Bill Powers, and Dick Broadwell hitched their horses in an alley and approached both banks. Citizens spotted them and spread the alarm. The cashier of the first bank lied about the safe, saying it was on a time lock, creating several minutes' delay in the robbery.

Townspeople opened fire through the bank windows. Bob and Emmet rushed out of the other bank and opened fire on the citizens, killing three. Marshall Charles Connelly tried to cut them off, and Grat dropped him. Stable owner John Kloeher, "the best shot in town," got Bob, Grat, and Bill; when Emmet was foolish enough to turn back to retrieve his brother's body, he too fell. Broadwell escaped on horseback but was found less than a mile away. When the smoke cleared, eight men were dead.

You will see the Dalton Gang laid out in a row on the sidewalk, as the men were placed for viewing after the shoot-out. The paintings on the buildings are designed to be viewed from across the street, or about 50 to 100 feet away. From the sidewalk, 3 or 4 feet away, the perspective is lost.

There are freestanding paintings inside some windows, and all of the paintings are within blocks of each other, so you can see them all on a comfortable walk. They include Colonel Coffey's Trading Post, a turn-of-the-twentieth-century streetcar, and the Natatorium, a huge bathhouse built in 1906 on the site of a natural spring.

You can pick up a list of mural locations and information about other interesting spots in town by stopping at the Tourist Information Station at 2108 Walnut St.

trivia

Old Route 66 cuts through the corner of Kansas from Galena to Riverton. It's a very short stretch, but you can still "get your kicks on Route 66" right here if you hurry. Kansas is the only state not mentioned along the route in the song of the same name. Trivia question: How many cities are mentioned in the song?

The ***Dalton Defenders Museum*** at 113 East Eighth St. (316-251-2550) honors the memory of the four men who died on the side of the law in the Dalton Raid on Coffeyville. The men were just average Coffeyville citizens—shoemakers and store clerks—as young as twenty-three. The museum is open from 10 a.m. to 4 p.m. Mon through Sat and 1 to 4 p.m. Sun to give you the rest of the story. Admission is $3 for adults, $1 for teens, or purchase a combination ticket also good at the Brown Mansion (described later) for $7.50 (adults) or

$3.50 (teens). Children age six and younger are free. Dalton Days re-creates the shoot-out the first weekend in Oct every year.

Enjoy good home cooking in the historic downtown area at **Lanning's Café,** 111 West Ninth St. (620-251-8255, open 7 a.m. to 9 p.m., seven days a week. It's a good spot for gossiping over morning coffee or enjoying a hearty dinner of chicken-fried steak or ribs. Another favorite: "chicken-fried chicken."

The magnificent **Brown Mansion,** located at 2109 South Walnut St., was completed in 1906; it remains as it was, the ultimate in grandeur. The porte cochere is topped with an ornate portico, and each room has a fireplace of different design. The full basement housed the butler's quarters, laundry, and walk-in icebox. The sixteen-room mansion has 20-inch-thick brick-and-concrete walls to serve as insulation for the gas heating system. Much of the original hand-carved furniture is still in use. There is a signed Tiffany chandelier in the dining room, believed to have been hung personally by the designer. Hours from Mar to Oct are 10 a.m. to 4 p.m. daily except Sun (1 to 4 p.m.) and Wed (closed). In Nov and Dec, visit 11 a.m. to 4 p.m. Sat or 1 to 4 p.m. Sun; the mansion is closed altogether in Jan and Feb. Admission is $6 for adults and $3 for youths age seven to seventeen. Children under age seven are free with an adult. You can also purchase a combination ticket for adults ($7.50) and teens ($3.50) good at both the Brown Mansion and the Dalton Defenders Museum. Call (620) 251-0431 for more information or visit www.coffeyville.edu.

trivia

The song about Route 66 mentions twelve cities. (You missed it by two, didn't you? Sing it again, only this time pay attention.) Remember: It "winds from Chicago to L.A. . . ."

U.S. Highway 75 will take you to the town of **Caney** and the privately owned **Safari Zoological Park,** 1.5 miles east of US 75 on old Highway 166. The park has a beautiful collection of animals, including white tigers, bears, wolves, and reptiles. Admission for a tour only is $14 for adults and $12 for children. Additional fees apply for hanging around to use the swimming pool, picnic area and gas grills. Park hours are Sat from 10 a.m. to 5 p.m. For more information, call (620) 879-2885 or check the Web site at www.safaripark.org.

Independence is the birthplace of former Governor Alfred M. Landon, Republican candidate for president in 1936 against Franklin D. Roosevelt. "Alf" lost the election by one of the greatest margins in American political history. His daughter is former Republican senator Nancy Kassebaum Baker.

Favorite son and playwright William Inge (*Come Back, Little Sheba* and *Bus Stop*) is honored in the annual William Inge Festival each April. His Pulitzer

Prize–winning Picnic and Academy Award–winning Splendor in the Grass depict small-town life in the Midwest. Call (620) 331-1889 or (800) 842-6063 for information, or visit the Web site at www.ingecenter.org.

The 124-acre *Riverside Park* at Penn Avenue and Oak Street is a fine example of Kansas fun. Carousel rides are still just a nickel. The Ralph Mitchell Zoo (cheaper than a nickel, it's free!) was home to Miss Able, the first monkey in space. She resided at Monkey Island until her blastoff in 1960. Peacocks wander the park at will, but the bears, cougars, and monkeys do not. A train will carry you around the park and to the miniature golf course called A Path Through the Past, where you can play through the history of the town for only a buck. The park is open 6:30 a.m. to 9:30 p.m. Mon through Sat, with shorter hours on Sun, from Easter through Oct. The Mid-Continent Band plays every Tues night at 8 p.m. in the band shell all summer. Visit www.forpaz.com.

The *Independence Science and Technology Center,* 125 South Penn Ave., invites visitors to mess around with echo tubes (tubes tubes tubes), an antigravity simulator (a great ride!), and the Van de Graaff generator (a hair-raising experience!). All for only $3. Hours are Mon through Sun from 1 to 5 p.m., and by appointment for evening or morning. Call (620) 331-1999.

Independence, population 11,000, receives more than 80,000 visitors for the Neewollah Festival (if you didn't guess, it's "Halloween" spelled backwards) in October when top performers in the entertainment world join street acts, concessions, and an artists' alley. Then there is the parade, one of the biggest and grandest parades you have ever seen, a two-hour festival of music and pageantry. Call (877) NEEWOLAH or check out www.neewolah.com.

Thirteen miles southwest of Independence on US 75 is a reproduction of the cabin made famous by Laura Ingalls Wilder's children's books and the television show based on them, **Little House on the Prairie.** Much research has been done to prove that the Ingalls family actually lived in a one-room cabin on this site from 1869 to 1871. An old post office and a one-room country schoolhouse have been relocated here. They are open from the end of Mar through Oct, Mon through Sat from 10 a.m. to 5 p.m. and Sun from 1 to 5 p.m. Admission is by donation. Call (620) 289-4238 or visit www.littlehouseontheprairie.com.

This is oil country. In 1891 several prominent citizens of *Neodesha* (pronounced *nee-O-da-shay,* an Osage Indian word meaning "the meeting of the waters") on US 75 invited an oilman to drill wells here in the hope of providing the city with a natural gas supply. The drilling revealed a treasure more valuable than the gold the conquistadores had searched for centuries before, and it changed the pastoral life of this part of the state forever. The Mid-Continent Field was producing more than half the nation's oil supply into the 1930s. It is now considered a National Historic Landmark. A replica of the first successful

Little House on the Prairie—
The True Story

Although author Laura Ingalls Wilder based her *Little House* books on her own life, she did make a few changes. The Ingalls family actually came to Kansas in 1869, lured by the Homestead Act, which offered 160 acres of free land to farmers. That means little Laura was just two years old, not eight or so, as in the book. And the homestead isn't 40 miles from Independence, but 12 or 13. But Pa Ingalls really did build a house and stable here with the help of Mr. Edwards. Other events described in the books are also documented: The Ingalls family encountered wolves and some tense moments with Native Americans, and they survived a prairie fire and malaria. They were treated by Dr. Tann, an African-American physician later buried in an Independence cemetery. The Ingalls family left Kansas a year or two later, after hearing that the government had changed its mind about allowing homesteaders here.

The site is owned by Bill Kurtis, a television news reporter most recently seen on A&E's *American Justice*, and his sister, Kansas state senator Jean Schodorf. The historic homesite was purchased by their grandfather in the 1920s, and Kurtis has bought about 2,000 acres surrounding it, with the dream of restoring it to prairie like that described by Wilder in *Little House on the Prairie*. Other attractions include horse-drawn wagon rides, a herd of buffalo, an Osage Indian village, and period farmsteads where visitors can spend the night.

commercial oil well west of the Mississippi stands 67 feet high and has a 22-foot-square base. It is called simply ***Norman No. 1*** and sits at First and Mill in Neodesha. For visiting hours, call the ***Neodesha Chamber of Commerce*** at (620) 325-2055. Okay, you gotta stop at ***Bumpy's,*** 1000 Main St., while you are in Neodesha. A surgeon in Orlando, Florida, told me about this place, which has an eclectic menu—from Philly sandwiches to juicy steaks to Mexican food. Hours are Tues through Sat from 2 p.m. until 2 a.m. Call (620) 325-2280.

Fredonia, near the Chautauqua Hills at the junction of U.S. Highway 400 and Highways 39 and 47, is about 20 miles from five lakes. The clock tower was built in 1886, and the time has rung out across the town every half hour ever since. A farmers' market opens Tues afternoon from June 15 through Oct 15 (and everything goes fast).

Just 1 mile south on Highway 39 and 1 mile west of Fredonia is the old ***Otto Grain Mill,*** which was powered by the Fall River. Below the dam is a low-water bridge where canoeing buffs can begin an easy 4-mile trip to an oxbow bend with shaded picnic tables. Locals caution that the water can be very fast following a heavy rain.

Altoona, east of Fredonia, is the place to try Mountain Oysters. What are Mountain Oysters, you ask? Let's just say it's a delicacy relying on hog castration. But perhaps you should taste now and ask owners Boby and Rhonda Roar later. Find the *Prairie Nut Hut* at 1306 Quincy St. (The name of the place leaves little doubt what the specialty is.) Hours are Tues through Sat from 11 a.m. until 8 p.m. Call (316) 568-2900.

The Martin and Osa Johnson Safari Museum, at 111 North Lincoln Ave., is in *Chanute's* beautifully renovated Santa Fe Depot. The museum contains the pictures and memorabilia of these world-famous photographers and explorers. It allows you to follow them from the South Seas through Africa, showing terrain untouched by civilization as well as animals now on the endangered list.

A re-created safari camp is only one of many unusual exhibits in the museum's *Imperato African Gallery.* There are ceremonial masks, swords, carved figures, textiles, musical instruments, and jewelry from four regions of West Africa. The gallery features the art and artifacts of more than sixty ethnic groups along with a dramatic, life-size Tyi Wara dance diorama. The Johnsons' feature films can be viewed in a thirty-seat theater.

The museum's *Selsor Art Gallery* is filled with original watercolors, oils, sketches, and lithographs by leading natural-history artists.

The museum's *Stott Explorers Library* (open by appointment only) has 10,000 books, journals, and manuscripts that form one of the country's foremost natural-history libraries. This research library specializes in early African exploration, ornithology, and primatology.

The museum shop offers art and crafts from Africa along with the Johnsons' original books and videos of the movies shown in the thirty-seat Snark Theater. The museum is open Mon through Sat from 10 a.m. to 5 p.m. Museum fees are

That's One Big Cat!

The state has always been proud of its big-cat population. Big catfish, that is. Fishermen used to talk about fish that were bigger than they were—with faded photographs to prove it. And scuba divers will tell you about spotting "cats" of terrifying size.

Well, fishing at Elk City Reservoir, northwest of Independence, is more exciting now since Ken Paulie caught a record 121-pound catfish in 1998. Think about that! That is a monster fish, and there might be some bigger ones lurking about. Before Paulie's catch, the previous record holder was a fisherman in Texas who caught a puny 92 pounder. Experts say that the Elk City Reservoir has become an old-age home for catfish, and once a cat reaches 15 pounds, the lake is its smorgasbord and it is rarely hooked and even more rarely landed. Paulie caught his by accident. He was fishing for crappie with a minnow.

$4 for adults, $3 for seniors and students, $2 for children six to twelve years old. Call (620) 431-2730. Check the museum's Web site at www.safarimuseum.com.

Chanute is filled with gracious houses and stately mansions of Queen Anne, Italianate, and other styles of architecture, especially on Highland and Evergreen Streets. These are all private homes, but they deserve a drive-by.

The **Chanute Art Gallery,** at 17 North Lincoln Ave. (620-431-7807), is an art museum known for its works by Kansas and regional artists. Among the permanent collection of 600 works are many by the Kansas Prairie Print-makers, a group of Depression-era lithographers. There are also changing monthly exhibits in the more than 1,500 square feet of gallery space, plus a classroom, library, and excellent gift shop featuring work by Kansas artisans. Hours are Mon through Fri from 10 a.m. to 4 p.m., Sat noon to 4 p.m. and Sun 1 to 4 p.m. Admission is free, but donations are welcome. See www .chanute.org.

The first thing you will notice about the **Bailey Hotel** at 822 Bridge St. in **Humboldt** are the elegant etched-glass doors on the building's south side. The walk to the lobby has many elegant touches, too—a red-carpeted stairway lighted with an Argentinean chandelier. The lobby features an embossed-tin ceiling and antique furnishings, as well as a fireplace with a handcrafted wal-nut mantel.

The rooms take you back to the days when this hotel was *the* place to stay. Each room is named after a local hardwood and decorated with a mix of antique furniture and replica pieces handcrafted from that particular hard-wood at Neosho Valley Woodworks by local artisan Pat Haire. All rooms include Jacuzzi bathtubs, showers, Egyptian cotton towels, embroidered terry cloth bathrobes, color cable televisions with remote, and telephones in both the sleeping rooms and the bathrooms. Room rates vary with each room and include a full breakfast. The kitchen offers a choice of European-style delica-cies or Kansas home-style cooking and all-you-can-eat buffets featuring fresh-baked breads, pies, and cakes. The hotel was recently purchased by Our Lady Queen of Peace Confraternity, and rooms begin at only $55 a night. Call (620) 473-3000, or visit the Web site at www.thebaileyhotel.com.

Iola boasts the oldest continuously performing community band in the state. The band performs nine summer evening concerts in the public bandstand downtown. While you're here, visit the **Old Jail Museum,** circa 1869, at 203 North Jefferson (620-365-3051). The museum offers tours May 1 through Sept 1, Tues through Sat, at 1:30 and 3:30 p.m. Admission is free. You might also stop at the Maj. Gen. Frederick Funston Boyhood Home at 14 South Washington Ave. Take in performing-arts programs at the **Bowlus Fine Arts and Cultural Center** at 205 East Madison. It's open Mon through

Fri from 8 a.m. to 4 p.m. Call (620) 365-4765 or go to www.bowluscenter .org. Iola has a handful of antiques shops, too.

Gary Hawk is a well-known watercolor artist whose western and wildlife paintings have been reproduced on everything from plates and Christmas ornaments to pewter and brass belt buckles. The *Hawk Designs Inc.* studio, 1415 North Kentucky, Iola, displays his rural, western, and wildlife art. Original paintings are sold at the studio, which is open by appointment. Call (620) 365-5343 or see www.hawk designs.net. Near Hawk's studio you'll find other treasures at *The Classy Attic* (15 West Madison Ave., 620-365-5343), which is open from 10 a.m. to 5 p.m.

astarisborn

Just west of Iola on U.S. Highway 54 is Piqua (pronounced *pick-way*), the birthplace of silent-film star Buster Keaton. His mother was passing through with a vaudeville team on Oct 4, 1895, when Keaton was born. Now there is a free Keaton fest in Iola every year to celebrate his birth. Keaton fans descend upon the town from as far away as New York and California to pay homage to the great clown of silent comedy. The festival is held the last weekend of Sept each year and includes film showings and speakers from the filmmaking industry.

weekdays (until 8 p.m. Thurs during warm months) and from 10 a.m. to 5 p.m. Sat. Call (620) 365-2440.

West of Iola on US 54 is *Moran,* and just outside Moran is *Hedgeapple Acres Bed and Breakfast* (4430 US 54), where you can discover the simple joys of country living. You can cast a line into two stocked ponds or take a peaceful stroll around the eighty acres. After a home-cooked supper, you can enjoy a cup of cocoa in front of the fireplace. A satisfying country breakfast will be waiting for you in the morning. All four guest rooms have private baths. They are $58 to $85, including both breakfast and dinner. Call hosts Jack and Ann Donaldson (620-237-4646) for reservations and directions. Visit their Web site at http://aceks.com/hedgeapple.

While passing through *Piqua,* search out *St. Martin's Catholic Church,* built in 1884. It has beckoned pioneers and brought comfort to weary travelers for more than 125 years.

At the crossroads of US 54 and 75 is *Yates Center,* called the prairie hay capital of the world. The rich grasslands need no irrigation and provide grazing for the livestock raised here. The town square surrounds the majestic three-story *Woodson County Courthouse,* built in 1895, and still has its original brick streets. The Historic Town Square is listed on the National Register of Historic Districts and showcases examples of restored Victorian architecture. Call (620) 625-3235 to see about a guided walking tour.

Kansas gardeners drive from as far as Wichita, Topeka, and Olathe to shop **Arnold's Greenhouse,** 1430 Hwy. 57 southeast, 4.5 miles west of **LeRoy.** What started as a hobby in 1977 when George and Rita Arnold built a 10-by-16-foot greenhouse in the backyard has mushroomed into a full-time business. You can't miss the huge display garden at the entrance, the 4,800-square-foot garden center, or the twenty-one greenhouses (covering a total of 80,000 square feet), one of which has a retractable roof. Arnold's carries about 3,500 varieties of plants and is known for its unusual perennials and exotic annuals that thrive in Kansas's hot summer weather. While always closed on Sun, open hours reflect Kansas gardening seasons: Mar, Apr, and May, open Mon through Sat 9 a.m. to 7:30 p.m.; in June through Oct, 9 a.m. to 5 p.m.; Nov through Feb, Mon through Fri 9 a.m. to 4:30 p.m., Sat open by appointment. Call (620) 964-2463 or (620) 964-2423 to request a catalog, or visit www.arnoldsgreenhouse.com.

Seventeen miles southwest of Yates Center on US 54 and Highway 105 is **Toronto Lake,** the state's only granite outcrop and scene of a very short gold rush in 1887. It's a Flint Hills fisher's paradise, containing some of the biggest white bass in the state. The state park here offers not only fishing but also swimming, RV camping (by reservation), and hunting (in season). The lush foliage attracts plenty of insects, so bring bug repellant. A vehicle permit is required; fee for camping. Call (620) 658-4445 for information.

The city of **Toronto** is on the east bank of the Verdigris River and the eastern edge of the bluestem region of the Flint Hills. It was called the "green city" because of the trees and grasses that grow abundantly around it. It was settled by farmers from Canada in 1869. A prehistoric cave containing pictographs was discovered in 1858 and is located about 12 miles north of town. You can head north on US 75 to Burlington.

Three miles north and 1 mile west of **Burlington** on US 75 is **John Redmond Lake,** where you will find 59 miles of shoreline and more camping areas. You can also swim, hike, bird watch, and hunt in season. Located in the middle of the huge Central Flyway, the reservoir is along the flight path for migratory geese and ducks. The park has 16 miles—Hickory Creek Trail—for hiking, horseback riding, or mountain biking. Call (620) 364-8613 for information.

At the upstream end of the reservoir, 18,500 acres are reserved for the **Flint Hills National Wildlife Refuge** (620-392-5553). Native grassland and hardwood timber with shallow marshes and flooded sloughs wait in the broad, flat Neosho River Valley, where native grasses ripple in the wind. Find out more at www.fws.gov/flinthills.

Northwest of Burlington and John Redmond Lake, the **Fall River State Park and Wildlife Area** (620-637-2213) stretches across Greenwood County. Both primitive camping and RV hookups are available. You can rent canoes in nearby Eureka or hike. The area is much as it was when the Wichita and Osage people hunted in the floodplains and upland areas surrounding Fall River.

Tucked between the timber area of the Chautauqua Hills to the east and the grasslands of the Flint Hills to the west, this area has open savannah scattered with black-jack oak and tallgrass prairies with an amazing diversity of plant and animal life. It is primarily designed for hiking, fishing, and hunting. If you prefer to shoot with a camera, visit the waterfowl observation blind, which has been constructed for people who want to observe and photograph the waterfowl that frequent the region's wetlands.

Hardwood forests are interspersed with shallow marshes and grasslands, creating a refuge for migratory waterfowl and dozens of other species as well. In the winter, golden and bald eagles ride the air currents over the marshes. Blue-winged teal, green herons, and wood ducks nest on the shores. In the fall, canvasbacks, redheads, and pelicans arrive to join the regular residents, the quail. The Wildlife Refuge office hours are from 8 a.m. to 4:30 p.m. Mon through Fri. A vehicle permit is required at the state park; camping is extra.

Lands of the Ottawa People

Founded in 1857 by a free-state colony from Kentucky, **Garnett** has several buildings from the 1880s (constructed with locally manufactured bricks) on the downtown square. West Fourth Street is called "The White Way" because of its lovely old ornamental streetlights.

Many of the town's prominent homes line the street. Two buildings on the National Register of Historic Buildings are the Harris House and the Anderson County Courthouse, completed in 1902. Of Romanesque design with red brick

Flint Hills Scenic Byways Etiquette

The state of Kansas asks that travelers on the scenic byways not pick flowers and native grasses or stray onto private land. The residents welcome visitors, so respect their privacy. Don't photograph the cowboys or their families, and stay out of the way of cattle drives (yes, they still have them). Climbing on fences or gates will not win you the love of the men and women who have to fix them. And it goes without saying: Don't litter the roadways or quiet little picnic spots you find. Speaking of roadways, it's best to obey the speed limits posted. Though it looks like a country mile of flat highway ahead of you, deer suddenly appear, and in the case of auto vs. deer, there is no winner. Death can, and has, come to both the deer and the driver. And, of course, the Kansas Highway Patrol is ever vigilant and sometimes hiding behind whatever is taller than the patrol car. The scenery is magnificent—enjoy it.

and white limestone, both were designed by George P. Washburn, a noted Kansas architect of the period. Garnett's **North Lake Park** is a 255-acre park with a 55-acre lake. The Garnett Water Reservoir is located 5 miles to the southwest and has fishing, boating, and camping. Be alert—you may see Amish driving horse-drawn buggies along the roadways. The city Web site is www.garnettks.net.

Maloan's Restaurant and Bar (785-448-2616) at 101 West Fourth Ave. is housed in an 1883 building that was originally a bank. The menu features grilled steaks, seafood, and chicken. Upstairs you'll find the spacious bar, open Wed through Sat evenings. The original brick walls and large windows provide a pleasant atmosphere. The outdoor deck that seats about thirty people is used when the weather is good. Lunch is served 11 a.m. to 1:30 p.m. Wed through Fri; dinner is 5 to 8 p.m. Wed and Thurs, 5 to 9 p.m. Fri and Sat. Maloan's is closed Sun through Tues.

The **Prairie Spirit Rail Trail** follows the right-of-way of the Leaven-worth, Lawrence, and Galveston (LL&G) Railroad Co., which was constructed as one of the first north-south rail lines in the state in the early 1860s. The trail travels from Ottawa to Welda and is 33 miles in length. (Plans call for it to eventually extend to Iola.) In Ottawa the Prairie Spirit connects to the 115-mile Flint Hills Nature Trail from Osawatomie to Herington. The 37-mile Landon Trail, which starts just south of Topeka, connects to the Flint Hills Nature Trail in Lomax.

The Garnett Public Library at 125 West Fourth Ave. has a lot more than just books. It is also the home of the **Mary Bridget McAuliffe Walker Art Collection.** Nearly 110 works make up the collection, begun in her honor in 1951 by her son, Maynard Walker, a New York art dealer who was born in Garnett and spent his childhood here. The gallery is a little jewel box done with beauty and taste. There is a changing gallery with new art moving through it and a community gallery featuring Kansas artists.

A Famous Outlaw Hides Out Near Garnett

During the Civil War, two cattle buyers from Kearney, Missouri, named Mr. Howard and Mr. Woodson were known to stay at the John Rutledge ranch 6 miles southeast of Garnett. Their true identities, however, were Jesse James and his brother Frank. The boys belonged to William Quantrill's guerrilla band, and they used the ranch as a hideout during the Civil War. A detective, who no doubt was hot on their trail, was found shot and burned in a haystack. The James boys, as usual, got the blame.

Artists whose works may be seen here include some very famous names: John Steuart Curry, Édouard Manet, Jean-Baptiste Corot, George Grosz, and Henry Varnum Poor, with an emphasis on early-twentieth-century American artists. The collection was not given the attention it deserved until two knowledgeable art dealers from California moved to Garnett and took it on as a project. Lighting was improved, the paintings were displayed to advantage, and artwork was sent to Kansas City's Nelson-Atkins Museum to be cleaned and restored.

trivia

Edgar Lee Masters (1868-1950), a great American poet and the author of *Spoon River Anthology*, was born in Garnett. A U.S. stamp was issued to commemorate him.

The Walker Art Collection Committee was formed, and the collection was appraised and catalogued. Contributors have added more than forty pieces to the collection, giving it breadth with many examples of different schools of art and different media. A gallery adjacent to the library holds it all.

Some of the artists represented are not so well known but are still highly accomplished, such as Luigi Lucioni and Van Dearing Perrine, a Garnett native who died in 1955 and whose works are sought by collectors in New York. The committee sees him as a source of pride and inspiration to young artists in the Midwest.

The Walker Art Collection may be seen from 10 a.m. to 8 p.m. Mon, Tues, and Thurs; from 10 a.m. to 5:30 p.m. Wed and Fri; and from 10 a.m. to 4 p.m. Sat. The library is closed Sun. For further information call (785) 448-3388.

The ***John Brown Historic Site*** (913-755-4384) at John Brown Memorial Park, Tenth and Main Streets in ***Osawatomie*** (a combination of the names Osage and Potawatomi, two Native American tribes of the area) on U.S. Highway 169, is the 1854 log cabin that served as the headquarters for the famous abolitionist when he was living in this free-state stronghold. In the spring of 1859, Brown planned a dramatic act that he believed would cause a general slave uprising. He and eighteen men (including his sons and five blacks) captured the federal arsenal at Harper's Ferry in Virginia. The expected uprising did not occur, and Brown was arrested and hanged in 1859. The cabin was originally built by squatters in 1854. It was dismantled and moved to its present site in 1912. Hours are Tues through Sat from 10 a.m. to 5 p.m. (if volunteers are available). There is no admission fee, but a $3 donation is suggested.

The Creamery Bridge, built in 1930, which spans the Marais des Cygnes River at Eighth Street, is one of two Marsh arch–triple span bridges in Osawatomie. The other spans the Potawatomi Creek at Sixth Street. Both are on the National Register of Historic Places. What makes these bridges unique is that they were designed and patented by James B. Marsh to expand and contract along with the bridge floor under varying conditions of moisture and temperature. The Creamery Bridge has a rainbow span reaching 140 feet into the air. Both bridges are open to traffic.

If you want to cruise by an absolutely magnificent Queen Anne home, head east on Carr Avenue just short of First Street and take a look at the **Mills House,** circa 1902. It was built by the man who drilled the Norman No. 1 oil well in Neodesha. This private home is on the National Register of Historic Places.

Another architectural gem is downtown on Sixth Street, between Parker and Lincoln Avenues. The **Old Stone Church** was built in 1861 of native stone hauled from the hills around the city by the Reverend Samuel L. Adair and his son Charles. Adair was the brother-in-law of the radical abolitionist John Brown. The minister was a gentler abolitionist and a mental health pioneer.

trivia

Snaggin' Days are from mid-Mar to mid-May. The Osawatomie Dam is one of only two places in Kansas to snag for the prehistoric spoonbill catfish in season. (Merriam-Webster defines *snagging* as: "to catch or obtain usually by quick action or good fortune." And that about sums it up. Snagging a spoonbill means going to the bottom of the lake, sticking your hand into a hole, and grabbing a very large fish.)

Midway Drive-In Theater at 29591 West 327th St. (Route 5) near Osawatomie in Paola is open from Memorial Day to Labor Day. It is the smallest of the drive-ins in the state, holding 240 cars. Call for coming attractions, (913) 755-2325.

If dining in **Paola,** try **Emory's Steakhouse,** which serves pork tenderloin bigger than the plate and prime rib so tender you can cut it with a fork. Hours are 11 a.m. to 9 p.m. Wed through Sat. Call (913) 294-4148 for reservations or see www.emeryssteakhouse.com for more details.

The Annual Roots Festival in Paola features a barbecue contest, and the winner goes to the American Royal event in Kansas City, Missouri. The American Royal barbecue event is a *big deal* to barbecue aficionados in the Midwest. For more information about the festival, look at the Web site, www.rootsfestival .org. To sample some of Paola's own sweet meats, go to the **BBQ Shack,** 1613 East Peoria St.. They have an award-winning sauce and feature such unique items as the "atomic buffalo turds," jalapeño poppers stuffed with cream cheese and marinated water chestnuts. The Shack is open Tues through Sat from 11 a.m. until 9 p.m. and Sun until 3 p.m. Check out www.thebbqshack .com or call (913) 294-5908.

Rutlader Outpost Complex is thirty minutes south of Kansas City, on Highway 69, 335th Street exit. Inside is a world of places to see. Enter the

Jayhawking? Where Does That Expression Come From?

According to the legend, Pat Devilin, a Free State Irishman, rode into Osawatomie one morning in 1856, with his saddlebags laden with considerable goods. As he tied his horse in front of a store, one of the men standing nearby said to him, "Pat, it looks like you have been foraging."

Pat, as he mounted the steps, replied, "Yes, I have been over in Missouri jayhawking." When asked what he meant by the expression, he said that in the old country a jayhawk was a bird that worried its prey before devouring it. This is the only known origin of the word.

Rutlader Antiques and Trading Co., an antiques and craft mall that is open Tues through Sat from 10 a.m. until 5 p.m. and Sun from 1 to 5 p.m. Call (913) 376-3350 or (913) 377-3350 or visit www.rutladeroutpost.com.

If you visit on the right Saturday of a summer month, you'll see the band of cowboy reenactors that makes its home at Rutlader Outpost. Hold onto your hat as they come out guns a-blazin' for a cowboy shoot-out.

Then at the Middle Creek Theatre, there is good live country music. Ticket office hours are 10 a.m. to 6 p.m. Mon through Sat, mid-Mar to Nov.

There's also a gift shop and RV park. Visit the Web site at www.rutlader outpost.com. The outpost is open Mon through Sat from 10 a.m. to 6 p.m. in the warm months. Call (913) 377-2722 or (866) 888-6779 toll free.

If you're staying in Paola, book a room at *The Victorian Lady Bed and Breakfast,* at 402 South Pearl St. Innkeepers Harry and Lue Ann Hellyer will offer you chocolates on your pillow and a gourmet breakfast in the morning, including one of their thirty-five scrumptious scone recipes. Guest rooms have queen-size beds and private baths. Rates are $125 to $135. Ask about their anniversary packages; your hosts can also arrange a horse-drawn carriage ride, massage, flowers, and gift baskets. Call (888) VICLADY or (913) 294-4652, or go to www.viclady.net.

A half-dozen antiques shops are in Paola, including *Pigeon West,* 14 South Silver (913-294-9094), and *Lucy Lockets Antiques,* 25 West Wea (913-557-5829). Call for hours—you never know when the owners will stick a

trivia

The Osawatomie State Hospital, erected in 1866, was the first mental health hospital built west of the Mississippi River.

You may have noticed that the streets in Paola running east and west are named for Native American tribes.

note on the door and head to an auction. That's the antiques business in action.

Ottawa, off Interstate 35 at U.S. Highway 59, lies in a saucer-shaped valley along the Marais des Cygnes River. There was a natural ford across the river at the site of Ottawa, and the land was given to many Native American tribes for reservations. In 1832 the Ottawa people gave their Ohio lands to the United States in return for 34,000 acres of what is now Franklin County and donated 20,000 acres of that land to a trust for the education of Native Americans; later, Ottawa University was formed. In 1867 a treaty was signed, moving the Ottawa

SELECTED CHAMBERS OF COMMERCE AND VISITOR BUREAUS

Chanute Office of Tourism
21 North Lincoln Ave.
Chanute 66720
(620) 431-3350

City of Garnett
131 West Fifth St.
P.O. Box H
Garnett 66032
(785) 448-5496

Coffey County Chamber of Commerce
110 North Fourth St.
Burlington 66839
(877) 364-2002

Coffeyville Convention and Visitors Bureau
807 Walnut
Coffeyville 67337
(620) 251-2250

Columbus Chamber of Commerce
320 East Maple St.
Columbus 66725
(620) 429-1492

Crawford County Convention and Visitors Bureau
117 West Fourth St.
Pittsburg 66762
(620) 231-1212

Franklin County Convention and Visitors Bureau
2011 E. Logan
Ottawa 66067
(785) 242-1411

Independence Convention and Visitors Bureau
322 North Penn Ave.
Independence 67301
(620) 331-1890

Osawatomie Chamber of Commerce
628 Main St.
Osawatomie 66064
(913) 755-4114

Paola Chamber of Commerce
3 West Wea
Paola 66071
(913) 294-4335

Yates Center Chamber of Commerce
108 South Main St.
Yates Center 66783
(620) 625-3235

to Oklahoma, and settlers flocked in. Ottawa University still offers scholarships to the dispersed Ottawa nation.

This area of rich farmland is known as the dairy capital of Kansas. Ottawa has a complete block of businesses listed on the National Register of Historic Places. The **Old Depot Museum** at 135 West Tecumseh St. near Main Street, housed in a former railroad depot built in 1888, features a Bleeding Kansas exhibit, Civil War displays, an old general store, period rooms, and an HO model railroad display. It is open Tues through Sat from 10 p.m. to 4 p.m. and Sun from 1 to 4 p.m. Admission is $3 for adults, $1 for students. Call (785) 242-1250 or see www.old.depot.museum.

Ottawa also has numerous antiques shops, a couple of good country restaurants, and a very good bakery and sandwich shop across from the courthouse. Pomona Lake is 16 miles west of Ottawa on Highway 368; and just 4 miles west on Highway 31, the Marais des Cygnes River valley becomes **Melvern Reservoir.** Adjoining the lake is 6,930-acre **Eisenhower State Park,** with a 12-mile equestrian trail and two nature trails.

In nearby **Kansas City,** barbecue is almost a religion, and people there consider themselves experts on ribs and brisket. Fights can erupt during conversations about sauces (to be or not to be sweet—that is the question). A goodly number of these fanatics drive to **Williamsburg,** 15 miles west of Ottawa just off I-35 (between Ottawa and Emporia) to eat at **Guy and Mae's** at 119 West William St., where the slab is served wrapped in foil and placed on newspaper. Plastic forks are presented for the coleslaw, potato salad, or beans (at 70 cents a serving). On a Kansas City country-music radio show, the question was asked, "Where's your favorite slab?" Guy and Mae's won hands down over all of the world-famous barbecue places in Kansas City. Hours are 11 a.m. to midnight Tues through Sat. Owners Diana Macoubrie, Judy Simpson, and Ty and Lori Thompson run this well-known barbecue gem. The ribs are served with their secret sauce on the side. You can take some sauce home in a container, but it's not sold commercially. Call (785) 746-8830.

Places to Stay in Southeast Kansas

BURLINGTON

Country Haven Inn
207 Cross St.
(620) 364-8260

CHANUTE

Safari Inn
3428 South Santa Fe Ave.
(877) 743-8713

COFFEYVILLE

Days Inn
820 East Eleventh St.
(620) 251-0002

FORT SCOTT

First Interstate Inn
2222 South Main St.
(620) 223-5330

GARNETT

Economy Inn
235 North Maple St.
(785) 448-6816

INDEPENDENCE

Appletree Inn
201 North Eighth St.
(620) 331-5500

Super 8 Motel
2900 West Main St.
(620) 331-8288

IOLA

Best Western Inn
1315 North State St.
(620) 365-5161

OSAWATOMIE

Landmark Inn
304 Eastgate Dr.
(913) 755-3051

OTTAWA

Comfort Inn
2335 South Oak St.
(785) 242-9898

PITTSBURG

The Extra Inn &
Breakfast Bar
4023 Parkview Dr.
(620) 232-2800

Places to Eat in Southeast Kansas

COFFEYVILLE

Phelps Hog Heaven
511 West Eleventh St.
(620) 688-6360

FORT SCOTT

El Charro
22 South Main St.
(620) 223-9944

INDEPENDENCE

El Pueblito
1721 North Penn Ave.
(620) 331-5860

IOLA

New Greenery Restaurant
1315 North State St.
(620) 365-7743

NEODESHA

Neodesha Family
Restaurant and Dairy
Queen
201 East Main St.
(620) 325-3929

OTTAWA

Poncho's Mexican Food
429 South Main St.
(785) 242-8227

PARSONS

Kitchen Pass Restaurant
and Bar
1711 Main St.
(620) 421-1907

SOUTH CENTRAL KANSAS →

Lush green fields of fall-planted winter wheat dot the landscape in central Kansas. Here cattle graze on the wheat until its winter dormancy, when intermittent snow insulates it from the cold. In early spring it once again colors the fields with startling splashes of green.

One-fourth of the nation's winter wheat grows here, a crop well suited to the state's mild winters, hot summers, and seasonal rainfall. September moisture is critical: too much causes root rot, but there will be no germination if it is too dry. A wrong decision in timing the planting of seed can be costly.

Kansas is at its most vibrant during the growing season. From late winter's brilliant green to summer's mellow gold, the wheat season is life to farmers. The harvest begins along the southern edge of the state and moves north, with wheat ripening one day later for every 15 or so miles. A hailstorm can wipe out a year's crop; a rainstorm can make the fields too muddy to work. Everything depends on the weather in a place where an innocent, blue morning sky can turn angry and destroy a season's crop in hours. During June harvests, crews and giant combines travel through the state. Only during the winter dormancy can the farmer rest.

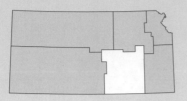

0   25 mi
0   25 km

N

Marion Lake

Marion

McPherson

Emporia

Newton

Arkansas R.

El Dorado Lake

El Dorado

Wichita

Eureka

Augusta

F L I N T   H I L L S

KANSAS TURNPIKE

Grenola

Elk Falls

Winfield

Sedan

Arkansas City

KANSAS

OKLAHOMA

The Mennonites introduced a new wheat to Kansas in 1874, the hard wheat favored for bread baking and able to withstand Kansas weather. Developed in Turkey and called Turkey Red wheat, the plant grew well on the dry steppes of Russia—but it's called Red because of its color, not its politics. Members of a German religious sect who had originally migrated from their native Germany to Russia in search of religious freedom, the Mennonites settled around Newton and McPherson. Here the "amber waves of grain" shimmer in the summer sun.

Flint Hills

Interstate 35 and the Kansas Turnpike follow the Old Chisholm Trail. **Wichita** lies where the Arkansas (pronounced *Ar-KAN-sas* in this state) River meets the Little Arkansas River. It is the center of the aviation industry, the second-largest business in Kansas, and its industrial jet set makes the city fly.

On Saturday, Wichita's old-fashioned trolleys, trimmed in mahogany and brass, connect major downtown hotels, museums, the stadium, convention center, and Old Town. The free service, called the Q Line, runs during peak hours. Call (316) 265-7221. Or, for trolley tours of historic Wichita areas, call River City Trolley and Charters at (316) 773-1931 or see www.rctrolley.com.

The city shines brightest during its annual ten-day **River Festival** that begins the Friday before Mother's Day weekend. Attracting crowds that exceed 300,000, it has become one of the premier events of its kind in the country.

It begins with the Sundown Parade, led by the reigning Admiral Windwagon Smith. He was the legendary seafaring Edward T. Smith, who came to Wichita one day and, faced with the sea of flat plains, decided that sails on a wagon would provide an inexpensive means of transportation.

You don't see too many windwagons today; it was a great idea, but on the rough prairie trails not too successful. (Maybe we should try it again on

AUTHOR'S FAVORITES

Chase County Courthouse	Tallgrass Prairie National Preserve
Elk Falls Pottery	Wichita Farm and Art Market
Exploration Place	Winfield's Vietnam War Memorial Wall
Lindsborg	Z-Bar Spring Hill Ranch
Sankey's 6N Ranch	

the glass-smooth Kansas Turnpike—it has potential.) Throughout the following week the city is a kaleidoscope of events, from an antique bathtub race on the river to a pops concert with fireworks. For information visit the festival Web site at www.wichitariverfestival.com.

Just west of downtown, along the banks of the Arkansas River, are the Museums on the River, a group of adjoining attractions that include Botanica—The Wichita Gardens, the Mid-America All-Indian Center, the Wichita Art Museum, and Old Cowtown, a living-history museum.

At 701 North Amidon is *Botanica—The Wichita Gardens,* a museum in bloom. The ten-acre botanical garden includes twenty themed areas ranging from the formal Shakespeare Garden to a riot of color in the Wildflower Garden. Visually impaired visitors are invited to touch and smell plants in the Sally Stone Sensory Garden's Living Plant Wall. Other areas not to be missed are the Margie Button Memorial Fountain and Rose Garden, the Woodland Walk, and the Butterfly Garden. In early summer, visit the Butterfly House, where more than 300 butterflies emerge from their chrysalises to fly freely among the flowers. Wear a bright color and stand still—one may alight on your shoulder. Be sure to bring a camera; the gardens offer many opportunities for photographers. A gift shop has unique ideas for plant lovers. The gardens are open Mon through Fri from 9 a.m. to 5 p.m. year-round. From Apr through Oct, extended hours include Sun 1 to 5 p.m., as well as Tues and Thurs from 9 a.m. to 8 p.m. Admission is $7 for adults, $3 for children age three to twelve, and $2 for kids age two and under. A family rate of $12 includes one or two parents and minor children. Call (316) 264-0448 for information, or visit the gardens' Web site at www.botanica.org.

Will the Real Buffalo Bill Please Stand Up?

On the highest point of the Highland Cemetery, at 1001 North Hillside in Wichita, rests an impressive monument. It is the final resting place of William Mathewson, also known as Buffalo Bill, the last of the old scouts. He spoke fourteen Native American languages, fought with Native Americans, and ultimately made peace with them. They knew the 6-foot-6-inch hero as *Sinpah Zilbah*, "the Long-Bearded Dangerous White Man." He is credited with a single-handed rescue of 155 men and a train of 144 wagons loaded with government guns and ammunition from a Native American attack. General Curtis said, "Nothing in the annals of history compares with the feats of bravery done by you." When a hard winter threatened settlers with starvation, Mathewson led buffalo-hunting expeditions. Grateful residents told of the sharp-shooting skills of "Bill the Buffalo Killer." Thus the legend of Buffalo Bill was born.

TOP ANNUAL EVENTS

MARCH

Wichita Lawn, Flower, and
Garden Show
(316) 946-2840

Prairie Chicken Booming
Grounds, Cassoday
mid-Mar to mid-Apr, reservation only
(620) 735-4252

APRIL

Tulip Time Festival
Belle Plaine; third weekend
(316) 488-3451

MAY

Annual Bluegrass Festival
Park City; first weekend
(316) 744-2026

Wichita River Festival
ten days, beginning Friday before
Mother's Day
(877) 934-3378

JUNE

Midsummer's Day Festival
Lindsborg; third Saturday
(785) 227-3706 or (888) 227-2227

JULY

Great Plains Powwow
Wichita
(316) 350-3340

AUGUST

Country Threshing Days
Goessel; first weekend
(620) 367-8187

SEPTEMBER

Arts and Crafts Fair
Hillsboro; third Saturday
(620) 947-3506

Scottish Festival
McPherson; last weekend
(800) 324-8022

Walnut Valley Festival
Winfield; third week
(316) 221-3250

NOVEMBER

Antique Country Christmas
Kechi
(316) 744-9287

The *Keeper of the Plains,* a 44-foot, five-ton sculpture, broods over the *Mid-America All-Indian Center,* at 650 North Seneca, overlooking the confluence of the Arkansas and Little Arkansas Rivers. Its sculptor, the late Blackbear Bosin, was known throughout the art world. The center is a nonprofit organization founded to serve the cultural and social needs of Native Americans, and it features a museum, gift shop, and Heritage Village. Native American tacos and fry bread are served Tues and Wed from 11 a.m. to 2 p.m., as well as 5 to 8 p.m. on the first, second and fourth Wed. Powwows are held here several times a year; the public is welcome to watch the dancing, done in traditional dress. Hours are Tues through Sat from 10 a.m. to 4 p.m. year-round. Admission is $7 for adults, $5 for seniors, $3 for ages six to twelve. Call (316) 350-3340, or visit www.theindiancenter.org.

You can't miss the huge outdoor sculptures on the grounds of the *Wichita Art Museum,* 1400 West Museum Blvd. Titled "Dreamers Awake," they are said to represent the universal struggles of the human experience. Judge for yourself. For information, call (316) 268-4921 or visit www.wichitaartmuseum.org. Hours are Tues through Sat 10 a.m. to 5 p.m. and Sun noon to 5 p.m. Admission is $7, $5 for seniors, and $3 for students and children age five to seventeen.

Old Cowtown Museum, 1865 Museum Blvd., brings back the feel of the Old West. Located in what was once Delano, a frontier town is re-created along the banks of the Arkansas River. More than forty authentically furnished buildings are on seventeen acres, including Wichita's first residence, the Munger House, and the city's first jail. Also featured are a general store, drugstore, saloon, one-room schoolhouse, blacksmith shop, livery stable, and five-acre farm. Periodic living-history programs show how folks of the 1870s worked and played. Special events include an 1870s Independence Day, Frontier Days, an old-time county fair, and a prairie Victorian Christmas. Old Cowtown is open 10 a.m. to 4 p.m. Tues through Sat from mid-Dec through mid-Apr; the rest of the year, hours are 9:30 a.m. to 4:30 p.m. Wed through Sat and noon to 4:30 p.m. Sun. Admission is $7.75 for adults, $6.50 for seniors, $6 for children ages twelve through seventeen, and $5.50 for children ages four through eleven. Call (316) 219-1871 for information, or visit www.oldcowtown.org.

For a grand place to stay in the museum district and convenient to downtown, check into *The Castle Inn Riverside,* 1155 North River Blvd. Known as the Campbell Castle, the building is listed on the National Register of Historic Places. It is a Scottish castle by a storybook river, yet it is close to the heart of the city. In this century-old castle, you can escape to the romance of another era.

Old West Fades Away

Wichita was a cow town. It is said that at any one time there were as many as 100,000 head of longhorn cattle passing through. Since it took about fifteen cowboys to move a herd, that meant that there were large numbers of cowboys passing through. Of course, gamblers, "fancy ladies," and con artists also arrived. Wichita tried to keep the peace by outlawing guns and prostitution, so the action moved across the Arkansas River to the little town of Delano.

Delano was a wild and wide-open town. According to legend, on Sunday morning the "ladies" would have nude races to the river to entertain the cowboys. Rowdy Joe Lowe and his wife, Rowdy Kate, ran the most unruly saloon in town.

The town of Delano doesn't seem to exist anymore. It has been eaten up by Wichita. But people still remember Delano. Yes, indeed, they do.

Sunlight shines through stained glass and glows on intricate woodwork and exquisite antiques. Twelve of its fourteen rooms have fireplaces. You can relax in the billiards room or explore the turret. On weekends, wine and cheese is served from 5 to 7 p.m. and an assortment of homemade desserts, coffee, tea, and liqueurs provide a fun end to the evening. A home-cooked breakfast awaits you in the dining room. As picturesque as it is, the hotel has all the amenities for modern travelers. The room rates are $125 to $275. Call (316) 263-9300 or (800) 580-1131 or visit www.castleinnriverside.com.

The sweeping curves on Wichita's downtown riverfront skyline are the modernistic pavilions of *Exploration Place,* 300 North McLean. Not just a children's museum, Exploration Place appeals to all ages. Tots love watching a wall of bubbles or exploring the sounds of wind chimes. Older kids and adults are drawn to the flight pavilion, where a shimmering wind wall is in constant motion and trying out flight simulators is a popular activity. You can even walk a virtual dog in the health exhibit or play minigolf. Live daily broadcasts are made from a local television station's weather lab inside the museum. In addition to a motion simulation theater (where the seats move in sync to the film), Exploration Place boasts a Cyberdome Theater, a cutting-edge use of interactive computer graphics. You can have a bite to eat at The WaterWay Café. General admission is $9.50 for adults, $8 for seniors, $6 for children ages four to eleven, and free for children under four. Additional charge for minigolf, Simulation Center, and Cyberdome Theater. Hours are 10 a.m. to 5 p.m. Tues through Sat and noon to 5 p.m. Sun. Call (316) 660-0600 or check out www.exploration.org.

The *Wichita–Sedgwick County Historical Museum,* at 204 South Main St., is housed in the old City Hall. The chiming of the clock in the tower of the 1892 limestone building can be heard for blocks. Inside is an 1880s Victorian home interior, a late-nineteenth-century drugstore, and an early auto repair shop with a Wichita-built 1917 Jones six auto. Hours are Tues through Fri from 11 a.m. to 4 p.m., Sat and Sun from 1 to 5 p.m. Call (316) 265-9314 or visit www.wichitahistory.org. Admission is $4 adults, $2 children six to twelve.

In the historic midtown you'll find Wichita's Calvary Baptist Church, at 601 North Water, now the home of the *Kansas African American Museum.* Inside this large brick building with beautiful wooden beams and stained-glass windows, you can view artifacts and displays that provide insight into the history of blacks in Kansas.

The museum displays a collection of African and African-American artifacts and publications and changing exhibits about sports and entertainment personalities and black leaders in the fields of medicine, the military, and education. The museum is also the site of holiday caroling and spiritual assemblies that bring the old church alive with the power of gospel music.

The museum is open Tues through Fri from 9 a.m. to 5 p.m., Sun from 2 to 6 p.m. Donations are encouraged. For more information call (316) 262-7651 or visit www.tkaamuseum.org.

There are some parts of town that are uniquely Wichita, so get off the main streets and head toward **Wichita's Old Town District.** The district is 6 blocks east of Wichita's present downtown center and extends about 0.5 mile east of the Arkansas River. It includes the 700 to 900 blocks of East Douglas Avenue. This revitalized century-old warehouse district has brick streets, boardwalks, and streetlamps. More than 200 businesses are concentrated here, including restaurants, antiques shops, nightclubs, movies, and even dinner theater. There is plenty of free parking, and the trolley runs in this district.

Hotel at Old Town, 830 East First St., is a converted 1906 warehouse—the largest in the world when it opened. The atmosphere is early 1900s, but the amenities are thoroughly up-to-date. Inside you'll find spacious suites where you can cook a meal in a full kitchen, listen to your favorite music on the CD player, or pop downstairs to the old-style piano bar off the atrium. If you're staying in Wichita a few days or a few weeks, make plans to "stay with history." For reservations and prices call (316) 267-4800 or (877) 265-3869, or visit the Web site at www.hotelatoldtown.com for a virtual tour of the hotel.

If you and the children want to enjoy something together, the **Museum of World Treasures,** 835 East First St. in Old Town, is the place to visit. Sure to delight the youngsters is one of only four complete Tyrannosaurus skeletons in the world. It is displayed doing battle with its prey, a 30-foot Edmontosaurus and eight other real dinosaurs. But there's more: two Egyptian royal mummies and painted sarcophagi, crown jewels and swords of royalty from Bali, a Hollywood exhibit, a sports exhibit, a 4½-ton chunk of the Berlin Wall, a museum of military history—and the list goes on. There's a children's activity center to keep 'em busy, too. Go to the Web site at www.worldtreasures.org or call (316) 263-1311. Hours are Mon through Sat from 10 a.m. to 5 p.m. and Sun from noon to 5 p.m. Admission is $8.95 adults, $7.95 seniors, $6.95 youths four to twelve.

Step over to 234 North Mosley St. in Old Town and enjoy the **Mosley Street Melodrama,** where villains abound and heroes save the day. It's dinner and fun in one cozy little place. Call (316) 263-0222 or visit www.mosleystreet .com for showtimes.

For drama on the bigscreen, visit the **Warren Old Town** (353 North Mead, 316-691-9700). The Warren Theatres have revolutionized movie experiences for Wichitans in recent years with luxury seating and state-of-the-art technology. The Old Town location, however, has a special twist: food and drinks. Enjoy a Cuban sandwich or alfredo pasta from the highly diverse Old Town Theatre Grill, along with an import beer or a bottle of wine—all while you enjoy the latest blockbuster from a comfy, reclining chair. Evening shows cost $10. For just five dollars more, though, you can enjoy the Director's Suite's leather recliners, full bar and prompt service at the touch of a button. Afterward, discuss the flick with a drink on the patio. The Director's Suite is for ages twenty-one and up. See www.warrenoldtown.com.

Near Old Town you'll find a rare culinary treat: *Nu Way Cafe* (1416 West Douglas Ave., 316-267-1131). This Wichita original has thrived since 1930 in this tiny, humble building. The star of the menu is the eponymous Nu Way sandwich, a pile of crumbly, well-seasoned ground beef on a hamburger bun with your choice of fixin's (try the classic, old-school version with mustard, onion and pickle). The Nu Way comes in medium and large sizes, and the restaurant motto, "crumbly is good," rings true. Other longtime menu items include pork loin sandwiches, homemade onion rings, fresh-cut curly fries, and tater tots. The prices are as good as the food—a combo meal, including a Nu Way, side and drink, runs around four bucks. The restaurant has four other locations throughout the city; visit www.nuwaycafe.com.

For another unique, fast-food experience, try *Dog-N-Shake,* a fixture of fried goodness since 1948. There are five locations; I can attest that the one at 8800 West Maple St. (316-722-3971) will serve you the most delicious, lovingly seasoned cheese fries to be found. Other fare includes ice-cream shakes of many flavors and variations on the hot dog (hence the name, Dog-N-Shake): chili dogs, chili cheese dogs, kraut dogs, spicy Polish sausage and corn dogs. Authentic cherry limemades can also be found here. Check out www.dognshake.com.

If you like dinner theater, this town has another. The *Crown-Uptown Dinner Theatre,* at 3207 East Douglas Ave, offers professional performances of Broadway shows each week, along with a buffet and bar. Dinner begins Thurs through Sat at 6 p.m. and Sun at 4:15 p.m. Performance follows. There is also a matinee on Thurs at 11:30 a.m. and a special children's matinee on Fri and Sat at 11:15 a.m. Call (316) 681-1566 for information or reservations, or visit www.crownuptown.com.

Across the river from Old Town is the *Historic Delano District.* Period lighting, historic plaques, and walking tours are in the works for this area. Practically a local institution is retailer *Hatman Jack's,* 601 West Douglas. "The largest selection of hats in the state" is no idle boast; you can choose from western hats, derbies, golf hats, and caps of all kinds. Jack Kellogg is one of only about thirty custom hatters in the United States. Hours are 10 a.m. to 5:30 p.m. weekdays, except Thurs, when the store stays open until 6 p.m. Sat hours are 10 a.m. to 5 p.m. Call (316) 264-4881 or (800) 347-4287, or visit www.hatmanjacks.com.

Need some camping equipment? Visit the *Coleman Factory Outlet Store and Museum* at 235 North St. Francis St., where you will find everything for the outdoors. There is also a museum display of vintage Coleman products (the earliest lanterns are especially collectible). Hours are Mon through Fri from 9 a.m. to 6 p.m., Sat from 9 a.m. to 1 p.m. Call (316) 264-0836.

The Clifton Square Shopping Village (3700 East Douglas Ave.) is a collection of shops in **College Hill**, a lovely nineteenth-century neighborhood. Shop for art, gifts, clothing, and collectibles, or find the only wine-and-jazz experience in College Hill. The stores are open Mon through Sat 10 a.m. to 5:30 p.m. Call (316) 686-2177 for tours or visit www.cliftonsquare.com for more information.

For a closer look at the animal kingdom, visit **Sedgwick County Zoo,** 5555 Zoo Blvd., just off Interstate 235 on Wichita's west side. It's consistently ranked among the top zoos in the country and is the number one outdoor attraction in the state. The 247-acre zoo is home to 2,700 animals from around the world. Exhibit areas include a gorilla forest, a tiger trek, a penguin cove, and a misty rain forest. The *Pride of the Plains* exhibit hosts African lions, meerkats, and warthogs, making it a favorite among young movie fans. Admission is $11.50 adults, $7 for children, $5 for seniors. The zoo is open 364 days a year (closing once in Sept to prepare for a fundraiser). Hours are 8:30 a.m. to 5 p.m. Mar through Oct and 10 a.m. to 5 p.m. Nov through Feb. Call (316) 660–WILD (9453) or visit www.scz.org.

The Inn at Willowbend (at 3939 Comotara St., near the intersection of Thirty-seventh and Rock Road on Wichita's northeastern edge) overlooks the championship Willowbend Golf Course. Steve Sonnoman is the innkeeper. Golf is the theme of this sprawling stucco building. Complimentary drinks are served at cocktail hour, and breakfast specialties such as banana buckwheat pancakes are available in the morning. There are forty-four rooms, all with private bath. British decor throughout the inn and paintings of Scottish golf courses keep golf in mind, and the massive fireplace in the St. Andrews' Lounge makes you feel as though you are right in the ancient golf club itself. Rates range from $89 to $159, depending on room size and day of the week; breakfast is included. Call (316) 636-4032 or (800) 553-5775, or visit www.theinnatwillowbend.net.

Red Barn Ostrich Farm Bed and Breakfast (6427 North Greenwich Rd.) offers guests an unusual setting 0.25 mile north of Highway 254. Early risers are rewarded by a view of 150 ostriches performing their sunrise ballet. And even if you don't get up early you can have a complete tour of Sue and Bob Johnson's farm. The Johnsons raise ostriches from eggs to yearlings. There are three guest rooms with private bath. For breakfast, steaming breads come straight from the oven every morning, and Sue's homemade jam and fresh fruits and juices are followed by a full specialty entree. Rooms are $75 per night. Call (316) 744-9800 or e-mail sue@redbarn.biz. Advance reservations are requested. The Johnsons sell ostrich leather goods, too.

For technological fun, head for **Laser Quest** at 2120 North Woodlawn 470, also in the northeastern part of Wichita. Play in swirling fog accompanied by space-age music and lighting. Don your LQ pack, get a personalized score-card, and go for it. Call (316) 652-9500 or visit www.laserquest.com. Hours are Wed and Thurs 6 p.m. to 9 p.m., Fri 4 to 11 p.m., Sat noon to 11 p.m., Sun 1 to 6 p.m. Admission costs $8.

The **Lake Afton Public Observatory,** 1845 Fairmount (316-978-3191), is 15 miles southwest of Wichita off Highway 42. Far, far away from city lights, the observatory's telescopes offer marvelous views of the moon, planets, and galaxies from one large 16-inch telescope and several small ones. See star clusters, double stars, and other celestial wonders. Photography night lets you bring your 35mm camera and some 200 or 400 ASA film and shoot the valleys and craters of the moon and the rings of Jupiter. The observatory also contains exhibits and displays. Drive west on U.S. Highway 54 (Kellogg Drive) to the Lake Afton sign. Go south 3 miles on Viola Road and 1 mile east on MacArthur Road. Follow the signs. There are programs on Fri and Sat nights from approximately 7:30 until 10 p.m. (times change slightly each month as the days lengthen). There is an admission charge of $4 for adults, $3 for children ages seven to twelve; children age six and younger are free. Call ahead for a recorded message of times and special events, (316) WSU–STAR, or visit www.wichita.edu/LAPO.

East of Wichita 1 mile north of US 54 (Kellogg Drive) on 159th Street in **Andover** is a golfer's dream: **Terradyne,** a Scottish-style eighteen-hole golf course at 1400 Terradyne Dr. This is a true Scottish course of rolling fairways with few trees and characteristic Scottish peaks, hills, and hidden bunkers. An experience every golfer should have until he or she can take that dream trip to St. Andrews (or Turnberry, or Royal Troon, or Murfield—dream on, golfers). The European-style clubhouse is reminiscent of St. Andrews with the Old World elegance of its marble floors and the dark, rich woodwork. **The Greens** restaurant is quite good, too. This is a resort hotel and country club, so hotel guests can play there if you call ahead for tee times at (316) 733-2582 or (800) 892-4613; or visit www.terradyne-resort.com.

Before you leave Wichita on a warm summer night, you might want to slip in to the **Starlite Twin Drive-In** at 3900 South Hydraulic St. (exit 2 from Interstate 135) for a movie or two (or three). Starlite has twin screens and double features. In fact, on Fri and Sat nights there is a bonus triple feature. This is a big drive-in that holds 1,300 cars. Call (316) 524-3267 or visit www.starlitefun .com to see what's playing.

East of Wichita on US 54, the little town of **Augusta** features the **C. N. James Log Cabin** at 305 State St. Built in 1868, the cabin was known as the Shamleffer and James General Store. It is one and a half stories tall and built of hand-hewn cottonwood logs from along the Walnut River. It is one of only two log cabins at their original site in the state. At one time it was Augusta's first school, with thirty-four students in the upper loft. It was the meeting place for the Baptist and Methodist churches and the Masonic Lodge. In the late 1870s, the loft was raised and it became a two-story cabin. Lap siding was added. Since then it has been a boardinghouse, residence, and woodworking shop. Now it is part of the **Augusta Historical Museum,** where you can also buy some of the top-selling books on Kansas. Museum hours are 11 a.m. to 3 p.m. Mon through Fri and 11 a.m. to 4 p.m. Sat and Sun. Call (316) 775-5655 or see www.augustahistoricalsociety.net. There is no charge, but donations are accepted.

Listed on the National Register of Historic Places is the **Augusta Theatre,** 523 State St., built in 1935 and featuring an elaborate art deco interior. It is host to movies, live theater, and music sponsored by the Augusta Arts Council. Call (316) 775-3661 for events information, or visit www.augustahistorictheatre.com.

Almost 4 miles east of Augusta on Highway 154 is a Spanish windmill. It serves no purpose other than as the quixotic target for a sharp, angular sculpture of a man on horseback.

If tilting at windmills piques your interest, you will want a closer look at the other unusual creations on **Henry's Sculpture Hill.** There are more than forty welded-metal sculpture scenes created by Franklin Jensen.

There is *Don Quixote,* of course, followed by his companion, *Sancho Panza.* Next is a scene based on e.e. cummings's poem "Chanson Innocente"—Pan leading four children. *Redbone,* the running larger-than-life bison, is made of strips of redwood decking attached to an angled iron frame. From the highway you can see a 24-foot-long praying mantis, which weighs as much as a small truck, preparing to strike a grasshopper; *Leo the Lion* pawing the air; an eagle turning to catch the wind; and a boy walking a cow home. There are more than one hundred sculptures, most outside, but some inside the barn.

All of this has evolved from Jensen's interest in literature and art (he was a high-school English teacher in Wichita). A few years ago he decided he needed more space and bought the twenty-eight acres. Several of the sculptures found there are visible from the highway. Visit www.sculpturehill.com for more information. East of Augusta, just south of Highway 96, is the town of **Beaumont,** a historic cow town. The **Old Frisco Water Tower** built in 1885 for the Frisco Railroad steam engines provided water for the railroad roundhouse and cattle-shipping operations. It is the last remaining railroad water tower in the state and is on the National Register of Historic Places. It is at Main and Eleventh Streets.

One mile south of Highway 400 (between mile markers 319/320) is the **Beaumont Hotel** at 11651 Southeast Main St. (620-843-2422). Beaumont used to be a magnet for cattle buyers visiting the surrounding big cattle ranches. In

1953, a 2,600-foot north-south native grass airstrip was carved out of the prairie so airplanes could come in. Now the Beaumont is a homing beacon to all pilots and travelers who want to touch down for just a cold drink, or for a hot bath, a great meal, and a night's sleep. The hotel's renovation and reopening was welcomed, and it is now listed on the National Register of Historic Places. Four suites with private baths, and seven bed-and-breakfast rooms, a homey screened-in porch, a dining room accented with period log furniture, and a gleaming kitchen make this a choice spot to land. The hotel is open daily as a bed-and-breakfast, and the café dishes up hearty menus Wed through Sun Mar through Dec. Visit www.hotelbeaumontks.com.

The Beaumont adjoins a 10,000 acre working cattle ranch and is near the Tall Grass Prairie National Park, so guests may also enjoy wagon rides and campfire cookouts, shop for antiques, or view works by local artists.

Café hours are Wed 11 a.m. to 3 p.m. and Thurs 11 a.m. to 8 p.m., Fri and Sat from 7 a.m. to 9 p.m., and Sun from 7 a.m. until 3 p.m.

This was always a personal favorite because we could fly into Beaumont in our Navion, taxi right up to the hotel, eat in the café, and spend the night deep in the Flint Hills. If you are flying in, the airport identifier is SM07. When you plan your flight, be sure to include the GPS coordinates for the Beaumont Hotel (SN07)—or DME off the 086° radial Wichita VOR (ICT) at 49 nautical miles. Unicom 122.9. Latitude and longitude coordinates are N 37–39.553/W 96–31.652.

Northwest of Andover on Highway 254 is the town of *Kechi* (pronounced *KEECH-eye*), birthplace of actress Kirstie Alley (her family operated Kechi Lumber) and the official antiques capital of Kansas. The town is filled with antiques shops, boutiques, food, fine arts, stained glass, and crafts of all kinds. Kechi was settled in 1865, and it still has a comfortable, small-town feel. There's even summer theater. About a dozen shops are open all year, with independent hours as posted.

One of these shops is *Karg Art Glass* at 111 North Oliver St. (316-744-2442), where you can watch glassblowers work their magic. Rollin Karg studied hot glass at Emporia State University, and he and his wife, Patti, decided to build their own furnace in Kechi. The large, open studio allows visitors to watch the blowers and learn how each piece is made. A gift gallery featuring sixty to eighty other artists has an exquisite collection of art glass. Glassblowers work Mon, Tues, Thurs, and Fri from 8 a.m. to 3:30 p.m. and Sat from 8 to noon. The gallery is open Mon through Sat from 8 a.m. to 6 p.m. and Sun from 11 a.m. to 4 p.m.

Other attractions are *Turkey Creek Weaving* and the *Kechi Playhouse* on North Oliver. Look at the town's Web site to get the full picture of what the town has to offer at www.kechikscoc.com, or call the chamber of commerce at (316) 640-3615. You can also visit www.kechikansas.org.

For modern man, the beaten path is covered with asphalt. But for the pioneers, the deep grooves worn into the earth by wagon wheels and horses' hoofs offered a certain amount of security. Getting off the beaten path was not a good idea. Today the ruts, called "swales," can still be seen in many places where the Santa Fe Trail crossed the prairie. If you think you are ready to get on that beaten path, ready for an adventure unlike any other today, then join the *Flint Hills Overland Wagon Train Trips,* which leave about five times a year from Cassoday, off the Kansas Turnpike (I-35) at the junction of U.S. Highway 177, for wagon-train trips across the central prairie.

Traveling away from modern roadways and through picturesque parts of the state, participants use horses, covered wagons, and coaches. Hearty meals (including coffee ground at the campsite and brewed in a sock—a clean one), evening entertainment (seasoned trail riders strumming guitars around the campfire, and maybe a tall tale or two), and a sunrise worship service are included in the tours. It is a once-in-a-lifetime adventure to see the glory of the Flint Hills "up close and personal."

The overnight trip is for nature lovers, for people who like to camp out and rough it, and who want to experience the life of the pioneers. Call (316) 321-6300, or visit www.wagontrainkansas.com for information. The cost of the overnight trip—round-trip first class (1878 style)—is $190 for adults and $150 for kids ages four to twelve. Toddlers ride free (and love it). You can go along as a trail rider with your own horse for $130.

The town of *Towanda* is 5 miles west of El Dorado on I-35 (exit 71). The *Paradise Doll Museum,* at 119 South Sixth St. (316-536-2678), is a repair facility for antique dolls. There are more than 5,000 examples on display, as well as regional craft items for sale. Owner Barbara Brush charges no admission. Her motto is "If I can fix it, I will," and she does—any kind of doll new or old. She lives nearby and will open by appointment. Official hours are Tues through Sat from 1 to 5 p.m.

trivia

Kansas ranks as the fourth windiest state. Only Massachusetts, Montana, and Wyoming are windier.

There are two and a half cows for each person in Kansas.

The *Kansas Oil Museum* is at 383 East Central in *El Dorado.* At the Texaco theater you can watch a video of one of the state's oil-drilling rigs in operation. There are also three working scale models of various rigs, and outdoors there is an oil field lease house furnished 1930s style. The house functions as a research facility and has extensive archives. The Teter Nature Trail is a 1.25-mile walking path through eight acres of wilderness with a diverse collection of plant and animal life. Visible from the path is a 100-foot steel oil derrick and rotary rig mast. Open from 9 a.m. to 5 p.m. Mon through Sat, from May through Sept. The rest of the year, hours are 9 a.m. to 5 p.m. Tues through Fri and noon to 5 p.m. Sat. Call (316) 321-9333 or visit www.kansasoilmuseum.org.

The *Coutts Memorial Museum of Art* (316-321-1212) is in the Bluestem Building in downtown El Dorado at 110 North Main and houses more than 1,000 original paintings, prints, drawings, and sculptures by such artists as Thomas Hart Benton and Frederic Remington. It is open 1 to 5 p.m. Mon, Wed and Fri, 9 a.m. to 5 p.m. Tues and Thurs, and noon to 4 p.m. Sat.

El Dorado State Park and Wildlife Area is nearby, between US 177 and I-35, and has a well-stocked lake. Hunting and fishing are allowed in season.

The town of *Cassoday*—the prairie chicken capital of the world—is on US 177, just off the Kansas Turnpike. From Towanda take Highway 254/US 54 east to US 177. There are cattle and horses in the pastures. There is nothing contrived or phony about Cassoday; this is a very real cow town. Beef and bread are the staples, and there are cowboys everywhere.

Cassoday is popular with upland game hunters and touring cyclists who can camp in the city park on their way through the Flint Hills. Lots of ranches dot the countryside. This is where cattle are brought in to "go to grass," sort of a last fling before they become prime meat. Herding cattle is not just cowboy history, it's the real thing, because cattle are brought from all over the country to graze on the rich bluestem grasslands of the Flint Hills.

If you want to see bull riding—the real thing, western style—the *Sankey Ranch* is the place to go in *Rose Hill,* southeast of Wichita. Bud Sankey and his two sons, Lyle and Ike, will teach you how to ride a bull. Why would

The Prickly Pear: Eat with Caution!

A surprise to most visitors is the common prickly pear cactus, which grows throughout the state in dry, gravelly soil. Flowers of the prickly pear are yellow, orange, or even red. The fruit of this cactus is edible and quite sweet, but it contains many small seeds. The secret is to chew lightly and swallow the seeds whole. A food source for early Native Americans, the prickly pear is still harvested for its fruit, which is sold in grocery stores. Proceed with caution, though. As the name warns, the fruit has many nasty little prickles on its skin.

anyone want to learn to ride a bull, you might ask? (Bud says, "For cash. Why else would anyone do it?") Well, maybe. But there are those who do it just for the excitement. For a mere $400 for three days, men come from all over the country to ride bulls. These are not wanna-be cowboys, they are professional men (doctors, lawyers, and CEOs), working men, young fellas who are looking at a career in rodeo, rodeo wanna-bes, and the occasional woman; people who just have to try everything. Bud admits he discourages women because his bulls are "just too rough" for them. Ladies, do you hear a challenge there?

Bud is justifiably proud of his sons. Lyle is the number-one instructor in the country and two-time National Finals Rodeo (NFR) Champion; four days in the arena with him will have you riding. With both indoor and outdoor arenas, there are no rain delays in this sport. Every ride is recorded so riders can see what they are doing wrong (a souvenir you can play and replay for your friends back home).

Ike is the top contractor for the NFR and offers world-champion bucking horses. You are in good hands at Sankey Ranch. So are the bulls. Bud says the bulls are worth a lot of dollars and they take good care of them. They work an eight-second shift, then get time off. Bud has been ranching here for twenty-five years. It is a professionally run operation.

Not so sure about that bull-riding thrill? Well, you can come to the ranch and just watch other people (who are braver than you) get flipped into the sawdust. Bud asks that you call ahead to arrange a time to watch, but you surely are welcome, he says.

Bud also has a full line of very good saddles and roping equipment for sale in the shop at the ranch. For dates, call (417) 263-7777 and talk to Lyle, or log on to www.sankeyrodeo.com, then get on the next plane to Kansas.

To find Sankey Ranch, take the Andover exit from I-35 West. Go right through Andover and cross US 54. Five miles south, turn east on 150th Street, then watch for signs leading to the ranch.

The last thing you expect to see in Kansas is the **Golden Gate Bridge.** But it's there, all right, crossing Cow Skin Creek in **Mulvane.** Larry Richardson, a mail carrier, and Barbara, his wife of almost thirty years, live nearby. Their cost of living isn't as high as it is in say, San Francisco, but their home at 1414 North Peaceful Lane is not as big a tourist attraction—yet. Larry and his dad, Norman (who worked as a machinist for Boeing), took nine years to built this incredible sight—totally by hand, mind you—and you won't believe it until you see it. It measures 24 feet to the top, is half a football field in length, used twenty-seven tons of concrete and 400 feet of continuous cable, and cost more than $5,000. (Makes you wonder if it has a working toll gate.) At 8 feet wide, it is probably one of the largest suspension bridges in Kansas. Larry told

Barbara, back in the '60s, that they couldn't get married until "[I] crossed the Golden Gate Bridge and got my service done." He was headed for Vietnam. Larry crossed that bridge in San Francisco and sent a post card home to Barbara, and that simple postcard was the model they used for this incredible feat. It has precisely the same dimensions as the original Golden Gate Bridge, only one-twentieth the size. There have been two weddings on the bridge, one with close to 500 guests, and since it is lighted at night, it was a beautiful setting. And a Model A car club motored there just to see it. There was even a group of ladies who called themselves a "bridge club," but they didn't play cards, they drove around looking at bridges. Finding the bridge is tricky because Peaceful Lanc isn't on any map except the 911 emergency map. So, since the bridge is actually on private property, calling ahead for directions is a good plan. To find the bridge go 3 miles west on Highway 53, turn south on Hillsdale Road, and go three-quarters of a mile to the low-water bridge, where you will turn right on Lynn Street (you will see a sign that says THS L DU). Best to call the Richardsons at (316) 777-1561 to get directions and meet this couple. They enjoy showing off the bridge and have shown it to thousands since the bridge was featured on the *Today Show*.

Wyldewood Cellars Winery (951 East 119th St.; 316-554–WINE or 316-554-9463) is south of Wichita, west of the turnpike (exit 33) west of Muluané in the town of *Peck.* It is the largest supplier of elderberry wine in the country. Take a guided tour and sample some of the delicious wine. The Marketplace features not only the wines but also other specialties, such as elderberry jelly and syrup and other Kansas products, including homemade fudge. You can send gift boxes home. The winery is open 9 a.m. to 6 p.m. Mon through Sat, noon to 5 p.m. Sun. If you paid a turnpike toll, the receipt is a credit toward your purchases. Call (316) 554-9463, visit www.wyldewoodcellars.com, or order by calling (800) 711-9748.

trivia

There is a Tourist Information Station in Belle Plaine on Interstate 35/Kansas Turnpike at milepost 25.7.

For the past seventy-five-plus years, thousands of tourists have descended on *Belle Plaine,* south of Wichita, to see the *Bartlett Arboretum,* at Highway 55 and Line Street. This twenty-acre garden planted in 1910 by the Bartlett family is now a mature arboretum with trees, shrubs, flowers, and grasses from all over the world.

The arboretum is unique in that it flowers in all growing seasons. In the spring, 30,000 tulips are bordered by 5,000 pansies. The garden contains fifteen varieties of flowering trees and shrubs. Summer annuals are planted in May.

Along Euphrates Creek, thousands of yellow water iris are naturalized, adding sunny color to the display.

Shade trees line the pathways, a cool relief from the hot Kansas sun. In the fall a brilliant panorama of chrysanthemums and changing foliage compresses the color of the country into the arboretum. Open by appointment only. For more information call (620) 488-3451 or visit www.bartlettarboretum.com.

Windswept Winery, 1227 Ninety-second Rd., is a family-owned and operated winery surrounded by vineyards in *Udall.* The Kansas-grown grapes and fruit are made into red, white, and blush wines. There's an apple and blackberry wine, too. Wander through the large and well-kept vineyards. Pick blackberries, in season, in the acre and a half of thornless blackberry plants, and enjoy the resident bluebirds. Each season has its beauty here. Enjoy a free tour of the winery and the surrounding vineyards, and stop for a free tasting of the many varieties of sweet wines. There is a gift shop as well. The winery is open daily from 1 to 7 p.m. weekdays, 10 a.m. to 7 p.m. Sat and 1 to 6 p.m. Sun. The winery is twenty minutes southeast of Wichita, 1¾ miles east of Twenty-first Road on Ninety-second Road. Visit the Web site for a map and more details; www.windsweptwinery.com, or call (620) 782-3952.

Along the peaceful western bank of the Arkansas River lies the small town of *Oxford,* southeast of Belle Plaine on U.S. Highway 160. It is filled with retirees and people who commute to nearby communities to work. The 113-year-old *Old Oxford Grist Mill* northeast of Oxford processed grain with the power of the river until recent years; artists travel here to capture the picturesque mill. Oxford also contains the oldest building and church in the county.

Winfield's Vietnam War Memorial Wall grew from the twenty-fifth class reunion, in 1988, of a young man killed in that war. Hal McCoy found a friend's name on the Washington, D.C., memorial and went to his classmates with his idea for a replica of that memorial. It was originally intended to honor the casualties among classmates, family, and neighbors in Cowley County. The project grew, the cost grew, but the people of *Winfield* would not let it fail. Classmates of Gary Bannon raised nearly $100,000, and on Veterans Day 1989, on behalf of the Winfield High School Class of 1963, McCoy presented the memorial honoring all servicemen and nurses from the state of Kansas who died in Southeast Asia. There are 778 names of servicemen and women who were killed or missing in action. It's in Memorial Park between Ninth and Tenth Avenues, along with a central white cenotaph honoring all veterans.

The *Walnut Valley Festival* has been held at Cowley County Fairgrounds on US 160 on Winfield's west side the third week in Sept for more than thirty years. It is four days of toe-tapping, knee-slapping, hand-clapping music. This is a true all-acoustic bluegrass music festival, even though bluegrass is only one kind of music you will hear. If you are a fan of western, Irish, folk, blues, or Cajun music, this festival is for you, too. Winfield isn't called the "Picker's Paradise" for nothing. Locals say it usually rains the weekend of the festival, and regulars come prepared. They say it is a must-do-at-least-once-in-your-lifetime event. Right up there with Woodstock. Once, the flooded Walnut River came up and lapped at the toes of those in the campground, but they unplugged their hookups and just kept on picking. Good thing the music is acoustic. Call (620) 221-3250 or visit www.wvfest.com.

The **Chisholm Trail Museum** is in nearby **Wellington.** In 1867 the Chisholm Trail, first marked by trader Jesse Chisholm for his wagons, wound from Abilene to San Antonio. It became a famous cattle trail, where more than a million head of Texas steers were driven to the shipping center of Abilene. Later, settlers moved in and fenced the land. The museum's collection has been donated by the descendants of those pioneers. Located at 502 North Washington St., 4 blocks west of US 160, the museum is open weekends spring and fall, and weekday afternoons in summer. It is closed in the winter because the building is difficult to keep warm. Call (620) 326-3820 for the current schedule.

West on U.S. Highway 81 is **Caldwell,** dubbed the Border Queen City by cowboys on the Chisholm Trail. **The Cherokee Strip Visitors Center and Museum,** (620) 845-2975, at the city park on West Central, retells the story of the Oklahoma Land Rush.

Eddie Morrison is a sculptor whose work is exhibited throughout the country. This Native American artist is the grandson of a Cherokee. He says he feels the presence of the Great Creator in every piece he makes. A half block off Main Street on Central, you can see an example of his work titled *Those Who Came Before*, a limestone relief depicting the cultures that have influenced this area. Call (620) 845-6666.

Other artists have left their mark in Caldwell. You can see *Cowboys Driving Cattle,* a 1941 mural by Kenneth Evett, a student of Thomas Hart Benton, on

How the Chisholm Trail Began

The only cattle Jesse Chisholm ever drove were oxen yoked to a freight wagon. He was neither a cowboy nor a cattleman. Born in 1805, Chisholm was the son of a Scottish father and a Cherokee mother. He established a trading post where Wichita now stands and cut a trail south to Mexico through Indian Territory. While Chisholm set the trail as a trade route, the "Chisholm Trail" opened the way to the railheads in Kansas, and in turn the eastern markets, for the great herds of Texas longhorns.

the south wall of the Caldwell post office at 14 North Main. Another mural is at the south side of Heritage Park at 102 South Main—a charming depiction of the historical progression of life on the plains by local artist Brenda Lebeda Almond.

Two miles south of Caldwell off US 81, watch for the **Ghost Riders of the Chisholm Trail.** These silhouettes are frozen in steel and concrete. The ghosts can be seen from US 81 on the windswept red bluff nearby. The life-size sculpture of a herd of longhorn cattle, a chuck wagon pulled by horses, and cowboys on horseback look startlingly real. So lifelike is the scene, observers are certain they have noticed both dust and sounds coming from the bluff.

This amazing piece of art has been named a Kansas Historical Attraction by the Kansas Historical Society. The ghosts will forever remind us of the great cattle drives of 1866 to 1886, when millions of Texas longhorn cattle passed here on their way to the other legendary railhead cow towns. Caldwell was the first stop on the trail after miles of Indian Territory, and it was so rowdy that in six years the town went through sixteen marshals. Today a church steeple graces the top of Mount Lookout, but in those days, it was the "border queens" who excitedly watched for the cattle herds approaching the town and the eager cowboys who rode with them.

Arkansas City (pronounced *Ar-KAN-sas*, remember?), east on US 166, was actually settled prior to 1870, but that was the year the sawmill and the flour and feed mills began operation. Nestled in a bluff at the confluence of the Arkansas and Walnut Rivers and at the north end of beautiful Kaw Lake, Ark City, as it is called locally, has played a vital role in the development of Indian lands to the south in Oklahoma.

Two of the most exciting races in the history of the country began here— the Run of 1889 and the renowned **Cherokee Strip Run,** for which 100,000 people arrived months months in advance to await the pistol shots signaling the start of the race at noon, Sept 16, 1893. Eager settlers raced south to claim land in modern-day Oklahoma, jockeying for position in every kind of trans-port you can imagine—oxcarts, covered wagons, bicycles, and horses of every description. In addition, thousands walked, or ran, to find homesteads.

South on US 77 at Arkansas City, you will find the **Cherokee Strip Land Rush Museum** on South Summit Street Road (31639 Hwy. 77, 620-442-6750, www.arkcity.org). More than 7,000 artifacts telling the history of the strip from the 1880s to the 1920s are housed here. It's open year-round Tues through Sat 10 a.m. to 5 p.m. Closed major holidays. Admission is $4.50 for adults, $3.50 for seniors, and $2 for kids ages six through twelve.

The **Chaplin Nature Center,** Route 1, Arkansas City (620 442 4133, www .wichitaaudubon.org), along the shores of the Arkansas River, combines 200 acres of magnificent woodlands, prairies, and streams into a beautiful preserve.

More Than One Hundred Years of Testimony

In the early twentieth century, passengers on the northbound Santa Fe out of Arkansas City could see the words CHRIST DIED FOR THE UNGODLY in large white stones. Then in smaller letters they could read the Bible citation from the Book of Romans, where these words are found. Today, the letters can be seen northbound on the U.S. Highway 77 bypass.

One man supposedly was responsible. Fred Horton was a young dispatcher who came to Arkansas City with his bride when the Santa Fe line crossed into Oklahoma, just south of the town, in 1889. His daughter Ruth tells how at the end of the day her mother would hitch their horse to the phaeton, and they would drive down to the south yards to her father. Every evening he went to the north hills to work on his project. He did it almost single-handedly.

Horton rebuilt his quotation three times over a thirty-year period to get it the size and shape it is today. Each letter is 18 feet high, 12 feet wide, and 3 feet deep. The quotation is about 475 feet long and is built of stone from the hillside on which it stands.

For more than a hundred years the stones have testified to Horton's beliefs. The Auxiliary to the Brotherhood of Locomotive Engineers undertook the project of having the text set in cement. Currently, the Jaycees keep it weeded and washed.

Here you can see, smell, hear, and feel nature with discovery trails, guided nature walks, bird counts, and a naturalist on duty. It is open Sat from 9 a.m. to 5 p.m. and Sun from 1 to 5 p.m. Weekday hours in July and Aug are 10 a.m. to 2 p.m. It is closed from the end of Nov to mid-Mar, but the free natural trails are open from sunrise to sunset every day of the year.

Grouse Creek, near *Silverdale,* is a lively stream with clear water. It runs through the *Kaw Wildlife Area.* There are no official campgrounds, but gravel bars provide good campsites. If the first riffle at the put-in is navigable, the entire stream may be floated without difficulty. If you follow Grouse Creek as it twists and turns beside the country roads, you will pass old ranches with stone houses and barns, limestone cliffs, and even a waterfall before you reach Oklahoma. Be sure to get landowners' permission if canoeing outside the public lands.

Henry's "Better Made" Candies (620-876-5423) is in its fourth generation of candy making in *Dexter,* northeast of Arkansas City on Highway 15. Evelyn Pudden and her daughters currently run the business, started in 1890 when Tom Henry began work in a candy shop in Boston at the age of ten. He was the inventor of the original Oh, Henry! candy bar. Now an average of

It's a Gas

Dexter is the self-proclaimed Wind Gas Capital of the World. Around 1903, in the heyday of wildcatting, folks here drilled for oil. They planned a celebration when the well came in, including a torch lighting. The well came in and grand torches were brought to ignite the gas, but the gas blew the torches out. The process was repeated with the same results. The oil folks were disappointed until some time later, when it was discovered that the "wind gas" was natural helium. It was the first discovery of helium in the United States. Soon the Navy began bringing dirigibles from the Olathe Naval Air Station and refueling virtually right out of the ground. Later the helium was used as a coolant in various nuclear projects.

65,000 pounds of candy, more than one hundred kinds (including taffy, fudge, and sugar-free candies) are made annually. The shop is open to the public seven days a week. Evelyn has been in this sweet business her whole life—she loves it. Look for a big red-and-white building on Highway 15. Hours are from 8 a.m. to 5 p.m. Mon through Sat and from 9 a.m. to 5 p.m. Sun. There are candy-making demos at 1:15 p.m. on Sun.

Dexter is in the southern part of the Flint Hills; every spring a redbud tour from Cedar Vale to Sedan runs over backcountry roads beside stone fences and clear creeks. It is an even prettier drive in the fall, when the oak trees turn russet.

The town of **Sedan,** at the junction of US 166 and Highway 99, is the hometown of "Weary Willy," probably the world's most famous clown. Behind the greasepaint was Sedan native Emmett Kelly. A museum in his honor has been created in an 1896 opera house on Main Street. *The Emmett Kelly Museum* houses memorabilia of the famous clown and his son Emmett Jr. You'll also find exhibits connected with D. W. Washburn, also known as Sparky the Clown. Washburn was a juggler, ventriloquist, magician, and pantomimist born in Chanute. Admission is free, but donations are welcome. Call (620) 725-3470 for hours or visit www.emmettkelly museum.com.

Sedan is also the home of the *Yellow Brick Road* (150 East Main St.), where you can put your name on an 8-by-10-inch brick in the Main Street sidewalk downtown. The road now has 10,000-plus bricks, with names from every state of the union and twenty-eight foreign countries, and a special brick for sister city, Sedan, France.

Old hardware stores are a piece of Americana, and *Ackarman's,* at 160 East Main (620-725-3103), has been a downtown gathering place since 1897.

The ***Chautauqua Hills Jelly Company,*** on Main Street in Sedan (620-725-4022), was founded when a group of thirty-three Kansans came together to help revitalize their community by beginning a new industry. The gourmet jelly brand is now distributed by ***Red Buffalo Country,*** whose gift store you can visit Wed through Sat from 10 a.m. to 5 p.m. Red Buffalo Country (www.theredbuffalo .com) is a multifaceted business owned by Bill Kurtis of A&E and History Channel fame. Red Buffalo Country manages lodging, organizes hunting trips and raises buffalo. At the ***Red Buffalo Ranch,*** you can ride wagons through the incredible tallgrass country or walk the miles of nature trails. A delicious chuckwagon dinner and old-fashioned entertainment will top off your evening. Red Buffalo is the Osage name for fire on the prairie—it comes like a red buffalo over the hills—and although burning is necessary for the prairie to survive, the winds can catch the flames and create a wall of flame 30 feet high.

Next stop is ***Elk Falls,*** where you can walk on the 1893 Iron Truss Bridge and have a wonderful view of the natural waterfalls. The bridge is a National Register of Historic Places site.

Tucked in the rolling landscape of the Flint Hills along US 160, Elk Falls is a natural limestone formation that can be seen from the old bridge that is closed to vehicles but open to walkers. The slow-running river picks up speed as it flows through shallow, rocky flats and down a slight decline, where it slows again before its sudden, powerful drop off the sharp limestone bedrock. Artists, craftspeople, and photographers come to the area to capture the beauty of this phenomenon. The falls can make an impressive roar, and impressive, too, is the deep boulder-strewn river canyon in which it is located. But this is Kansas—it is called Elk Trickle in dry years.

The town of Elk Falls calls itself "the world's largest living ghost town" and, like Sedan, offers you immortality on its own famous road: You can write your name on a piece of gravel with a permanent marker and become part of

"Here Lies Prudence Crandall and Her Brother Hezekiah"

The Elk Falls Cemetery is interesting to history buffs. The cemetery was started before Elk Falls became a town, when a party of the famous Buffalo Soldiers camped in the vicinity. Several fell ill and died and were buried here. In the northwest corner of the cemetery, there are simple markers inscribed A SOLDIER. Several Union soldiers and one Confederate soldier also rest here. So do Prudence Crandall—shunned in Connecticut for opening a school for black girls, she homesteaded in Kansas—and America L. King, one of America's first female mayors.

history. The sense of humor displayed in their brochure makes you want to find the town and see just what kind of people live here. This is a beautiful little community in the Kansas Ozarks, with a population of under 120, so you can ask for directions anywhere. There are no addresses or street signs. See www.elkfallspotttery.com.

The center of the artistic community seems to be the **Elk Falls Pottery Works** (620-329-4425), operated by Steve and Jane Fry, who were drawn here not only because of the area's natural beauty but also for the excellent earthenware clay in the Elk River. For stoneware clay they travel to Barton County. The Frys use a potter's wheel with a foot-powered wooden treadle wheel. Call for hours.

Jane designs jewelry at the Elk Falls Piecemakers—tiny, 1½-inch square pins of porcelain with old-fashioned quilt patterns.

This energetic couple has also opened the **Sherman House Bed and Breakfast** a few blocks away at Tenth and Montgomery This lovingly restored 1870s building was a popular stop for passenger trains passing through Elk Falls in 1879. The spacious rooms offer visitors their own secluded guest house for exploring rural Kansas. (The owners live nearby.) The large, upstairs Bunkhouse Room is great for families with children—it sleeps six and is provided with games and "family-friendly" videos. The Bunkhouse has a queen-size, rustic pole bed for the grown-ups, and the kid-size tack room and tepee have a campfire night-light—they're gonna love it. The skylight in the Prairie Flower Suite lets you look at the stars. Then, wake up to your choice of French toast with sausage, buttermilk pancakes with eggs and bacon, a breakfast burrito or "breakfast in bread"—a homemade loaf filled with smoked turkey, scrambled eggs and cheese. Rooms are $75 per couple, $10 extra for each additional person. Call (620) 329-4425.

A side trip north on Highway 99 from Elk Falls will take you past **Howard,** where you can find whimsical outdoor sculptures made from cast-offs. **Hubbell's Rubble People** are sure to bring a smile to your face. These large metal sculptures represent the Tin Man, Batman and his motorcycle, and an outhouse tumbled by a tornado. While in Howard, you'll want to stop at **Batson's Drug Store,** 102 North Wabash. Sit down at the counter in front of a '50s-vintage soda fountain and enjoy ice cream for 40 cents a scoop, sodas, sundaes, and old-fashioned limeades. Hours are Mon through Fri 8:30 a.m. to 5 p.m. Call (620) 374-2265 or (620) 374-2270.

Lodging is available at the Cattle Baron Inn, 516 East Randolph, a 1910 Victorian decorated with beautiful woodwork and stained glass and furnished with antiques. Innkeepers Dr. Robert Black, a veterinarian, and his wife, Shirley, also own some acreage with a lake about 7 miles from their home and invite guests to ride up there on four-wheelers and enjoy the countryside. The Blacks also have horses to ride some of the time, and other times, mares and new colts to visit. A nearby blueberry farm keeps the kitchen supplied, so there are always blueberry pancakes or muffins for breakfast. Rooms are $65 to $90. Call (620) 374-2503.

Check out the **Benson Museum** at 145 South Wabash in Howard for a look at Elk County's heritage. You can call (620) 374-2333 for an appointment to see a Country Schoolhouse and Teacher's Quarters, for a nostalgic look at the "3Rs" of the 1800s. The museum features Bertha's Dolls, a collection of more than 3,500 dolls amassed by a longtime Elk Falls resident during her 82 years.

There's more to do in this tiny town of 750 people. You can eat at **Poplar Pizza,** which has a varied menu, not just pizza, at 202 South Wabash (620–374-2525). Hours are Tues through Thurs 11 a.m. to 9 p.m., 11 a.m. to 10 p.m. Fri and Sat, and Sun 11 a.m. to 2 p.m. If you are in a hurry, there's **Toots** (620-374-2345), a drive-in on Highway 99 with window (or inside) service for a quick burger. Toots is open Mon 10 a.m. to 10 p.m. and Tues through Sun 6 a.m. to 10 p.m.; during the winter, the place closes at 8 p.m.

Take that burger for a serendipity picnic: Coming from the north on Highway 99, turn left at the south end of town (there is a sign by the vet's office) and follow the gravel road as it goes down a hill, crosses a creek, and climbs back up again leading to **Polk-Daniels Lake,** a pretty little sixty-five-acre lake surrounded by stone bluffs. This quiet little spot was a 1936 WPA project, and like most WPA projects, there are handcrafted natural-rock shelters and birdbaths. A permit is needed to fish or boat on the lake, but it's the perfect place for a picnic. Oddly, a person can water ski on the lake, but swimming is not permitted. I guess you have to be pretty good to attempt that.

If you're headed back west on US 160 from Elk Falls, the next stop will be **Moline** to see one of the oldest suspension bridges in the state. It was built at the turn of the twentieth century to give a view of the Wildcat Creek and stair-step cataract falls. You can walk out confidently, but cautiously, to enjoy the view yourself.

Nearly every community in the state has a landmark grain elevator, a necessity for farmers and ranchers as a place to sell grain or purchase feed. Some of the elevators in smaller communities have closed because of modern technology, and often they stand as a sad reminder of a declining economy.

The elevator at Grenola, the next stop on US 160 westbound, is one of those. Historical records show Grenola (the cities of Greenfield and Canola were merged) to have been a thriving community of more than 3,000 people. The grain elevator, built in 1909, stood next to the Santa Fe Railroad tracks. The Grenola Historical Society heard that the railroad was going to demolish the building, and it swung into action. The society had been looking for a permanent location for the **Grenola Museum** to display local historical artifacts, and so it bought the elevator for $200 at the sheriff's auction in 1989. The price was right and included the platform scales, the office safe, and other property at the site. What it didn't include was the land under the elevator.

The group raised the money to purchase the land, and cleaning and restoration of the elevator began. Removing the accumulated grain dust and grime was a major project, but by opening day in May 1990, the museum was ready.

Displays in the museum show the history of the area—a covered wagon, a surrey with fringe on the top, an old grocery wagon, and an antique automobile all were donated. The museum's displays include an old country kitchen, a doctor's office, and a one-room schoolhouse with a potbellied stove and original slate boards from other schoolhouses in the area. Old desks and a piano complete the theme. Most of the museum's collection is displayed in the long feed-storage room that extends from the main elevator. Microfilm readers with reels containing newspapers dating from 1879 and Elk County census records, as well as old pictures and photographs, are found in the office. Call (620) 358-2820 for hours or to make an appointment.

Across the street from the elevator is a park with a gazebo of stone that came from old stone houses in the Flint Hills, and a building dating from 1924 with a mural depicting a cattle drive and the railroad.

In October, Grenola celebrates Oktoberfest, highlighted by a free "bean feed" that begins at 5 p.m. The beans, some 150 pounds of them, are cooked over an open fire in four huge cast-iron pots hanging on tripods. Locals fire up the pots in the park and help with the cooking, seasoning, and tasting of the beans, stirring with a long paddle or hoe. With the announcement "Beans are ready," people line up with bowls in hand. Cooks in the community supply plenty of corn bread to go with the beans. Hay bales serve as seating for those who do not bring lawn chairs. The festival wraps up with a street dance.

There is a canoe trail at the Fall River Highway 99 Bridge to the Climax boat ramp. The length is 12 miles; it takes about six to eight hours to complete the trip.

Cattle Country

Hawthorne Ranch is about 8 miles north of **Eureka,** off US 54. Sally Hawthorne owns this 960-acre spread and invites you and the kids to try the **Hawthorne Ranch Trail Rides** (620-583-5887). She provides the horses and the tack and even beginner riding lessons for $25. The ride lasts about two to two hours; trips leave in the morning and afternoon. The ranch is on the edge of the Flint Hills, mostly grassland with ponds and creeks. Sally will point out The

Dome (a trail marker for Indians), Turkey Knob, and other interesting trail sights. She always leads each trail ride, which is limited to four people. Primitive camping facilities, including a picnic table and an outhouse, are provided, and there is a pond for fishing and swimming. Lessons and rides are from 9 a.m. and 1 p.m.

Hamilton, on Highway 99, is the place to find if it's a hot day and an honest-to-goodness vanilla root beer sounds good. At ***Holmes' Soda Fountain and Sundries,*** 101 East Main (620-678-3341), Donita Edwards can make you a malt or a genuine cherry Coke. The drugstore has been at that spot since 1929. Hours are from 6 a.m. to 6 p.m. Mon through Fri, 6 a.m. to 4 p.m. Sat, and from 7 a.m. to 2 p.m. Sun.

The Chicken House (620-475-3386) at 8 East Hwy. 99 in the town of *Olpe* is well known as having the finest fried chicken around. Owners Leonard and Theresa Coble have been frying chicken there for more than forty years. The brick building is newer than that, though, because in 1974 the restaurant was struck by lightning and burned to the ground. They rebuilt, and now the restaurant seats 320 people, who drive in from every town in a 50-mile radius for the fried chicken, the homemade onion rings, the famous sunny wheat, nut, and honey breads, and the homemade pies. The Chicken House is open Mon through Sat from 11 a.m. to 9 p.m.; closed Sun.

Emporia, on I-35, lies on a low ridge between the Cottonwood and Neosho Rivers. This once-treeless plain is now a forest of maples. The surrounding valley is still blanketed with pastures of bluestem. The town is filled with beautifully preserved old homes. Unique to Emporia are the early houses built by the Welsh settlers in the style they had known in Wales—simple, clean lines reminiscent of an earlier period. The Howe house on East Logan Avenue is a good example of this Welsh heritage. Other houses are Italianate, Queen Anne, and post–World War I bungalows.

At the ***White Rose Inn Bed & Breakfast*** at 901 Merchant St., you'll begin your stay with afternoon tea. Later retire to a private suite with your own bathroom and sitting room. In the morning the scent of fresh-baked muffins, biscuits, or coffee cakes will lure you to the dining room, or you can have your breakfast in bed if that's your mood. Owners Sheri and Scott McGuire and manager Shannon Foxen are happy to pamper you totally. They can arrange a manicure, pedicure, or massage in the privacy of your room in this quiet Victorian home. Four suites are available, all with private bath. Doesn't a weekend alone (or not) sound just lovely? Rates are $89 to $149. Call (620) 343-6336 or (800) 288-6198. You can also visit www.whiteroseinnemporia.com.

Shop the ***Dalton Gang Antique Mall*** (502 Commercial St., 620-342-9217)—housed in a former bus barn—from 11 a.m. to 6:30 p.m. Tues through Sat and 1 to 5 p.m. Sun.

Veterans Day—A Kansas Connection

Veterans Day has its origins in Emporia. In 1953 local citizen Alan J. King proposed that Armistice Day be changed to honor not only World War I veterans but also those who served in all wars and conflicts. Veterans Day was celebrated in Emporia that year.

The next year, Kansas congressman Ed Rees took King's proposal to Washington. President Dwight D. Eisenhower, also a Kansan, signed the bill proclaiming November 11th as Veterans Day. The holiday was first observed nationwide on November 11, 1954.

If you work up an appetite while shopping, stop for lunch nearby at the *Commercial Street Diner*, 614 Commercial St. (620-343-9866). It's all home-style food—from buttermilk pancakes to tasty chicken sandwiches. Hours are 11 a.m. to 2 p.m. Tues through Fri.

Prairie Passage is a collection of stone sculptures designed by Richard Stauffer and produced by the 1992 Kansas Sculptors Association Team Carve. The design reflects the city's role as gateway to the Flint Hills. The pylons—made of cottonwood limestone quarried in Chase County—range from 10 to 15 feet high and weigh between five and nine tons. They are clustered in four pairs of "echoing images."

The sculptures are silhouettes with incised lines of varying depth and thickness done by feather wedging, chiseling, drilling, and masonry sawing. For more information contact the Emporia Convention and Visitors Bureau at (620) 342-1803 or (800) 279-3730, or visit www.emporiakschamber.org.

You can tour history in Emporia starting at the *Emporia Gazette*, 517 Merchant St., and follow the literary and cultural heritage left by the famous editor William Allen White, well-known small-town sage. The memorial drive passes the White home and ends at the *William Allen White Library* at Emporia State University, Twelfth and Commercial Streets, which houses the world's largest collection of public and private memorabilia of this Pulitzer Prize winner. The memorial library is open year-round: Mon through Thurs 7:30 a.m. to 11 p.m., Fri 9 a.m. to 6 p.m., Sat 9 a.m. to 6 p.m., and Sun 2 to 11 p.m. Call (620) 341-5207 for extended hours.

Emporia also has a fine zoo at 75 Sodens Rd., near South Commercial Street. Here you can see animals in their natural habitats, with nearly 400 specimens of birds, mammals, and reptiles, from your car or walk-through areas. You'll also see game native to Kansas prairies—bison, white-tailed deer, prairie dogs—as well as longhorn steers and other exotic species. The drive-by area is free year-round from dawn to dusk, the walk-through Oct through Apr from

10 a.m. to 4:30 p.m. The zoo extends its hours until 8 p.m. from Mother's Day through Sept on Wed and Sun. Call (620) 341-4365 or visit www.emporia.ws.

The *Lyon County Historical Museum* at 118 East Sixth Ave. (620-340-6310) is housed in the former 1904 Carnegie Library, with leaded-glass windows and an unusual water fountain in the foyer. Rich oak woodwork embellishes the main part of the building, now used for exhibits. A growing collection of archives is housed at 225 East Sixth Ave. There is the Gallery of Gifts, where most items for sale are made by Kansas artists, craftspeople, and manufacturers. The museum is open Tues through Sat from 1 to 5 p.m. Archive hours are Tues through Fri from 10 a.m. to 4 p.m. Visit www.lyon countymuseum.org.

The *National Teachers Hall of Fame,* at Visser Hall, Room 114 at Emporia State University, annually recognizes five teachers who have demonstrated commitment to the profession. We all remember special teachers who changed our lives. Now there is a way to memorialize these teachers. For more information, call (620) 341-5660 or visit www.nthf.org. Hours are 8 a.m. to 5 p.m. Mon through Fri.

If you visit in June—and call early for tickets—you'll find a unique way to experience the Flint Hills about thirty miles southwest of Emporia. The *Symphony in the Flint Hills* (known to Kansans as "Symphony on the Prairie"), held the second Sat in June, brings the Kansas City Symphony to the treasured grasslands of Kansas. The terrain is rugged; organizers greet you on horseback and direct you to a parking area, after which you traverse a walking trail of wildflowers and native grasses or hitch a ride on a flatbed trailer. Those arriving early will enjoy educational activities about the Flint Hills, its history and its cowboys; horse-drawn wagon rides into the prairie; and a musical story circle and petting zoo for children. Barbecue is served for all. And then, the main event, beginning before 7 p.m., just as the heat is backing off: the powerful sounds of a professional symphony, echoing across one of the most gorgeous landscapes in America. Afterward, some people stick around to dance to old-time acoustic music in a huge tent. Tickets cost $60; call (620)273-8955 or visit www.symponyintheflinthills.com.

The *Flint Hills Rodeo* has been coming to *Strong City,* west of Emporia on U.S. Highway 50, since 1937 and is the oldest consecutive rodeo in the state. The Sept event draws cowboys and cowgirls from near and far to try to qualify for the National Finals Rodeo. From barrel racing to bareback broncs to bull riding, events at the Flint Hills Rodeo generate a lot of excitement.

The Rodeo Parade begins in Cottonwood Falls and ends in Strong City at the rodeo grounds. For more information, call Chase County Convention and Visitors Bureau at (620) 273-8469 or check out www.flinthillsrodeo.com.

South of Strong City on Highway 57 is tiny **Cottonwood Falls,** where you can bed down for the night in comfort at the **Grand Central Hotel and Grill** (215 Broadway). The two-story hotel, built in 1884, has undergone a major renovation but still has a western flair. The ten large suites upstairs—named for the surrounding ranches—are not just comfortable but "cushy," complete with concierge service. Iron beds with thick down comforters and white terry robes give you the feeling that you are at a spa. You'll be very pampered here. The restaurant serves a big continental breakfast each morning. White linen covers the tables for elegant lunches and dinners. For rates, call (620) 273-6763 or visit www.grandcentralhotel.com.

If that's too rich for you, The **1874 Stonehouse,** Mulberry Hill in Cotton-wood Falls, might be more your style. This two-story limestone home is about 2 miles east of town. There are four upstairs guest rooms, with private bath, overlooking the surrounding sixty acres. On the grounds is a 1-mile walking trail. Guests are invited to use two rooms on the main floor—the parlor, where music or satellite TV is available, and the fireplace room, where you can curl up with a book. Breakfast is served here daily. Rates are $105 to $170 per night. Billie and Joe Altenhofen invite you to check their home page on the Web at www.stonehousebandb.com or call (620) 273-8481 or (866) 464-3214.

The **Chase County Courthouse** in Cottonwood Falls holds the distinction of being the oldest in the state still in use. The French Renaissance–style limestone structure was completed in 1873 and is especially noted for its walnut spiral staircase stretching from the first to the third floors. Tours are offered noon to 4 p.m. Sat and Sun. For information call (620) 273-8469.

trivia

Chase County rock has been used around the world. The stone arch bridges in this area are enduring examples. One built in 1886 stands 1.5 miles southwest of Emporia on the Cottonwood River.

The **Fiber Factory** at 209 Broadway in Cottonwood Falls is a weaving shop featuring turn-of-the-twentieth-century looms. Carol and Charley Klamm are the weavers; they make rugs, place mats, baby blankets, and scarves, to name a few. Since they live right there, they are open "until fairly late at night" and often "don't bother to open on Sun." Since they sometimes are gone, if you are making a special trip to see them, calling ahead would be a good plan (620-273-8686).

Stop in the **Emma Chase Café,** 317 Broadway, for "A Bite of the Old West," where the menu has everything from beef to buffalo. "Miss Emma" is Sue Smith, who loves to brag on the "fabulous pies" and great entertainment. The café is well-known for hamburgers and features bison burgers, which you should try if you have not tasted this western treat. There are too many monthly special events to list: Bluegrass pickin', gospel singing, and rock 'n' rolling all have their own breakfast day. Cyclists, bikers, and antique auto fans have one, too. There's even a fly-in from the local airport. Friday nights are music-filled—outdoors, weather permitting—and then stay for the fish fry; Sat nights feature professional entertainers. The café is 9 a.m. to 2 p.m. daily, and on Friday evenings from 5 to 8 p.m. for fried catfish dinner. Call (620) 273-6020 or check the Web site, www.emmachasecafe.com.

Next door is the **Prairie Maid Emporium** at 319 Broadway. There is plenty to see in this shop. Begin with hand-poured, heavily scented, long-burning Prairy Fyre Candles, then choose among the Gifts in a Jar, which can be anything from elderberry jam to Miss Emma's pepper jam. Over in the corner is Fudd's Fudge (named after Sue's uncle) and all the chocolate you could ever want, and on to Nancy's Fancies, purses and pillows all created by hand. Greeting cards, kitchen gadgets—and "Tea at Three" happens every third Tues: tea is served by Miss Emma herself. Hours are 9 a.m. to 3 p.m. Tues through Fri and 8 a.m. to 5 p.m. Sat and Sun. Call (620) 273-6020.

Since 1927, **Jim Bell & Son Clothes,** 322 Broadway (620-273-6381), has been in Cottonwood Falls. It is 8,000 square feet full of high-quality western wear—among other things—for the entire family. Cowboy hats, boots, jeans—you name it, you can find it here. Jewelry and gift items are just another part of the collection. It's a shopper's dream come true. Hours are Mon through Fri from 10 a.m. until 6 p.m., Sat from 10 a.m. to 5 p.m. Visit the Web site for more shopping, http://jimbellandson.com.

The **Roniger Native-American Artifacts Museum** (620-273-6310), behind the impressive courthouse at 315 Union St., was a gift from George and Frank Roniger, who had a fine collection of Native American artifacts. There's a story behind the museum: When the brothers offered their collection to the Smithsonian, that institution wanted a large amount of money to mount and display it, so the brothers decided to spend the money to build a museum for Chase County instead. It is open from 1 to 5 p.m. Tues, Wed, Fri, Sat, and Sun, and by appointment. Admission is free; donations are welcome.

Shop **the Gallery at Cottonwood Falls,** 313 Broadway (620-273-6100), for art, glassware, pottery, Navajo and Hopi crafts, homespun wool sweaters, and antiques. The store specializes in rare clocks and early American furniture. The place also features the Friendly D's Coffee Shop, new in 2009, which offers java, baked goods and sweets. Hours are 7 to 10 a.m. Mon through Wed and 7 a.m. to 5 p.m. Thurs through Sat.

Two miles north of Strong City on US 177 is the historic **Z-Bar/Spring Hill Ranch,** the crowning achievement of cattleman Stephen Jones. Built in the 1880s with hand-cut native limestone, the eleven-room house is Second Empire–style of the nineteenth century. The massive three-story barn is impressive in its own right. You can see the Lower Fox Creek School, a one-room schoolhouse located on a nearby hilltop. Water to the house was provided by a spring on the hillside; thus the name Spring Hill Ranch. It is a National Historic Landmark.

The former ranch lands, now the ***Tallgrass Prairie National Preserve,*** were once the hunting grounds of the Kansa and Osage. The hills and prairie streams are home still to thirty-one species of mammals and nearly 400 species of plants, 130 kinds of birds, and numerous reptiles and amphibians. The National Park Trust purchased the 10,894-acre remnant of tallgrass prairie to preserve it for future generations.

There currently are no picnicking areas, camping facilities, flush toilets, or potable water here. It is recommended that you wear comfortable outdoor clothing as well as shoes suitable for negotiating uneven walkways, steep stairs, and unpaved footpaths. Your reward will be a close-up look at a vanishing prairie ecosystem. The trail winds across rolling hills, over a spring-fed stream lined with cottonwood and hackberry trees, and through a fascinating array of grasses and flowers. Be prepared for tiny insects and small animals—bobwhites and killdeer—that make the prairie their home.

The lonely stretch of land can be beaten with lightning and walls of hail; it can be quiet and beautiful with nothing but grass and the little shade offered by the occasional cottonwood tree. The bright yellow of the prairie ragwort and the blue wild indigo scatter primary colors in the sunshine. You can hike the 1¾-mile trail to the Lower Fox Creek School, an 1884 one-room schoolhouse restored with period blackboards, desks, and books. The school is open by reservation. The former ranch house is open for free group tours. The Second Empire–style house has a bookstore and living-history demonstrations on roping, quilting, and other skills essential for survival on the prairie. The historic ranch headquarters and Southwind Nature Trail are open daily except holidays 9 a.m. to 4:30 p.m. Visitor information is available on the back porch of the ranch-house headquarters, including a ten-minute orientation video. Free group tours are available by reservation; be sure to call two weeks in advance.

A 7-mile bus tour led by National Park Service rangers will take you through the backcountry, where you will learn about the prairie's intricate system of plants and animals and the geological history of the Flint Hills. From late Apr through the end of Oct, a one-hour-and-thirty-minute tour is available every day of the week at 11 a.m., 1 p.m., and 3 p.m. The cost is $5 for adults and $3 for children under age eighteen. Advance reservations are recommended, but arrangements can be made the day of your visit if space is available. For more information or arrangements for wheelchair access, call (620) 273-8494 or visit the Web site at www.nps.gov/tapr.

You hear a lot about the Harvey Girls in Kansas. When Frederick Harvey opened his first restaurant in Topeka and then went on to become the first restaurant chain in America, everyone wanted to keep a bit of that fame at home. So it is in *Florence,* where Harvey opened his first restaurant and hotel, the Clifton Hotel. *The Harvey House Museum,* 221 Marion St., was once a railroad stop; now it houses a unique museum/restaurant where the Florence Historical Society serves authentic dinners to parties of twelve or more. You can sample a five-course meal served the way the famed Harvey Girls would have served it, complete with costumes that replicate the uniforms. The people at Harvey House had to have everything ready when the train arrived, but "fast food" then meant vintage claret and quail in aspic—served in a setting that would rival restaurants anywhere—but served quickly so the train could depart on time. To make tour or dinner arrangements or for more information, call (620) 878-4296 or visit www.florenceks.com.

The comfortable atmosphere at *Shippy's Town and Country Café* on US 77 has a stream of loyal patrons who travel that roadway. Caroline Spencer, owner, offers specials every day and employs some of the best cooks in the area. The cafe is open from 6 a.m. to 2 p.m. Sun and Mon, and from 6 a.m. to 8 p.m. the rest of the week. Call (620) 878-4487.

This region is the beginning of the Western Plains and buffalo country. The Santa Fe Trail crossed the county from east to west; the Chisholm Trail crossed it from southwest to northeast.

Nestled in the beautiful valley of the Cottonwood, *Marion Lake* is near the Cottonwood Crossing of the Santa Fe Trail; the deep wagon ruts can still be seen, although they are barely visible through the grass and prairie flowers. The lake is excellent for fishing, and there is hunting in public hunting areas, as well as picnicking, camping, boating, and hiking.

It's a very pleasant drive on U.S. Highway 56 west. The lake takes its name from the nearby town of *Marion,* settled in the 1860s in the fertile Cottonwood Valley at the western edge of the Flint Hills. The lake is surrounded by native hardwoods, wildflowers, and flowering shrubs. Here the seasons' colors change from spring redbud, flowering catalpa, and Osage orange to the beauty of the fall sumac. You can fish for largemouth bass, white bass, and walleye in well-stocked coves and hunt in specified areas for pheasant, mourning dove, and deer.

The *Marion Museum,* 623 East Main St., is tucked into a century-plus-year-old church near Central Park. Built in 1887 as a Baptist worship house, the museum features ornate wood ceilings and stained-glass windows that reflect a time of hymns and sermons while telling the story of the history of Marion. The first twenty-three settlers came into the area in five covered wagons, stopped on a bluff above the park, and saw Cottonwood Valley to the west. Soon after that, they discovered a freshwater spring coming out of the bluff and decided that this was a fine place to stay. They lowered their wagons and horses into what is now the park, and the town of Marion grew from that camp. The museum is open from the first of May to mid-Oct, Tues through Sat from 10 a.m. to 2 p.m. and Sun from noon to 2 p.m. Call (620) 382-9134.

A country home overlooking a private lake and the surrounding 480 acres of wildlife is a bed-and-breakfast owned by Kent and Alice Richmond. *Country Dreams Bed and Breakfast,* 2309 Clover Rd., has five guest rooms, and all have private connecting baths and queen-size beds. Guests are invited to use the family room and the native stone fireplace and satellite television system. A full country breakfast is served, and other meals may be arranged in advance. Rooms are $75 per night on weekends. Horses can be stabled in a nearby barn. Call (620) 382-2250 or (800) 570-0540 for rates. The home is 3 miles north of Highway 150 at the 7-mile marker. Visit their Web site at www .countrydreamsbedandbreakfast.com.

Ernest Hett was the founder of *The Copper Shed,* 1832 East 140th St., 5 miles south of Marion and 1.5 miles west on County Road 140. The shed and a barn nearby are worth a drive to visit. The smaller sculptures represent all that is beautiful about the state and are often mounted on parts from antique farm machinery. The windmill, for example, is mounted on the sickle section from an old hay cutter.

You can visit the barn and watch them work or just browse in the shed, where the Nelsons' works and the works of other Kansas artists are displayed among antiques and collectibles that are also for sale.

Not only metal sculptures, but wheat weaving and sprays, black walnut bears, driftwood Santas, and various kinds of fancywork are also for sale in the shed. Collectors can find bunnies, bears, geese, chickens, ducks, and handmade dolls. There are metal and wooden puzzles and painted skins and leaves. Kansas souvenirs, sunflowers, mugs, antique tools, and kitchen utensils are next to tole-painted cream cans and saw blades. It's all here.

The Copper Shed is open by chance or by appointment. Call ahead (620-382-2041).

Melting Pot

The town of *Hillsboro,* on US 56 west of Marion between Emporia and McPherson, is a Mennonite community and headquarters for the Mennonite

Back from the Brink of Extinction

Before the1800s, experts estimate the number of buffalo at 120 million. Buffalo were once the most numerous of any large mammal on earth. By the turn of the twentieth century, only twenty-two buffalo could be found in the United States. You read that right—twenty-two. A few conscientious ranchers took it upon themselves to save the animal from extinction. Buffalo have made a remarkable comeback and are now bred for their high-protein, low-fat meat (half the calories of beef). They are resistant to many of the diseases that plague the cattle industry and can endure the harshest of winters. They also tolerate the intense summers of the Midwest. Buffalo cows have been known to live for forty-two years and bear thirty-eight calves, which certainly makes breeding easier. These animals weigh in at about a ton and can run 35 miles an hour.

Brethren of the United States. Tabor College, a private Mennonite school, is here.

The *Pioneer Adobe House Museum,* at 501 South Ash St., is the only adobe house that has been preserved. A team of people led by Emil Bartel built special tools and moved the delicate structure, made of mud and straw bricks, to the corner of D and Ash Streets where it now stands. The bricks were made by either horses or humans walking in the mud and straw mixture, which was then poured into wooden molds and set in the Kansas sun to bake. Most adobe houses had a standard floor plan with a grass-burning oven in the kitchen (yes, that's *grass*, not gas). There was a dining room, living room, parlor, and three bedrooms to house the large pioneer families.

Along with the adobe house and barn, the museum complex also contains the Kreutziger Schoolhouse (complete with iron bell and potbellied stove), which was moved to Hillsboro in 1965 from a small town in Canada. Call (620) 947-3775; office hours are 10 a.m. to noon and 1:30 to 4 p.m. Tues through Fri.

The Friesen Dutch Mill was reconstructed from one original photo of the mill. Inside, the millstone grinds the flour and occasionally a decorative cloth bag of flour is available for purchase. Credit for the reconstruction goes to college professor Richard Wall, a handyman who became an amateur millwright during the project.

The *Ebenfeld Mennonite Brethren Church,* located 5 miles southeast of Hillsboro, is believed to be the first organized Mennonite Brethren congregation in North America, begun in 1874 when two Mennonite Brethren families immigrated from south Russia due to religious intolerance and set aside Sunday as a day of worship. The *Historic Mennonite Brethren Church,* built in 1893 and now located on the campus of Tabor College, is believed to be the oldest existing Mennonite Brethren church structure in North America. It is a simple, plain white church with a Roman-arched ceiling and Roman-arched windows.

The **William F. Schaeffler House,** at the corner of Grand and Lincoln Streets, was built in 1909. The house was very "modern" in its day and had features that still make it fascinating to visitors. There is a dumbwaiter from the kitchen to the basement for canned goods, fireplaces that are strictly decorative, inside bathrooms for use at night or when someone was ill, and carbide gas that ran to each room of the house for lighting. The dining room holds a twelve-place china set, and the library is filled with stackable oak shelving containing many valuable books. Call the Hillsboro Historical Society at (620) 947-3775 for an appointment for a tour.

The **Mennonite Heritage and Agricultural Museum** at 200 North Poplar in **Goessel,** on Highway 215, tells the history of the Mennonite immigration. These peace-loving settlers came to this area in 1874 seeking freedom to live their faith in the lifestyle they had chosen.

The Mennonite Immigrant Historical Foundation has constructed an eight-building museum complex with a Wheat Palace (which contains a full-scale replica of the Liberty Bell made entirely from Turkey Red wheat), Immigrant House, school, bank, barn, and other buildings. The museum is closed during the winter months. Call (620) 367-8200 for hours and admission rates.

Six miles north of **Canton** lies a 4,000-acre midgrass prairie, fenced to contain 200 bison and 50 elk. The preserve also contains a forty-six-acre fishing lake with campsites and a boat ramp. It is open year-round Mon through Fri from 8 a.m. to 5 p.m.

The **Maxwell Wildlife Refuge,** 2577 Pueblo Rd. in Canton, lets you see the prairie the way our ancestors might have seen it. Herds of buffalo and elk roam free. You can experience all the sights and sounds of the native Kansas prairie while riding in a modern version of a covered wagon—a tram, which departs from the visitor center and winds across a trail right into the territory of the buffalo herd. A tour guide recounts the region's history and points out prairie wildlife along the way. The best time is in the spring, when the buffalo calves are born among the wildflowers in the shade of the cottonwood trees.

This 2,500-acre prairie preserve has the largest buffalo herd on a refuge in the state. Tours are available year-round by reservation. The preserve is situated 10 miles east of Interstate 135 on US 56, then 7 miles north of US 56. Rates are $8 for adults, $5 for children age four to twelve, and free for those under four. Call (620) 628-4455 for more information.

Although **McPherson** does have a bagpipe band, its name has more to do with history than nationality. Civil War soldiers from this area served under Gen. James "Birdseye" McPherson, killed in battle in Atlanta; the town is named in his honor.

Even if you can't stay two years to complete a degree in antique auto restoration at **McPherson College,** you can still get a tour of the program facility (Jay Leno is one of its supporters) by calling (800) 365-7402 or visit www.mcpherson.edu.

Vaniman Mansion is now the home of the **McPherson Museum** at 1130 East Euclid St. (620-241-8464, www.mcphersonmuseum.com), on US 56. This elegant three-story home is furnished in 1920s style with hand-crocheted lace-edged curtains. Among the numerous exhibits are the very rare skeleton of a prehistoric giant ground sloth, the largest collection of Indian pottery outside the Smithsonian, and the world's first man-made diamond. Mr. Vaniman's collection of mounted birds and animals also is on display. The museum is open from 1 to 5 p.m. daily except Mon and legal holidays. Admission is $3 for adults, $2 for students, and $1 for children twelve and under.

In 1868 a group of Swedish immigrants made a new home in America's heartland, in the valley of the Smoky Hill River. The result is **Lindsborg,** off I-135 on Highway 4. It is a community that calls itself "Little Sweden, U.S.A."

Old World facades adorn every building, and bright red, wooden Dala horses (pronounced *DAW-la*) are prominently displayed in front of most residences. You must buy yourself a Dala horse (Dalahäst) when you visit Lindsborg. It is one of the most traditional Swedish items, passed on from generation to generation.

The **Swedish Country Inn** (800-231-0266) at 112 West Lincoln is in the former Carlton Hotel, now an authentic Swedish bed-and-breakfast; Becky Anderson is the innkeeper. The cream and baby blue, two-story brick building half a block from downtown is trimmed in copper accents. There are nineteen rooms, and all have private baths. A truly Scandinavian feature is the redwood sauna in the lower level. The pine furniture and accessories are imported from Sweden, and hand-quilted spreads adorn every room. A typical Scandinavian buffet breakfast of specialty breads, pastries, cheese, and meats is served every morning. This scrumptious buffet is open to the public Mon through Fri from 7 to 10 a.m., Sat and Sun from 7 to 11 a.m. Breakfast is included in room price for hotel guests. Rooms range from $69 to $120 (for a suite sleeping up to six people). The building is air-conditioned, and bicycles (including two tandem bikes) are available for guests to tour the town. Visit the Web site at www .swedishcountryinn.com.

Each room in **Seasons of the Fox** has been decorated to represent one of the four seasons. An elevator can take you up to the Jacuzzi on the secluded upstairs deck. The price includes a three-course breakfast, afternoon

Lindsborg Is a Festival Town

Of all the places in the state I have visited, Lindsborg is at the top of the list as a family favorite. It is a perfect weekend trip from most urban areas, and whenever I visited, there was something there for everyone in my family.

The entire town is a tribute to the Swedish pioneers from Varmland, Sweden, who settled in the Smoky Valley in 1868. My favorite time to go is during one of the many festivals, when townspeople walk in the streets dressed in Swedish costumes and tourists become Swedish for the weekend. I end up buying brightly colored Dala horses that have become the symbol for this town.

It's a good idea to go hungry for a few days before arriving so that you can load up on potato sausage, meatballs, and Swedish tea ring while you watch the folkdanslag (folk dancers) perform to Swedish folk music. Lindsborg resembles Sweden as it was a century ago.

If you are interested in art, Lindsborg's many galleries will keep you busy anytime. During the festivals, large tents located off Main Street are filled with wares made by area craftspeople. Midwestern baskets, paintings, pottery, wreaths, and wheat weavings are for sale.

Parades are another great part of festival weeks. Some comical floats celebrate silly things like *lutefisk*, a dried stock fish eaten at Christmas. I've also seen a 30-foot motorized Viking ship, complete with fur-clad Vikings. Any of the festival weekends makes a perfect getaway.

"samples," and evening snacks—and an exercise room to work it off. Innkeepers are Michael J. Fox and Sue Schlegel. This bed-and-breakfast is at 505 North Second St. across from Bethany College and a few blocks from downtown. Rates are $90 to $125. Call toll free (800) 756-3596 or visit www.seasonsofthe fox.com.

Rosberg House, 103 East State St., is a beautiful three-story Queen Anne home that offers yesterday's charm with today's comforts. Each guest room is decorated with its own unique theme and offers private bath, cable TV, and a private phone line equipped with data ports. That's the "today's comforts" part of the equation, as is the whirlpool bath. The charm of yesterday lies in the fireplace, private sitting areas, breakfast at your convenience, and outdoor swimming pool. Rates are $79 to $169. Call (785) 227-4189 or toll free (888) 215-5234. You can also check out www.rosberghouse.com.

There is no shortage of places to stay in Lindsborg, but it makes such a great day trip or weekend getaway that people flock here.

Hemslöjd, at 201 North Main St. (785-227-2053 or 800-779-3344, www .hemslojd.com), is a shop filled with custom-made Dala horses, Swedish candelabra, and etched glass. In fact, it's among the world's top importers of Dala horses from Sweden. You can watch craftspeople work in the Dala Horse Factory, established in the early 1980s. It is open from 9 a.m. to 5p.m. Mon through Fri.

Lindsborg is best known for its three major festivals: In December it is Santa Lucia Day, honoring a Sicilian who, according to Swedish legend, brought food and drink to hungry Swedes during a famine in the Middle Ages; Midsommardag (Midsummer's Day) in June; and the Svensk Hyllningsfest in October every odd-numbered year.

You can step into the Old World charm of *The Courtyard* at 125 North Main St. and find mouth-watering pastries, antiques, and arts and crafts. The *Courtyard Bakery and Kafe* under the skylight is the spot for lunch, with home-baked Swedish delicacies, gourmet coffee, deli sandwiches, salads, soups, and anything from the bakery display—cookies, pastries, and breads baked daily. Hours are Sun from 12:30 to 5 p.m. and weekdays from 9 a.m. to 7 p.m. Call (785) 227-4233 or (888) 268-7893.

In the same building you'll find the *Courtyard Gallery* (785-227-3007), which features handblown glass paperweights by Rollin Karg, decoy ducks and carved songbirds by Eugene Fleharty, and paintings, sculpture, pottery, art glass, and woodcarving by Great Plains artists. Hours are 10 a.m. to 5 p.m. Mon through Fri, 1 to 8 p.m. Sat and 1 to 4 p.m. Sun. Visit www.courtyardgallery.com.

For some unusual clothing, look for *Elizabeth's Handwoven Artwear* (888-215-7329) at 110 North Main St. The fabric is woven on three looms in the back of the store; you can watch weaving demonstrations and the making of handwoven clothing. Choose your own yarn colors for a custom-made item. Hours are 10 a.m. to 3 p.m. Mon through Fri and 1 a.m. to 5 p.m. Sat. Call (785) 227-2757 or see www.elizabethshandwoven.com.

The *Olive Springs School House Gallery* (785-254-7833) is the studio of Maleta Forsberg, whose love of all creatures great and small is evident in her art. She and numerous pets live next door to the gallery on 120 acres 10 miles southeast of Lindsborg. The gallery is a restored schoolhouse built in 1885. It's 7 miles east of Lindsborg, Roxbury exit 72 on I-135, at the corner of Twenty-fourth Avenue and Smoky Valley Road. It's open by appointment; visit www.maletaforsberg.com.

Lindsborg has many, many galleries and artists in residence—far too many to list here—but you can pick up the *Lindsborg Visual Arts Directory* from the Lindsborg Arts Council at 101 North Main St. (785-227-3032). Listed are galleries and studios of artists who specialize not only in paintings but also in ceramics, fiber art, folk art, graphic art, photography, jewelry, metalsmithing, sculpture, stained glass, and woodcraft.

The ***Messiah Festival of Music and Art*** has been an annual event at Bethany College in Lindsborg since 1882. Through the years the festival has grown to international fame. It begins on Palm Sunday and continues through Easter Sunday. Tickets may be purchased by mail or phone (785-227-3311).

The ***REO Antique Auto Museum*** at Lincoln and Harrison Streets, near Old Highway 81, specializes in REOs dating from 1908, but it also has other cars, bringing the total to forty. This is the private collection of Quintin and Florence Applequist. A donation is requested. Call (785) 227-3726 for hours.

The ***Old Mill Museum*** (785-227-3595, www.oldmillmuseum.org), in the park at 120 Mill St., began on the first floor of the circa 1898 Smoky Valley Roller Mill, but the present complex consists of twelve buildings. They feature Native American artifacts as well as the Swedish culture of the town. The Swedish pavilion, which was brought to St. Louis from Sweden for the 1904 World's Fair, has a huge maypole standing in front of it. An 1870 log cabin, 1880 depot (and Santa Fe locomotive), and other nineteenth-century buildings are also here. It is open yearround, Mon through Sat, from 9 a.m. to 5 p.m. and Sun 1 to 5 p.m. Admission is $2 for adults, $1 for children six to twelve years old.

Take time to visit ***Anderson Butik Scandinavian Shop*** at 134 North Main St. (785-227-3268 or 800-782-4132, www.andersonbutik.com). It is one of the leading suppliers of Swedish gifts and foods by mail in the country. The Scandinavian tour office is in the Swedish timber cottage, at 125 North Second, transported to Lindsborg from Siljansnäs, Sweden. It is made of pine logs from Swedish forests. The joints that form the cross-sections were hand cut with an ax; the exterior surfaces of the timbers were cut by hand with a hatchet for the Old Country look. Wooden pegs were driven into the timbers to hold them tightly and give stability to the walls. After every log, door, and window was numbered, the cottage was dismantled and shipped to Lindsborg. Hours at the shop are 10 a.m. to 5:30 p.m. Mon through Sat and 12:30 to 4 p.m. on Sun.

West of Lindsborg on Highway 4 is ***Marquette.*** This 1880s town with its carefully restored Main Street is fun to visit. Be sure to visit ***Marquette City Sundries*** at 104 North Washington for ice cream served at an old-fashioned marble-topped soda fountain dating at least from 1901. Hours are 10 a.m. to 7 p.m. daily except Sun, when it's open noon to 6 p.m. Phone (785) 546-2234.

A few miles north of Lindsborg stands ***Coronado Heights,*** a butte with an incredible view from which the Spanish explorer Coronado looked over miles of prairie in 1541. It is believed that this part of the Smoky Hills is the northernmost point in Kansas that Coronado traveled. This hill stands alone on the prairie. In 1936 the WPA built a castlelike structure atop this point, from which you can see a tapestry of farmland, wildflowers, wheat fields, and lonely clusters of trees.

Inside the structure are an enormous stone fireplace and two large picnic tables. Stairs wind up through the tower to the open rooftop. A path leads down from the plateau of the butte to more picnic tables and heavy, stone fireplaces. The park is splashed with wildflowers, yuccas, soapweed, and prairie grass.

The small town of **Hesston** is a good spot to stop and stretch your legs. Spend some time at the **Dyck Arboretum** at 177 West Hickory St. at the south end of Main Street. In addition to 180 types of trees, shrubs, and woody plants, it features 380 types of flowers in perennial gardens and wildflower displays. There is also a bird-watching area and a pond with an island garden. Tours can be arranged. The visitor center is open from 9 a.m. to 4 p.m. Mon through Fri year-round and 1 to 4 p.m. Sat and Sun from May through Oct 15, but the public garden is open every day until sundown. The suggested donation when visiting is $2 for adults, $1 for children age twelve and younger. Call (620) 327-8127 or visit www.dyckarboretum.org.

Newton lies amid gently rolling hills at the junction of US 50 and I-135. There, an elegant, sixteen-room Victorian home is one of several attractions honoring the strong Mennonite heritage in the Newton area. The **Warkentin House** at 211 East First St. is a highlight. Call (316) 283-3113 for hours.

Other buildings in town that appear on the National Register of Historic Places are the **Neal House,** at 301 East Fourth St., and the **Bethel College Administration Building.** Bethel College, at North Main and Twenty-seventh Streets (in North Newton), is the oldest Mennonite school in America. It was chartered in 1887 and is the home of the **Kauffman Museum,** 2701 North Main St., highlighting the strong Mennonite heritage here. The museum displays the culture of the Mennonite settlers. Other exhibits include the natural history of the Central Plains and the mammals and birds of North American prairies. The museum is surrounded by an award-winning "living prairie," which has more than one hundred species of prairie grasses and flowering plants, streamside woods, and a farmstead. It is open Tues through Fri from 9:30 a.m. to 4:30 p.m., Sat and Sun from 1:30 to 4:30 p.m. year-round. Admission is $4 for adults, $2 for children ages six to sixteen. Call (316) 283-1612 or log on to www.bethelks.edu/kauffman.

The Old Parsonage Bed and Breakfast at 330 East Fourth (316-283-6808), in Newton's oldest neighborhood, was the parsonage for the First Mennonite Church. It is a cozy yet spacious home filled with family heirlooms and is just a short walk from the Warkentin House. You can also visit nearby Bethel College to see the Kauffman Museum. Rates include breakfast. Call for more information.

Here's an interesting way to get off the beaten path. At **Country Boys Carriage and Prairie Adventures** (office at 1504 South Rock Rd., Newton),

The Wickedest City in the West

Like all of the other cow towns on the Chisholm Trail, Newton was bloody and lawless, and it was nicknamed "the wickedest city in the West." Newton was the western terminus for the Atchison, Topeka, and Santa Fe Railroad, and the railhead brought a horde of gunslingers, gamblers, "soiled doves," cowboys, and railroad crews to town. Peace officers often worked both sides of the law. Bully Brooks was marshal of Newton in 1872. Two years later he was hanged as a horse thief in nearby Sumner County.

you can rent your own covered wagon, carriage, surrey, or hayrack. The Prairie Adventure features Flint Hills wagon-train trips ("Experience the pioneer life on a covered wagon without all the hardships!" they say) and group trail rides throughout the summer (bring your own horse). Cost is $50 per person. The overnight experience costs about $170 for adults, $75 for children ages five to twelve; it includes a steak dinner. (If your idea of camping out is a Motel 6, deduct 20 percent from the adult rate and come for one day, Sat.) Trail riders are charged $100, to follow the wagons and camp overnight, but you must have your own horse and feed for the horse. Call (316) 283-2636 for reservations, or visit the Web site at www.kscoveredwagon.com.

The place to stop for a meal is ***The Breadbasket*** at 219 North Main St. (316-283-3811), where you can have a good old-fashioned Mennonite buffet on Fri and Sat evening. The bakers start at midnight, and by morning the bakery is filled with mouth-watering pies, muffins, breads, cookies, sweet rolls, and, of course, zwieback. Breakfast is an incredible choice of pastries, fruit, biscuits and gravy, pancakes, sausage, and on and on. Lunch sandwiches are on freshly baked buns. Hours are 6:30 a.m. to 5:30 p.m. Mon through Thurs, 6:30 a.m. to 8 p.m. Fri and Sat; 10:30 a.m. to 2 p.m. Sun. Visit www.newtonbreadbasket.com.

trivia

Stop by the Newton Convention and Visitors Bureau at 500 Main Place, Suite 101, and pick up a historical driving tour of the area, or check out the Web site at www .infonewtonks.com. Call (316) 283-2560 or (800) 899-0455.

The High Street Company is a unique little gift and antiques shop at 315 North High St. Vicki Stobbe will help you explore every nook and cranny of this former 1910 neighborhood grocery, filled with gifts, antiques, and collectibles. Hours are Mon through Fri from 10 a.m. to 5:30 p.m. and Sat from 10 a.m. to 5 p.m. Call (316) 283-1080 or visit www.highstreetco.com.

The *Carriage Factory Gallery* (316-284-2749, www.carriagefactoryart gallery.com) at 128 East Sixth St. is a 110-year-old stone building originally built for manufacturing carriages. It now shows a variety of art by twenty-two area artists, sponsored by the Newton Fine Arts Association. Hours are 11 a.m. to 4 p.m. Tues through Sat; closed Sun and Mon.

Going east on US 50 will bring you to downtown *Peabody's* Walnut Street, and it is like a visit to the past. It's not just the friendly atmosphere and nice little shops, but in addition, there is the *Peabody Historical Complex* (104 East Division), which includes the *1881 Morgan House.* It was the home of the first editor of the *Peabody Gazette,* W. H. Morgan. Hours are from Memorial Day through Labor Day, Wed through Sun from 1 to 4 p.m., or by appointment by calling (620) 983-2815. Just south of the Morgan House is the *Printing Museum,* which displays printing equipment from the turn of the twentieth century, including that of the last newspaper in the state to print with "hot type." The equipment is all operational, which makes it one of a kind. Call (620) 983-2174 for hours and admission information.

The *Kansas Learning Center for Health* at 505 Main St. in Halstead, slightly south of US 50, is home to "Valeda," the talking, transparent woman. This place is fantastic! It contains more than twenty exhibits depicting the healthy human body and the way it functions. You can test your lung capacity with a breathometer, listen to your heartbeat on a heart monitor, and look into a giant mouth to inspect the taste buds. There are a giant tooth and an eye, with each part illuminated as it is described. One exhibit explains how chromosomes work and why boys and girls are different (and who decides the sex of a baby), and you can see the development of a child from egg and sperm to baby.

Admission is $2; there are also group rates available. The center is open Mon through Fri from 9 a.m. to 4 p.m. Call (316) 835-2662 or (800) 798-2124 for more information, or visit www.learningcenter.org.

Places to Stay in South Central Kansas

ARKANSAS CITY

Best Western
3232 North Summit St.
(620) 442-7700

LouAnn's Campgrounds
9423 292nd Rd.
(620) 442-4458

ELK FALLS

Silver Bell Motel
406 Second St.
trailer hookups
(620) 642-6145

EMPORIA

Candlewood Suites
2602 Candlewood Dr.
(620) 343-7756

Emporia RV Park & Campground
4601 U.S. 50
(620) 343-3422

Guesthouse Inn
2700 West Eighteenth Ave.
(620) 343-2200

HILLSBORO

Country Haven Inn
804 Western Heights Circle
(620) 947-2929

LINDSBORG

Coronado Motel
305 Harrison St.
(785) 227-3943

Viking Motel
446 Harrison St.
(785) 227-3336

MCPHERSON

Econo Lodge
2111 East Kansas Ave.
(620) 241-6960

NEWTON

**Best Western
Red Coach Inn**
1301 East First St.
(620) 283-9120

WICHITA

Candlewood Suites
570 South Julia St.
(316) 942-0400

Comfort Inn East
9525 East Corporate Hills
(316) 686-2844

Comfort Suites (airport)
658 Westdale Dr.
(316) 945-2600

The Kansas Inn
1011 North Topeka St.
(316) 269-9999

LaQuinta Inn
7335 East Kellogg Dr.
(316) 685-1281

**Econo Lodge Inn and
Suites Airport**
600 South Holland Dr.
(316) 722-8730

WINFIELD

Comfort Inn
Highway 27 at Quail Ridge
(316) 221-7529

Places to Eat in South Central Kansas

ARKANSAS CITY

Brick's Restaurant
301 South Summit St.
(620) 442-5390

BENTON

**Prairie Rose
Chuckwagon Supper**
15231 Southwest
Parallel St.
(316) 778-2121

BURNS

Burns Café & Bakery
106 East Broadway
(785) 726-5528

CALDWELL

Last Chance Bar & Grill
30 South Main St.
(620) 845-2434

DURHAM

Main Street Café
517 Douglas St.
(785) 732-2096

EL DORADO

Carl's Place
127 North Main St.
(620) 321-0855

FLORENCE

Chuck Wagon
503 Main St.
(785) 878-4382

LINDSBORG

Swedish Crown
121 North Main St.
(785) 227-4800

MARION

Stone City café
211 East Main St.
(620) 382-2656

Wagon Wheel Express
202 West Main St.
(620) 382-3544

MCPHERSON

Neighbor's Café
204 South Main St.
(620) 241-7900

NEWTON

Charlie's
200 Manchester Ave.
(620) 283-0790

PEABODY

Coneburg Inn
904 Peabody Ave.
(620) 983-9000

WICHITA

Red Bean's Bayou Grill
306 North Rock Rd.
(316) 687-1778

Stroud's
3661 North Hillside St.
(316) 838-2454

SELECTED CHAMBERS OF COMMERCE AND VISITOR BUREAUS

Arkansas City Convention and Visitors Bureau
P.O. Box 795
Arkansas City 67005
(620) 442-0236
www.arkcity.org

Caldwell Chamber of Commerce
P.O. Box 42
Caldwell 67022
(620) 845-6666
www.caldwellkansas.com

Emporia Convention and Visitors Bureau
719 Commercial St.
P.O. Box 417
Emporia 66801
(620) 342-1803
www.emporia.com

Hesston Chamber of Commerce
115 East Smith St.
Hesston 67062
(620) 327-4102
www.hesstonks.org

Hillsboro Chamber of Commerce
109 South Main St.
Hillsboro 67063
(620) 947-3506
www.hillsboro-kansas.com

Lindsborg Chamber of Commerce
104 East Lincoln St.
Lindsborg 67456
(785) 227-3706 or (888) 227-2227
www.lindsborg.org

Marion Chamber of Commerce
203 North Third St.
Marion 66861
(620) 382-3425
www.marionks.com

Mulvane Chamber of Commerce
P.O. Box 67
Mulvane 67110
(620) 777-4850
www.mulvanechamber.com

Newton Chamber of Commerce
500 North Main St.
Suite 101
Newton 67114
(316) 283-2560
www.infonewtonks.com

Wichita Convention and Visitors Bureau
515 South Main St.
Wichita 67202
(316) 265-2800
www.gowichita.com

Winfield Convention and Tourism
123 East Ninth Ave.
Winfield 67156
(620) 221-2421
www.winfieldks.org

SOUTHWEST KANSAS →

The crops growing in Kansas today reflect the prairies of yesterday. Strips of trees known as gallery forests grow along meandering rivers and creeks, much as they did long ago. The tallgrass prairies of eastern Kansas now grow tall corn. The midgrass prairies are sown in wheat, and in the western part of the state, the short-grass prairies have prevailed because there is not enough rain to support tall grasses. Today steers roam where buffalo once covered these grasslands for miles in every direction. The short-grass prairie has become pastureland with vast uninterrupted sweeps of sky, resembling a tranquil, waterless sea.

The buffalo herds dwindled because they interfered with the building of railroads and the settling of the western part of the state. A herd of four million was reported near Fort Larned as late as 1870, covering an area 50 miles long and 25 miles wide. During the 1880s almost all of these creatures were destroyed for sport as well as for the hides and meat. Folks going through the territory by train would even shoot from their windows, leaving the carcasses for the vultures. The Native Americans were gradually replaced by cattlemen.

In dry grasslands elsewhere, several acres of land are needed to provide enough feed for one animal. But the big

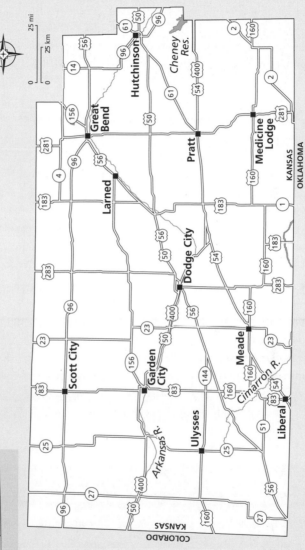

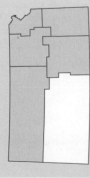

and little bluestem grasses of western Kansas are rich in nutrients; today over 300,000 head of cattle are brought here from southwestern states to fatten before being taken to market.

Cities such as Abilene, Dodge City, and Wichita sprang to life as great herds of longhorn steers were driven from Texas up the Chisholm and other trails to be shipped east to market on the new railroads. They were wild, disorderly cow towns before the farmers came to share the Great Plains with the cattlemen. Between Copeland and Sublette the road enters boundless level plains. During the summer months the mirage is a common phenomenon here; travelers often see large lakes in the distance, which vanish as they are approached. Before this country saw a plow, it was thickly covered with buffalo grass. Although it may resemble the "Great American Desert" that Zebulon Pike reported the Great Plains to be, this section of Kansas has the largest share of minerals and natural resources to be found in the state.

The Great Plains owe their flatness to the erosion of the Rockies before and during the Ice Age, when streams deposited huge loads of sand and gravel as thick as 300 feet over western Kansas. Along with these deposits came large quantities of underground water, which can be used for irrigation of crops.

The Wild West and Chalk Hills

We begin our tour of southwest Kansas in *Dodge City,* the meanest, wildest town in the old Wild West. Dodge was called "Hell on the Plains," and with good reason. Gunslingers worked both sides of the law—occasionally at the same time. Marshal Henry Brown of Dodge City once rode with Billy the Kid.

The famous *Boot Hill Cemetery* was originally at Fourth and Spruce Streets, on a bluff 100 feet above the Arkansas River. In 1872 two cowboys had

AUTHOR'S FAVORITES

Cynthia's Pizzaria	Parman Brothers Limited
Dodge City	Stan Herd's Earthwork
Fort Larned National Historic Site	Stauth Memorial Museum
Kansas Cosmosphere and Space Center	Trail Rides
	Yoder
Mid-America Air Museum	

a gunfight while camping here. The dead man was unknown and, wrapped in his blanket, was buried where he fell, boots and all; thus Boot Hill was born. The frequent and sudden deaths of unknown cowboys and buffalo hunters filled the cemetery quickly. Historians say that the burial in 1878 of Alice Chambers, a dance-hall girl, was Boot Hill's last. In 1879 the bodies were moved to Prairie Grove Cemetery.

On the site of the old Boot Hill Cemetery now stands the **Boot Hill Museum,** a re-creation of Dodge City in the 1870s. Lining historic Front Street, where lawmen Wyatt Earp and Bat Masterson once walked, are an 1865 Fort Dodge jail, the Santa Fe Depot, and a nineteenth-century blacksmith shop. Call (620) 277-8188 or visit www.boothill.org.

During the summertime, daily entertainment includes melodramas, old-fashioned medicine shows, stagecoach rides, reenactments of gunfights, and a real crowd favorite, the Long Branch Saloon Variety Show, where Miss Kitty's cancan girls kick up their heels. Get a reservation for this show. Afterward, stop in for a buffalo burger and ice cream at **Beatty & Kelly's Restaurant and Old Fashioned Ice Cream Parlor,** also part of the museum complex.

Hours at the museum are 8 a.m. to 8 p.m. daily from Memorial Day to Labor Day. The rest of the year, hours are 9 a.m. to 5 p.m. Mon through Sat and 1 to 5 p.m. Sun. Summer admission is $8 for adults, $7.50 for seniors and students; off-season is 50 cents less. The Boot Hill Museum also has a research library, open by appointment, where history buffs can see scores of old photos, maps, and other documents of the period.

You can relive the legend in Dodge. The **Dodge City Trolley** visits places where history was made along the Santa Fe Trail. Tours are daily, and schedules are in the information center. See www.visitdodgecity.org.

Two museums share a building at 603 Fifth Ave., across the street and west of Boot Hill. The **Kansas Teachers' Hall of Fame** is not only a memorial to the state's teachers but also a museum containing early classroom items. No admission charge. Also at this location is the famous **Gunfighter's Wax Museum.** Life-size gunfighters buried with their boots on create a scene you won't soon forget. Admission is $3 for adults, $1.50 for children ages six to thirteen. Both museums are open daily Memorial Day through Labor Day, Mon through Sat 10 a.m. to 5 p.m., Sun 1 to 5 p.m.; call (620) 225-7311 for additional hours.

Santa Fe Trail Tracks, situated west of the city, is part of the original wagon trail used by westward-bound travelers between 1821 and the 1880s. It is 9 miles west of Dodge City on U.S. Highway 50 and is listed on the National Register of Historic Sites. Here 140 acres are set aside to preserve the finest remnants in existence of the Santa Fe Trail. The deep swales left by the wagons can still be seen quite clearly, especially in spring, when the prairie grass is short. Officials ask that you stay on the walkways in order to help preserve the ruts.

For a hearty steak, head to **Casey's Cowtown** at 503 East Trail St. (620-227-5225). Inside, the place has an Old West feel, circa 1890s. After dinner, spend some time looking at the restaurant's collection of antique stained glass and western art. On summer weekends and during Dodge City Days (late July or early Aug), enjoy an outdoor barbecue and dancing. Hours are 11 a.m. to 10 p.m. If sundown finds you in Dodge, the **Boot Hill Bed and Breakfast** at 603 West Spruce St. might have a bed for you. This elegant Victorian home across the street from Boot Hill is owned by Kurt and Enid Scadden. The B&B's popularity is due in part to the breakfast served its guests; a previous owner, a former Ritz-Carlton pastry chef, left some of his recipes, and the Scaddens have added some of their own. In addition, the landscaped yard has a gazebo (a favorite for weddings). The 6,000-square-foot mansion has five rooms available, all with private baths. One is a honeymoon suite, which comes with a romantic package. Rooms range from $99 to $175. Check out the Web site at www.boothilldodgecity.com, or call (620) 225-0111.

After checking in on a summer evening, drive to **South Drive-In,** 1019 West McArtor Rd., for a double feature. The theater was built in 1947, and its one large screen has withstood all the weather that Kansas has thrown at it. In fact, it's the oldest operating outdoor cinema in the state. Three hundred cars can get in, and for $10 you can stuff in the entire family. The screen is lit up from Apr to Oct on Sat and Sun nights. Call (620) 225-4301 for the playbill.

A short trip south from Dodge City on U.S. Highway 283 and west on U.S. Highway 54, you'll find the town of **Meade,** the perfect place to "get away"—at least, the Dalton Gang thought so. The **Dalton Gang Hideout,** at 502 South Pearlette, is only one of many spots the outlaws used, but this one has been preserved, restored, and furnished as it was in the nineteenth century, complete with secret passages and a tunnel leading from the house down the hill to the barn.

trivia

Dodge City, with an average daily wind speed of 14 miles per hour, is the windiest city in the United States.

cityofmany names

Dodge City has had many nicknames over the years: Buffalo Capital of the World, Cowboy Capital, Queen of the Cow Towns, Wickedest Little City in America, and Beautiful Bibulous Babylon of the Frontier, to name a few.

Fort Dodge: A Home for Soldiers

The Fort Dodge site was once used as a campground for wagon trains. The fort was established in 1865 to protect the wagon trains as well as mail carriers. Fort Dodge was abandoned in 1882. Eight years later it was deeded to the state of Kansas so that the adobe and sod buildings could be used as a soldiers' home. Most were veterans of the Civil War and Mexican and Indian wars. Today the fort's quiet, tree-lined walks and dignified buildings are still home to Kansas soldiers. A small museum and self-guided tour of the grounds relate the history of the fort. It's 6 miles east of Dodge City on U.S. Highway 400. Leave a message at (316) 227-2121 if you'd like more information.

The tunnel is cool and quiet in the middle of a Kansas summer; at the south end of the passageway in the loft of the barn is the *Dalton Museum.* It's filled with a fascinating collection of pioneer items, including the W. S. Dingess Antique Gun Collection. Hours are Mon through Sat 9 a.m. to 5 p.m., Sun 1 to 5 p.m. The museum is open yearround from 9 a.m. to 5 p.m. Mon through Sat and 1 to 5 p.m. Sun. Admission is $4. Call (620) 873-2731 or (800) 354-2743.

The *Meade County Historical Museum,* 200 East Carthage (620-873-2359), contains replicas of a one-room schoolhouse, an early church, a general store, a blacksmith shop, a sod house, a doctor's office, and a barber shop. Truth be told, our favorite exhibit is a unique two-headed calf. Outside, a windmill and early farm equipment join the 1976 Bicentennial time capsule; but the place is a time capsule in itself. It is open 9 a.m. to 5 p.m. Mon through Sat, 1 to 5 p.m. Sun. Admission is free.

You can spend the night in a peaceful country farmhouse northeast of Meade on US 54 near the town of *Fowler.* Dean and Mary Reese will welcome you to *Creek Side Farm* at 26131 A Rd. They offer deer and pheasant hunting in season. The farm, built in the 1930s along the banks of Crooked Creek, now raises its main crop in a lush greenhouse filled with bedding plants. Two guest bedrooms with double and queen-size beds with private baths and ceiling fans await you, and a full country breakfast will be served on the enclosed porch that overlooks the farm, or in the dining room, if the weather's not right. Rooms are $45 to $65. Call (620) 646-5586 for reservations or for more information.

The *Neon '57* at 102 East Fifth St. in Fowler is an old fifties-style diner and gift shop, open 9 a.m. to 4:30 p.m. Mon through Fri, 10 a.m. to 2 p.m. Sat. Call (620) 646-5775 or go to www.neon57.com.

Just 10 miles west of *Kismet* you will see the *Mighty Samson of the Cimarron,* the largest railroad bridge of its kind. It's officially known as the

Rock Island Bridge and is 1,200 feet long, rising 100 feet above the Cimarron River.

From US 54 take East Cedar Street to 567 East Cedar, where the **Coronado Historical Museum** contains exhibits concerning the Spanish explorer who came here in 1541. Overseeing the artifacts and exhibits with typical explorer's aplomb is a bronze statue of this famous adventurer. The museum is open Tues through Sat from 9 a.m. to 5 p.m. (7 p.m. in summer) and Sun from 1 to 5 p.m. (6 p.m. in summer). Call (620) 624-7624.

The **Mid-America Air Museum** (620-624-5263), located on the former Liberal Army Air Field (now the municipal airport on US 54 and 83), at 2000 West Second St., has more than ninety airplanes on exhibit. The airfield was the training ground for more than 5,000 B-24 Liberator commanders during World War II, and the idea for the museum was born during a reunion in 1986. The 86,000-square-foot building is devoted to aircraft exhibits and displays. The facility also features a 6,000-square-foot Aviators Memorial Chapel, a library, and a gift shop, as well as a 200-seat theater.

pancake
boulevard

In Liberal, US 54 is called Pancake Boulevard in honor of the international pancake race held here every Shrove Tuesday. Women from the town run a quarter-mile course flipping a pancake. The winner's time is compared with the winning time from a similar race held in Olney, England, on the same day. The race makes TV news nationwide and abroad—a welcome and entertaining change from the usual fare.

Aircraft on display include a 1929 Pietenpol, the oldest vintage aircraft in the collection. This high-wing monoplane was powered by a Ford Model A engine. The restoration area, a popular part of the exhibit, is open to visitors. Another favorite is the TBM Avenger like the one flown by former President George Bush during World War II and named for his fiancée, Barbara Pierce. Bush was the Navy's youngest aviator when he received his wings in 1943; he went on to earn the Distinguished Flying Cross and three air medals.

The museum is open Mon through Fri 8 a.m. to 5 p.m., Sat 10 a.m. to 5 p.m. and Sun 1 to 5 p.m. Admission is $7 for adults, $3 for seniors and students, free for children five and younger.

What would a trip to Kansas be without a visit to Oz? At **Dorothy's House and the Land of Oz,** you can walk the Yellow Brick Road and see Dorothy and Toto, Dorothy's house (with the Wicked Witch's feet showing beneath it), Scarecrow, Tin Man, Cowardly Lion, winged monkeys, and talking trees. The address is, of course, 567 Yellow Brick Rd. Summer hours are 9 a.m.

Is It the Prairie or the Plains?

What is the difference between the plains and the prairie? One hundred degrees lon-gitude, a line that runs north-south near Dodge City, is the approximate dividing line between the two. To the east of the line are the tall grasses—the prairies—and to the west are the short grasses—the plains. The former are better for crops, and the latter for grazing.

to 6 p.m. Mon through Sat, 1 to 5 p.m. Sun. From Labor Day to Memorial Day, hours are Tues through Sat 9 a.m. to 5 p.m. and Sun 1 to 5 p.m. Admission is $5 for adults, $3.50 for seniors and for children ages six through eighteen. Call (620) 624-7624 for more information.

The **Baker Arts Center** at 624 North Pershing Ave. is known as the Cul-tural Oasis on the Prairie for good reason. It is an art-education facility in a 5,000-square-foot, three-floor building. There are four galleries, a workshop area, and a Discovery Center for children. Visiting the galleries is free; fees are charged for workshops. Gallery hours are Tues through Fri from 9 a.m. to noon and 1 to 5 p.m., Sat from 2 to 5 p.m. The center is closed Sun. Call (620) 624-2810 or visit www.bakerartscenter.org..

Twenty-five miles southwest of Dodge City on U.S. Highway 56 is the little town of **Montezuma.** Every small town has its surprises, and Montezuma's is the **Stauth Memorial Museum** at 111 North Aztec St. The visitors who come each month outnumber the 900 souls who live in this town. Claude and Donalda Stauth were world travelers for thirty-eight years, and "Donnie" was a profes-sional photographer. Many of her slides have been made into laser videos featur-ing children, animals, or famous places. The focal point of the 10,000-square-foot museum is the permanent exhibit, *Around the World*, which showcases some of the 10,000 slides and many "off-the-back" artifacts collected in their travels. These are items that people owned and used, such as the Croatian skirt com-pletely covered with detailed embroidery and edged with handmade lace. There are musical instruments of all kinds, such as a thumb piano from Cameroon. Statues of ivory and ebony are from Papua New Guinea and Indonesia.

Built to Smithsonian specifications, the museum has hosted dozens of national and international traveling exhibits. This is a not-to-be-missed place. Hours are Tues through Sat 9 a.m. to noon and 1 to 4:30 p.m., Sun 1:30 to 4:30 p.m. Call (620) 846-2527, or visit www.stauthmemorialmuseum.org. Admission is free, but donations are welcome.

If you're passing by on US 50, stop in at **Clark Pharmacy** at 101 South Main St. in Cimarron, 16 miles west of Dodge City. The building dates from the

1930s or 1940s and still has the original tin ceiling. It also has an old-fashioned soda fountain of the same era. Call (620) 855-2242 to check hours or log on to www.clarkpharmacy.com.

While in Cimarron, call ahead (620-855-7718 or 800-261-6251) to arrange a visit to the **Kansas Wheat House** at 102 South Main St. and try some of Shirley and Dave Voran's Wheat Nubs, and other wheat snacks and confections. They also offer bread mixes ranging from jalepeño-cheddar to chocolate-raspberry and gift baskets of Kansas items. You can see several of the products at www.kansasgrown.com. A personal favorite—partly because of the name, mainly because it involves chocolate—is the Cow Patti, made of wheat, soy nuts, and sunflower seeds, bound together with a caramel base and coated with chocolate. It's as nutritious as chocolate can be and a very funny gift as well; a small tin is $19.95. You can order it online and have it shipped to your friends on the coasts who have never seen a real cow patty—with love from the "flyover states."

A good option for accommodations is the **Cimarron Crossing Bed and Breakfast,** 307 West Ave. A (US 50) on the edge of Cimarron. This charming 1907 home was built by Joan and Gerald Vogel's great-aunt and great-uncle, who followed the Santa Fe Trail as far as this corner of Kansas before deciding they'd gone west far enough. The house is furnished in period antiques and reproductions (you'll have to look closely to see that the kitchen stove isn't a wood burner), with modern amenities including central heat and air-conditioning and a hot tub in the herb garden. Rooms (four, all with private baths) include a hearty country breakfast with locally grown and homemade treats such as jelly made from Kansas peaches. Rates are $60 to $90. For reservations call (620) 855-3030 or (888) 829-3232, or visit the Web site at www.cimarroncrossing.com.

trivia

The Cimarron Route was a shorter road to Santa Fe than the Santa Fe Trail, but water was dangerously hard to find. Travelers sank a wagon bed into the quicksand to let the water seep through and fill the wagon. A wagon bed still marks the old route today at Wagon Bed Spring.

East of Cimarron on US 50, a historical marker points out wagon-wheel ruts (called swales) remaining from the Santa Fe Trail.

Garden City lies in beef country. You'll see feedlots and packing plants, but some unexpected pleasures, too. The **Lee Richardson Zoo** at Finnup Park at Fourth and Maple Streets was founded in 1920. You can walk or drive through the zoo in your car, a "wild experience" the easy way. The park also boasts the largest free, outdoor swimming pool in the world, occupying half a city block and holding two and a half million gallons of water. There are picnic areas, tennis courts, horseshoe pits, and a formal garden. The free zoo is open daily from 8 a.m. to 6:30 p.m. from Apr 1 to Labor Day and until 4:30 p.m. the rest of the year. Call (620) 276-1250 or visit www.garden-city.org.

Long before cattle were king in this part of the state, bison roamed the prairie. You can see the state's oldest publicly owned herd of the massive creatures at the 3,670-acre **Finney Game Refuge,** south of the Arkansas River bridge on US 83 near Garden City. Male bison can reach 6½ feet high and 9 to 12 feet in length and weigh more than a ton. The herd usually numbers about 150. This stretch of prairie is also home to lesser prairie chicken, quail, ground squirrels, jackrabbits, and deer. For the safety of the public, no self-guided tours are allowed, but a guided tour can be arranged by calling Friends of Finney Game Refuge at (620) 276-9400 or the Finney County Convention and Tourism Bureau at (888) 445-4663, ext. 9400. There is no charge, but donations are welcome.

trivia

Garden City is the proud owner of the world's largest hairball. It is at the Finney County Museum. (I am not making this up.) It was found in a cow's stomach at the packing plant.

Garden City's **Mercer Gallery** offers a simple place to enjoy a range of quality art exhibitions. Two rooms are filled with paintings, sketches, engravings, sculpture, and hand-thrown ceramics, done by students and some well-known Kansas artists. Located in the **Pauline Joyce Fine Arts Building** at Garden City Community College, 801 North Campus, the new gallery was a dream turned into reality by Garden City resident Maxine Mercer Porter in memory of her late husband, Clyde Mercer.

The gallery is open from 2 to 5 p.m. Sun and from noon to 4 p.m. Mon through Fri during the college year (Sept through May). For more information call (620) 276-9644.

Fred and Kathryn Askren opened a bed-and-breakfast in their twenty-two-room brick Victorian mansion, circa 1909, at 501 North Fifth St. in Garden City. **Sunnyland Bed and Breakfast** is indeed a mansion, with a ballroom that will seat seventy-five people, seven bedrooms all with private baths (and named for Bible verses), and a chef who will do wedding receptions and other events. Prices are $85to $125 a night with a full breakfast. You can visit the Web site at www.sunnylandbandb.com, or call (620) 276-0500 or (866) 453-0500.

Bob and Adrian Price have a quiet little place in **Deerfield** about 7 miles east of Lakin, which is 48 miles from the Colorado border on US 50. Their little log cabin sits on a private fishing pond. It is the perfect spot to just get trivia

An old Jewish cemetery is 4 miles north of Garden City on Kansas Avenue and 4 miles west on US 83, at the southeast corner of Chmelka and Lowe Roads. Four grave sites are still visible. Several Jewish colonies were formed in this part of the state in the early 1880s, and the land was permanently deeded for a cemetery in 1892.

away and enjoy some quiet time. There is no phone, no television (and in fact, no kitchen or bathroom; there is an outhouse and water outside), but lots of birds, fish, geese, and ducks. Bob will take you hunting during the season, and ice-skating is always a possibility in the winter. Call (620) 426-6291 for more about this secret retreat. Bob calls his hunting operation **Oasis Hunting,** and he is an outfitter for trophy whitetail and mule deer, pronghorn antelope, and even prairie dogs. You can hunt upland game such as prairie chickens, sandhill cranes, pheasant, dove, and quail. Ducks and geese are plentiful, too. If you want a taste of the outdoor life of Kansas, prices are $100 a person for a half day for upland birds and water fowl (two-person minimum) and $2,600 for five days of deer-hunting. That includes meals (some of which involve Adrian's homemade tortillas) and lodging. Bob's Web site, www.oasishunting.com, will fill in the details and hunting permits can be obtained there.

West of Garden City in **Lakin** is the **Windy Heights Bed and Breakfast** at 607 Country Heights Rd. This B&B is a modern home on a nine-hole public golf course. With some advance notice, you can have dinner waiting for you when you're through playing. A continental or full breakfast is served in the kitchen or dining room, or outside on the terrace overlooking the golf course. Or have breakfast in bed, if that's your mood. Hosts Chuck and Dianne Jaeger have three rooms with private baths. Rooms are $50 to $60. Call (620) 355-7699 or www.windyheightsbandb.com.

Lakin is a rural community made up of farmers and ranchers. But for a small town, it has some interesting places, including Charlie's Ruts, the Santa Fe Trail ruts still visible four miles east of town.

Next head south on Highway 25 to **Ulysses**—actually, new Ulysses. Old Ulysses gave itself away in 1909, when all the buildings in town were loaded on skids and moved 3 miles to the present site so that the lots could be deeded back to bondholders. George W. Earp (first cousin to Wyatt Earp of Dodge City) became (old) Ulysses's first peace officer in 1885. The town's hotel was cut into three sections for transport. One section is now part of the **Historic Adobe Museum,** 300 East Oklahoma (620-356-3009), which features artifacts from the tribes of the High Plains and memorabilia of the Santa Fe Trail. Call for hours. **Fort's Cedar View** (620-356-2570) is a bed-and-breakfast that sits on twenty acres of landscaped grounds 0.75 mile northwest of the junction of Highway 25 and U.S. Highway 160, 1675 West Patterson Ave., Ulysses. It is a quiet getaway with an indoor pool and fireside room. This modern brick-and-cedar home has four rooms, one with private bath.

Owner Lynda Fort invites guests to think of the place as their own. Breakfast can be whatever guests want, from homemade cinnamon rolls to a full meal. Often the entire house is rented for business meetings. Rates are from $80 to $100 per night. Call (620) 356-2570 or visit www.fortscedarview.com.

At Highway 25 and US 56 is *Hugoton,* probably the cleanest, most all-American little town you will ever see. If you'd like to stay here, try the *Shady Lane Bed and Breakfast,* at 110 North Main St. Neal Gillespie hosts guests at his World War II–vintage home, which has been completely renovated and lies down a shady tree-lined lane on the northern end of Hugoton.

All four rooms have a king-size bed, large TV set, private phone line, and private bath. There's even a spa off the outdoor deck. Rates are $50 to $80. Call (620) 544-7747.

Elkhart is southwest of Hugoton, in the southwestern corner of the state. The *Morton County Historical Society Museum* on US 56 in Elkhart (620-697-2833) brings the covered-wagon experience alive in your imagination as you walk through. You can imagine Coronado's quest on the prairie, the Native American's life following herds of buffalo, and the freight wagons hurrying to reach the only available water on the Cimarron Cut-Off at Middle Springs. As the covered wagons came, sod houses were built in the treeless plains. The red caboose in front of the museum symbolizes the end of the Santa Fe Trail. Hours are Tues through Fri 1 to 5 p.m. Visit www.mtcoks.com.

Stop by *Jim-n-I's* (620-697-9886) on US 56 (next to the El Rancho Motel). This restaurant owned by Jim and Janelle Shultz has a delightfully varied menu. Rotisserie chicken, burgers, and a noon buffet are available weekdays; Fri and Sat

The Pride of Morton County

Morton County is the smallest county in the world to have not one, but two Olympic medal winners: Glenn Cunningham ran on the 1932 and 1936 indoor track teams and won a silver medal in 1936 in the 1500 meters; in 1938 he set an indoor mile world record with a time of 4:04.4 and was selected as the outstanding track performer in the one-hundred-year history of Madison Square Garden. Thane Baker won the silver medal in the 200 meters in 1952 at Helsinki. In 1956 in Melbourne he won a gold medal as captain of the 400-meter relay team, a silver in the 100 meters, and a bronze in the 200 meters.

Stocking Your Wagon

I have traveled across Kansas many times, and I have learned that "gettin' outta Dodge" takes some forethought. If you look at a map of the state, you will realize that in western Kansas, it can be a long way from one town to the next. So check to see that your gas tank is full and your spare tire is inflated. Measure the distance between your starting point and destination. Just "eyeballing it" will leave you in the middle of nowhere at sundown. If you are traveling with children (and even if you are not), it's a good idea to use a public restroom whenever one appears.

Weather is a serious factor in Kansas. There are thunderstorms with "posthole diggers"—that's what they call lightning around here—and thunder that will scare you to death. Blizzards seem to come from nowhere; there are floods and, of course, tornadoes. Pay attention to weather watches and warnings. For example, a tornado watch means the conditions are right for a tornado; a tornado warning means one has been spotted in the area. It's a good idea to have a map, walking shoes, water, a first-aid kit, snacks, sunglasses, and, in winter, blankets and some heavy clothing. And you will want binoculars and a camera!

night, folks come for the prime rib and smoked chicken and ribs, and free Wi-Fi if you have your laptop along. Hours are 6 a.m. to 9 p.m. seven days a week.

Ten miles north of Elkhart on Highway 27 is the *Cimarron National Grasslands,* open year-round during daylight hours. The USDA Forest Service maintains the ecosystem here; a self-guided tour allows visitors to familiarize themselves with the natural history of the region. You'll begin to get an idea of what it was like when the first pioneers crossed that wide-open grassland. The 108,000 acres have been reclaimed as a complete ecosystem of native wildlife and plants. This is the largest area of public land in the state and is a great experience for campers, hikers, and hunters. There are elk and antelope along the 19-mile companion trail that parallels the preserved trail ruts. Call (620) 697-4621 for information.

Go north on Highway 27 to *Johnson City* to find David and Steve Parman's most unusual shop. They create kaleidoscopes for collectors at *Parman Brothers Limited,* 106 South Main (620-492-6882, www.kaleido.com/parman .htm), at the intersection of Highway 27 and US 160. A tube-shaped optical toy, the kaleidoscope produces changing symmetrical patterns as loose bits of handblown glass are moved about under a set of mirrors.

Parman kaleidoscopes, made of imbuia (a Brazilian wood), oak, and walnut with optical-quality lenses, sell for low prices, as kaleidoscopes go. The Parmans offer fifty models in a range of sizes for $47 to $200, and kaleidoscope collectors snap them up. The miniscopes, which weigh less than eight ounces, have the same optical quality as the larger ones and are made of beechwood, walnut, and imported wenge, a black wood. Hours are from 8 a.m. to 5 p.m. Mon through Fri (when the owners are home).

Syracuse was once one of the most favored towns on the High Plains, a green oasis on the prairie. People in distant towns drove here to enjoy the cool beauty of its graceful poplars, weeping willows, and other trees.

At 208 North Main St. is *Cynthia's Pizzaria,* the most popular place in town. They make a sauerkraut and vegetable pizza that is so good, you will want to carry one away with you. It is very good cold. The place is packed with senior citizens, high-school students, and local farmers searching out a breakfast pizza. Everyone eats here. Call (620) 384-5928. Hours are 11 a.m. to 1:30 p.m. and 4 to 8:30 p.m. Mon through Thurs and to 9:30 p.m. Fri and Sat.

The *Horace Greeley Museum* (620-376-4996) is located in the old Greeley County courthouse in the small town of *Tribune* at Highways 27 and 96. Built in 1890 of post rock (local limestone), the structure is listed on the National Register of Historic Places. There's no proof that either the museum or the county is named for the *New York Tribune* newspaperman who penned the famous words "Go West, young man." But there is a connection; the founder of Tribune, C. K. Gerard, worked with Greeley in New York before editing his own newspaper here.

The jail that was once part of the courthouse is still there, as well as a restored courtroom. A late-1800s kitchen and schoolroom and an early-1920s filling station have been added. Among the displays on the museum's three floors is a collection of Old West branding irons. Hours are Thurs from 9 a.m. to 4 p.m. and by appointment.

Following the Civil War, there was a soldier's colony in Tribune. Eager to settle the West, the government offered soldiers 160 acres of land if they settled and "proved up" the property—building a house, farming or raising cattle, and staying a set number of years. The settlers could also file a tree claim, receiving an additional 160 acres for planting trees. Many of these Civil

Prairie or Forest?

In the early part of the twentieth century, the U.S. government designated a significant amount of the state's prairie as the Kansas National Forest. Beginning with 30,000 acres of seedling trees in 1905, the project had expanded to 800,000 acres by 1915 and looked very promising. But weather runs in cycles, and when a dry cycle set in, most of the trees soon died and the land reverted to prairie.

The Squaw's Den Battleground

In 1878 Chief Dull Knife and Little Wolf of the Northern Cheyenne escaped from their reservation near Fort Reno, Oklahoma, with 235 followers, including women and children. Their escape took them through western Kansas, and on Sept 27 the men, women, and children of the Cheyenne Nation made a stand against the U.S. Army on the bluffs of Beaver Creek, just south of what is Lake Scott State Park today. This encounter with the cavalry was the last Indian battle in the state. The site became known as Squaw's Den Battleground because of the cave in which the Cheyenne women and children hid during and after the battle. Colonel William H. Lewis was wounded during the fighting and died en route to Fort Wallace, making him the last casualty of the Indian wars in Kansas. Ask at the state park office for directions to the historical marker.

War veterans lived out their days here and are buried in a GAR (Grand Army of the Republic) cemetery in northwest Greeley.

Lake Scott State Park (620-872-2061) is 12 miles north of Scott City on US 83. Steep canyons and bluffs seem oddly out of place in Kansas, but then, so does Lake Scott, a cool, wet haven and one of the few large lakes in southwest Kansas. Lake Scott is in the spring-fed Ladder Creek Valley. It is a lush oasis in a land where water is scarce. The valley is carved into the white stone of the Ogallala bluffs and watered by the Ogallala aquifer. Lake Scott's water is a natural beauty surrounded with cottonwood, elm, and walnut trees. It is much the same as the Native Americans and later the pioneers saw it. The Ogallala aquifer has provided an important and reliable water source for thousands of years. The Plains Apache people lived part of each year in the valley in the 1600s, enjoying shelter, wild fruits and berries, and easy water. Bison and antelope on nearby plains provided supplies of meat and hides. Visit www.naturalkansas.org/lake.htm.

Within Lake Scott State Park is the *Steele Home Museum.* Built in the shadow of the bluffs, the native sandstone home of the Steele family still feels the steady breeze of western Kansas after more than a century. Except for a covered porch and a few rain gutters for protection, the home looks just as it did so long ago. Inside the restored house is some of the original furniture that traveled to Kansas by covered wagon, along with other period pieces.

Herbert Steele came with his parents, brothers, and sisters in a covered wagon to the land and filed claim to it. Eliza Landon, a Tennessee school-marm, lived with her family on a timber claim nearby. When Herb and Liza united their frontier families in 1892, they purchased a section of ranch land with natural springs trickling from the bluffs. The couple hand-quarried blocks of sandstone from the land and built a two-story house near the cool bed of Ladder Creek.

Liza's kitchen and workroom were in a dugout surrounded by sod to protect her from the summer's heat and winter's chill. The back door was at ground level and provided a view of the cherry, apple, and peach orchards. Two living rooms and two bedrooms, also at ground level, faced the bluff. The walls of porous sandstone and mortar are more than a foot thick, insulating the house and trapping warmth from the kitchen below in winter. The rock floor of the springhouse built around the bubbling spring just north of the house provided refrigeration for the milk and cream from the dairy cows and for eggs from the chickens, kept in the quarried-stone chicken house on the bluff.

Rugs handwoven by Liza grace the floors; her iron kettle still hangs over the coals on the range where buffalo chips fueled the fire. Near the window in the sitting room stands a bookcase made by the Steeles' only son, Roy, who died when he was twenty. Two daughters died in infancy.

The Steeles' reputation for hospitality was well known, and their door was always open, the spring providing a cool drink to visitors. They sold nearly 800 acres of their land to the state to create a park, and the house was preserved

TOP ANNUAL EVENTS

APRIL

Mennonite Quilt Auction & Relief Sale
Hutchinson
(620) 665-7406

MAY

Wildflower Tour
Medicine Lodge; second Saturday
(620) 886-3721

MAY–JUNE

Beef Empire Days
Garden City; first two weeks
(620) 278-6807

JULY

Pretty Prairie Rodeo
Pretty Prairie
(620) 459-4653

JULY–AUGUST

Dodge City Days
Dodge City; last week
(620) 227-3119

AUGUST

Heritage Day
Yoder
(620) 465-2515

SEPTEMBER

Kansas State Fair
Hutchinson
(620) 669-3600

Peace Treaty Pageant
Medicine Lodge
(620) 886-9815

in their honor. The spring still bubbles cool water for travelers. The home can be viewed by appointment.

El Cuartelejo Pueblo Ruins, also at the park, is an important archaeological site occupied by the Taos and Picuris Indians from 1650 to 1720. It is the northernmost Indian pueblo in the Americas. It was also the first white settlement in Kansas. Rick Stevens, park manager, can tell you all about it. Vehicle permits to enter the state park are $3.70. Camping is extra. There is no charge for viewing the museum or pueblo ruins, but donations are welcome.

US 83 from Lake Scott north to Oakley cuts through the Chalk Hills, which contain the fossils of not only fish and sharks—which you might expect if you know the geology of the region (once an inland sea)—but also flying reptiles and swimming birds. The Smoky Hill River eroded its way down through the chalk, exposing prehistory at a glance.

Patrycia Ann Herndon's Studio/Gallery is in an 1888 landmark bank building in *Dighton,* east of Scott City along Highway 96. She records her surroundings in western Kansas in watercolor, pastel, or pencil. Her realistic interpretations can be seen in her studio/gallery, known as the *Old Bank Gallery,* at 146 East Long St. Call (620) 397-2273 for hours.

The *Lane County Historical Museum* at 333 North Main St. has something a little different in the *Bachelor Exhibit.* The museum features a dugout; inside, a mechanical man—whose creator does special effects for movies— sings "Lane County Bachelor," a late 1800s song, at the press of a button. Close by the museum in the park is a full-size sod house, furnished the way these dwellings were when settlers lived here. Virginia Johnston is the museum curator and can be reached at (620) 397-5652. The museum is open Tues through Sat 1 to 5 p.m. year-round, and Sun from 2 to 5 p.m. Memorial Day to Labor Day. Admission is free.

If you happen to be on Highway 4 north and east of Dighton you will find the town of *Utica,* with the *Wertz Street Social Emporium* at 222 East Wertz. The restaurant serves top-notch steaks and German cuisine. It is only 17 miles south of Castle Rock. For hours and specials call (785) 391-2342.

Ness City is the next stop eastbound on Highway 96. It's the home of the *Prairie Mercantile,* featuring Kansas products. The Mercantile is at 102 West Main St., inside the native stone Ness County Bank building, which is on the National Register of Historic Landmarks. The building has been called "the finest and most imposing structure west of Topeka." In 1890 it was the skyscraper of the plains. All money earned in this shop is used to restore the building. (Everyone in the shop is a volunteer.) Hours are from 1 to 5 p.m. Mon through Fri. Call (785) 798-3337.

Cheyenne Bottoms

The **Barbed Wire Museum** in the heart of Post Rock Country displays more than 500 varieties of barbed wire. It is located in Grass Park at 120 West First St., a complex with three museums in **La Crosse,** on U.S. Highway 183. The second museum, the **Rush County Historical Museum,** is housed in an old Santa Fe Railroad Depot and focuses on local history. The third, the **Post Rock Museum,** is in a restored stone house. It was built around 1883 and serves to tell the story of the stone used for fenceposts—there were precious few trees in southwest Kansas—and the tools used to quarry it. All three muse-

> ## trivia
>
> American white pelicans are among the thousands of migrating birds that stop at Quivira or nearby Cheyenne Bottoms in the spring and fall. The endangered whooping crane has been seen here, too.

ums are generally open May through mid-Sept, Mon to Sat 10 a.m. to 4:30 p.m. and 1 to 4:30 p.m. Sun. There is no admission fee, but donations are requested. Call 785-222-9900 or go to www.rushcounty.org/barbedwiremuseum.

US 183 is a north-south road that rolls with river valleys and is lined with hills. It cuts right through the middle of **Liebenthal.** You often can see many out-of-state license plates in front of the old Liebenthal State Bank building at 401 Main St. They come for **Pat's Beef Jerky** (785-222-3341). People stop at Pat's every time they pass through to stock up on jerky, bologna, or summer sausage.

A strange business to be in an old bank building? Well, the structure was empty for years. It was closed during the Depression. But the building remained because on one corner of it is a small marker saying that right there is an exact point on maps, a benchmark for the "U.S. Coast and Geodetic Survey" (now the National Geodetic Survey). Anyone who moves that circular piece of brass is in trouble with the Feds.

Pat Carver got into the business by accident. He was messing around with jerky, trying to invent new marinades and seasonings, and he started giving it away. His friends loved the stuff, and before he knew it, he was in business. Now Pat's turns out 22,000 pounds of jerky a year. Call for hours. You can also order through their Web site at www .patsbeefjerky.com.

> ## trivia
>
> In Great Bend you can see the Kansas Quilt Walk, a site that has seven historic quilt patterns built into the sidewalks around the courthouse square. Rocky Road to Kansas, Kansas Dugout, Windmill, and the other patterns are described in a self-guided walking-tour brochure available from the local visitor bureau.

"Tanking" on the Arkansas River

The sport of *tanking* on the Arkansas River (pop quiz: How is that pronounced?) originated here. What is tanking? Well, it started as an annual race. People dragged big round aluminum horse tanks down to the river, where they were painted and decorated with streamers and balloons, then raced from Syracuse to the town of Kendall, 10 miles east. When there's enough water (Colorado and Mother Nature control the water in the Arkansas River), you can float to Lewis Landing, 5 miles downriver.

Great Bend, at US 56 and 281, derives its name from the sweeping curve made here by the Arkansas River as it loops through southwest Kansas. The town was settled in 1871, two years after the abandonment of old Fort Zarah, and the railroad reached it in 1872 on its way west. The Southern Hotel was the first building in Great Bend, and the town soon became the railhead on the Chisholm Trail. For a time, its boisterous saloons and dance halls made it a hot spot among cowboys and railroad freighters.

Bob Mix is one of the artists featured at the Grassroots Art Center in Lucas. His creatures are welded from scrap and junk metal. Bob and wife Beverly's yard is filled with quirky vehicles, which they actually drive in parades wearing Beverly's handmade costumes, the skeletons of various animals and primitive fish, a saber-tooth tiger, and other creations. They love to show people around their menagerie, which is at 801 Fourth St. in Great Bend, but be sure to call for an appointment and to get directions if you don't want to spend a lot of time wandering around the neighborhood. There are few through streets. Call (785) 525-6118.

The *Barton County Historical Museum and Village* (620-793-5125) lets you walk into the past. A five-acre outdoor village includes a pioneer home, church, schoolhouse, post office, and railroad depot from the late 1800s and early 1900s, and a wood-vane windmill. Inside, see Native American artifacts, farm implements, and exhibits spanning history from the Paleozoic period, the Santa Fe Trail, and World War II. During the war, Great Bend was a training base for the B-29 Superfortress bomber, with its top-secret Norden bombsight (its crosshairs were made of spider webs). The village is located south of Great Bend on US 281 just south of the

trivia

Just east of Great Bend, along the Arkansas River from Raymond to Sterling, is a 20-mile canoe route that takes from eight to twelve hours to run. If you prefer a shorter trip, Section 2, from Sterling to Hutchinson, is 15 miles long and takes five to six hours.

Arkansas River bridge. The museum is open 10 a.m. to 5 p.m. Tues through Fri year-round, with weekend hours of 1 to 5 p.m. Sat and Sun from Apr to Oct. Admission is $2 for ages sixteen and older.

Just west of Great Bend, near Tenth Street and Patton Road, at 5944 West Tenth St., is the *Kansas Oil and Gas Hall of Fame and Museum.* Exhibits on geology, drilling and refining oil, and a Hall of Fame of industry leaders are housed in the main building. Tours are by appointment; call (620) 793-7033 or (620) 793-5742.

The *Shafer Art Gallery* at Great Bend's Barton County Community College displays the bronze western sculptures of internationally known Kansas artist Gus Shafer and other artworks. Open 10 a.m. to 5 p.m. Mon through Fri and 1 to 4 p.m. Sun. Call (620) 792-9342 or visit www.bartonccc.edu/gallery.

Seven miles northeast of Great Bend on Highway 156 or 2 miles east of US 281 is an immense, 19,000-acre wildlife area, the *Cheyenne Bottoms Wildlife Management Area.* Cheyenne Bottoms is the largest inland marsh in the United States. Hundreds of thousands of migrating waterfowl can be seen here each March and October. It also provides a safe roost for bald eagles in winter. As many as 300 species, or three-fourths of all the birds sighted in the state, visit the Bottoms, and it has been designated as critical habitat for the endangered whooping crane. Hunting of nonprotected birds is permitted in season. Call (877) 427-9299 or go to www.cheyennebottoms.net for more information.

There are several antiques shops in *Ellinwood* on US 56, so walk along the brick streets and explore them. Ellinwood is a sleepy little town of about 2,200, but it has a most interesting history. You can actually see some of that history by stopping by the old Hotel Wolf at 1 North Main, home to *James Elliott Antiques,* (620) 564-2400. Inside the same building but around the corner at 104 East Santa Fe is *Starr Antiques* and owner Bill Starr. Jim's shop specializes in art glass, chandeliers, and fine antiques, while Bill's leans more to country antiques and collectibles. The men travel the Midwest buying and selling, so the shops always have something new.

Jim and Bill are not just businessmen but history buffs as well. They will tell you the story of Ellinwood and take you down below to see the circa 1890 underground town left over from the days of the Santa Fe Trail. The town was settled by German immigrants from Munich, who brought with them the custom of building one town aboveground and an entirely different town below it. On the tour you will see the original barbershop, bathhouse, and harness shop from that era. Jim will tell you the stories of the underground town the women of Ellinwood never entered—except for the "soiled doves," who worked the bathhouse there. Because the Santa Fe Trail was a freight trail and the new railroad soon followed, bringing lots of men looking for some

R&R, the town had plenty of, shall we say, male-oriented businesses—"Sample Rooms," as the saloons were called—two in the Hotel Wolf, and seven of them underground. But hear the whole sordid tale from Jim. The tour begins at the Hotel Wolf, which is on the National Register of Historic Places, and costs $5 for adults. Call (620) 564-2400 for store and tour hours.

Dozier Winery, 2.5 miles west on Main Street, across the bridge, and 2.5 miles south to 323 Southeast 80 Ave., is where Bruce and Nina Dozier make twelve varieties of wine. Not just grape wine, but apple and plum wine as well. They even have a gourmet cooking wine made of peppers. The Old Depot Gift Shop there carries any wine accessories you might need as well as wine racks, gift baskets, and the wine itself. The shop is open seven days a week from 1 to 6 p.m. Call (620) 564-0195, www.dozier-winery.com.

The Old Township Hall in *Alden,* west of Highway 14/96 and southeast of Great Bend, was built in 1905, and the Santa Fe Depot was constructed in 1884. This place has history going for it. The *Prairie Flower Craft Shop,* 205 Pioneer St. (620-534-2405), features wicker creations of every description; floor to ceiling, wall-to-wall bolts of fabric; as well as gift items, quilting supplies, and works of art by local craftspeople. Call for hours.

Three miles south and west of Alden you'll find the Arkansas River again. It is a beautiful waterway here, lined with stately cottonwoods and drooping willows. Drop a line, hike on the nature trails, or canoe on this historic stream, and look sharp—wildlife abounds. Beaver join green and great blue herons along the slow-moving river. Bald eagles survey the icy waters in winter as the river slides slowly past long sandbars.

Perhaps you don't think of conquistadores when you think of Kansas, but you should in *Lyons,* on US 56. At 105 West Lyon, the *Coronado-Quivira Museum* (620-257-3941) contains artifacts from Coronado's trip to Kansas. In 1541, more than seventy-five years before the Pilgrims arrived at Plymouth Rock, Francisco Coronado and his expedition arrived in Kansas with just one thing in mind—gold. His party brought a force of 300 Spaniards and 2,500 horses, along with slaughter animals, a cannon, and the other necessities of sixteenth-century travel.

His journey took him to the land of the Quivirans, but no gold was found. Coronado's legacy to the Indians was the horses they began using instead of travois pulled by dogs. There were no

trivia

In 1946 Earl Kelly of Stafford bought a rooster he called Just Bill for $100. Just Bill became famous when he won a contest the next year to become the crowing rooster for Warner-Pathé Newsreels. He beat out several thousand other roosters because he could crow on cue—with the urging of Kelly, waving his arms.

finer riders than these Plains Indians. The museum is open Tues through Sat from 9 a.m. to 5 p.m.Admission is $2 for adults, $1 for children ages six to twelve.

On US 50 between Hutchinson and Kinsley is the little town of *Stafford,* the gateway to the Quivira National Wildlife Refuge. Four bed-and-breakfasts here form the hub of a retreat center. *Henderson House Bed and Breakfast,* at 518 West Stafford, is a 1905 two-story with a dozen stained- or beveled-glass windows, original brass light fixtures, and an ornate staircase. The house is on the National Register of Historic Places. It has four rooms, all with private baths. Rooms are $75.

The second of the trio, *Weide House,* is at 302 North Green. It dates from 1904 and offers five rooms ranging from $65 to $85. The third accommodation is the 1905 *Spickard House,* just down the street at 201 North Green. It has three rooms, all with private baths. Meals for guests at all three bed-and-breakfasts are prepared in the commercial kitchen here and served in two dining rooms that seat up to forty people. Rooms at the Spickard are $55 to $65. The latest addition to the complex is the Littlefield House, 216 North Green, a recently restored 1903 home with six rooms ranging from $60 to $90 per night.

All of them include breakfast. Meeting or event space is available in a 1913 church at 113 Green, also part of the retreat center. Call innkeeper Marie Thompson at (316) 682-5803 or (800) 888-1417 for reservations or information. Visit the Web site at www.hendersonbandb.com.

trivia

The line of longitude that marks the change from central time to mountain time wanders down the western end of the state. The towns of Syracuse, Tribune, Sharon Springs, and Weskan are on mountain time.

The *Quivira National Wildlife Refuge* is located 13 miles northeast of Stafford. Public hunting of waterfowl, pheasant, and quail is permitted in season on 8,000 of the refuge's 22,135 acres. The Quivira Refuge is an intact ecosystem. Because of the salinity of the water, the marshes have not been depleted, as many freshwater marshes have. It is a gold mine for nature photographers because it provides a habitat for migrating birds on the Central Flyway, and almost one-half of all the shorebirds east of the Rockies stop at Quivira in the spring. The main roads in the refuge allow excellent viewing opportunities from a car, but birders and wildflower enthusiasts prefer the two hiking trails and the service roads. The northern part of the refuge is dominated by the Big Salt Marsh, where thousands of ducks, geese, and sandhill cranes can be seen as they migrate in spring and fall. Prairie dogs, coyote, white-tailed deer, northern bobwhite, and wild turkeys also call Quivira home. The visitor center is open Mon through Fri from 7:30 a.m. to 4 p.m. The refuge is open sunrise to sunset. There is no entrance fee. For more information, call (620) 486-2393 or visit www.fws.gov/quivira.

In 1939 the *Saturday Evening Post* turned up the fact that **Kinsley** was exactly halfway between San Francisco and New York City—1,561 miles from either city on US 50. Not about to let an accident of geography go unnoticed, the town adopted the nickname Midway USA. Now local boosters are giving the old moniker a new twist by making Kinsley the home of the new **National Center for Carnival Heritage.** During the 1900s, six family-owned carnival companies operated out of Kinsley. What had long been part of the town's heritage is now housed in the **Carnival Museum,** located in a renovated downtown department store building at 200 East Sixth St. Former carnival workers have donated to the project various items, including some of the canvas backdrops used by burlesque queen Sally Rand, who once appeared in carnival shows. One carousel is already operating there. Call (620) 659-2201.

Larned is located at the junction of US 56 and Highway 156, midway along the historic Santa Fe Trail. By the 1850s the stream of soldiers, wagon trains, mail coaches, and miners headed for the goldfields of California, and later Colorado, and the mail stations built on their hunting grounds were too much for the Native Americans to tolerate. Established as a military post in 1859 to protect travelers on the trail, Fort Larned served as a base for operations against the Plains Indians, who saw the wagon trains as trespassers.

The **Official Santa Fe Trail History Museum and Library** tells the story of the Santa Fe Trail. The East Gallery displays the prehistoric days of

The Caches

A marker 2.1 miles west of Dodge City on US 50 is all that is left of a well-known landmark and rest stop on the Santa Fe Trail. The marker indicates the location of the Caches, pits that supposedly were dug out of the ground. According to legend, a trading party set out from Missouri in late 1822, but their pack train was caught in a blizzard near this site. They lost most of their pack animals and were stranded for three months. In early spring of 1823, they dug pits to cache their goods and left for Taos, New Mexico, to purchase mules. On their return trip, they were attacked by a war party of Pawnees. They survived and dug up their goods and returned to Taos. The pits were left open and were a landmark on the trail for many years.

the trail when buffalo covered the plains and Wichita Indians living in grass hunting lodges followed the herds.

Mexican independence from Spain in 1821 opened trade for American and Mexican businesses, helping to blend the cultures of the three countries. The Santa Fe Trail was a two-way route filled with commercial freight wagons—Conestoga, Murphy, and Osnaburg wagons—pulled by oxen (the beast of choice as they were less likely to be stolen by the Indians and didn't need the grazing and rest that mules and horses required). Settlers established homes, then ranches and farms, along the ruts of the trail despite the dangers of Indian attack and weather extremes. Military forts were established along the trail to protect the caravans.

The trail had two routes: the mountain route began near Franklin, in western Missouri, and went through Kansas and Colorado, then ended in what is now Santa Fe, New Mexico; about 900 miles long, it took approximately seventy-two days, or two and a half months. The cutoff route began in Missouri, passed through Kansas and the Oklahoma panhandle, and ended in New Mexico; it was about 800 miles long, taking approximately sixty-two days, or two months. Arrival of the railroad—a cheaper and faster way to transport goods—near Santa Fe in 1880 ended the Santa Fe Trail's heyday.

Along with the indoor displays and library, the museum features an outdoor setting with sod and dugout houses and a one-room schoolhouse with living-history presentations during the year.

The Santa Fe Trail Center is located 2 miles west of Larned on Highway 156. This fine regional museum has archival and research facilities. A replica sod house and dugout—a practical solution to Kansas's extremes of heat and cold—are on the grounds. The museum focuses on the history of commerce and trade along the Santa Fe Trail and civilian life near Fort Riley. The exhibits trace transportation from the covered wagon to the railroad. Hours are 9 a.m. to 5 p.m. daily (closed Mon from Labor Day through Memorial Day, and closed for Thanksgiving, Christmas, and New Year's Day). Admission is $4 for adults, $2.50 for students twelve through eighteen, $1.50 for children six through eleven, and free to preschoolers. School groups with teachers get a 50 percent discount. Call (316) 285-2054 or go to www.santafetrailcenter.org for more information.

Fort Larned National Historic Site has been magnificently restored to its original condition. All but one of the sandstone buildings were constructed after the Civil War ended, when more time could be spent on the "Indian Problem." The fort was constructed in the shape of a quadrangle.

Six miles west of Larned on Highway 156, a 100-foot-tall wooden flagstaff still towers over the fort, miles from any interstate highway. The fort attracts

trivia

In 1859 the U.S. Army established a small post of dugouts and tents along the Pawnee River near the Santa Fe Trail. The post was originally named Camp on Pawnee Fort but later was called Camp Alert because of the need to be on guard against Indian raids. The post later was moved and renamed Fort Larned.

more than 40,000 visitors a year, despite the same isolation it endured so long ago.

Neatly arranged around the still-intact original parade ground, nine sandstone buildings dating from 1866 to 1868 and a blockhouse stand guard along the Pawnee River, just as they did more than a century ago. Forty interior rooms are restored and furnished in period style, including crowded troops' quarters, where broad bunk beds in the barracks slept four men, two up and two down. A gloomy blacksmith shop and a nineteenth-century post hospital are startlingly real. The isolation of the fort, the relentless wind, the hot sunshine, and the endless flat plains are also striking. The park shows the stark reality of life on the prairie for those who were daring enough to brave the Santa Fe Trail.

One barrack has become a visitor center, with audiovisual programs, and a museum. The museum has grim photographs, archaic tools, and old uniforms; one case details the role of the Buffalo Soldiers—the black men of the Tenth Cavalry stationed at Fort Larned.

Park rangers and volunteers give tours and living-history programs. Admission is free. It is open from 8:30 a.m. to 4:30 p.m. daily except Thanksgiving, Christmas, and New Year's Day. Call (620) 285-6911, or check the Web site at www.nps.gov/fols.

The **Central States Scout Museum** at 815 Broadway has one of the best collections of worldwide Boy and Girl Scout memorabilia in the country. Admission is $1 for youth, $2 for adults. Scout troops and other groups can

Where's the Stockade?

One of the most frequent questions asked of National Park Service personnel at Fort Larned concerns the lack of a stockade surrounding the fort.

There never was a stockade here. It wasn't necessary. The Plains Indians didn't attack the fort. They were guerrilla fighters, ambushing small groups of soldiers traveling to and from the fort. Because the prairie in the 1860s was nearly treeless, building a stockade would have required shipping logs from Colorado or Missouri.

Those "Amber Waves of Grain" Explained

Besides wheat, the important crops of central and western Kansas are alfalfa, sorghum, barley, and broomcorn. Sorghum is a tall, grasslike plant that looks somewhat like corn. The grain, leaves, and stalks are used as cattle feed. The juice of one kind of sorghum is used for making molasses. Broomcorn is related to sorghum. Brooms and brushes are made from the stiff branches of the plant. Broomcorn is grown in the irrigated areas of southwestern Kansas.

stay overnight at a Boy Scout camp 1 mile out of town that has a dormitory; the charge is $4 per person plus a $10 utility charge. Call for reservations. The museum is open from 9 a.m. to 5 p.m. Mon through Sat and noon to 5 p.m. Sun. Call (620) 285-8938 or (620) 285-6427.

Outside Larned is a unique spot that is really off the beaten path. Vicki Dipman has built a barnlike, two-story structure and filled it with antique English and American furniture, lamps, and art glass. Daughter and son-in-law Sandi and Jeff Bates have joined this growing business, which also includes kitchen remodeling, interior design, and custom-made lamp shades and rugs. *Memories Restored* is worth searching out: Go 1.25 miles west of the historic site on Highway 156, then 3.25 miles north. Hours are from 10 a.m. to 5 p.m. Tues through Sat. Call (620) 285-3478.

Heartland Farm in Rush County is eighty acres of homestead, organic gardens, and cropland owned and operated by the Dominican Sisters. It is a ministry of healing and simple living and is open to people as a retreat. Stay in a rustic one-room cottage, and try your hand at organic gardening or explore holistic health, conservation, and alternative energy sources, including solar power.

Meals created with natural whole foods are not strictly vegetarian but emphasize a naturally healthy diet. A small herd of alpaca call the farm home, too. The alpaca is smaller than a llama and has a more gentle nature. Now the sisters spin and knit the fine alpaca. Two interesting buildings also are here, built of straw bales and stuccoed over to look like adobe. Inside one of the 1,600-square-foot buildings is an art studio, where the sisters make pottery and spin alpaca fleece. Therapeutic massage is available for $40 per hour. Suggested offering is $15 a day for lodging and $10 for a full day of meals. For information call (620) 792-1232. No one is excluded from sharing the experience of Heartland Farm because of financial stress. Bartering of contributed services and extended time payment may be prearranged.

Amish Country

Hutchinson lies on the north bank of the Arkansas River. Built in a level valley, the town boasts long, straight streets. The discovery of salt led to almost a dozen salt plants by 1888. In fact, the Morton Salt Stabilized Highway was built accidentally between the Morton plant and Main Street as salt spilled from trucks onto the soft road. It soon became a satisfactory road for heavy trucks.

A shallow inland sea covered the land here 300 million years ago, slowly receding, drying, and concentrating its salt near Hutchinson; the area has the world's largest salt deposit—100 miles by 40 miles, 325 feet thick, mined from underground passages. It yields 44.1 million tons of salt each year; that'll salt a lot of homegrown tomatoes!

If you're a golfer, then Hutchinson has something special for you. The ***Prairie Dunes Golf Club,*** 4812 East Thirtieth Ave., is one of the top fifteen courses in the country. It was designed by Perry and Press Maxwell. The course is designed like a Scottish links course and offers "a touch of Scotland" in Kansas and also what is reputed to be the world's most difficult hole—number 8, a long par 4 that is 422 yards of rolling hills.

Prairie Dunes is a private club but has reciprocal privileges: If you belong to another private USGA facility, you are welcome here, but you must call ahead for a tee time. There is a fine restaurant here with a very large selection of unusual dishes. Call (620) 662-0581, or visit the Web site at www.prairie dunes.com.

The ***Kansas Cosmosphere and Space Center,*** at 1100 North Plum, is affiliated with the Smithsonian Institution in Washington, D.C. The

Pretty Prairie's Big Rodeo

South of Hutchinson, in the quaintly named, minute town of Pretty Prairie, you can enjoy the state's largest nighttime rodeo. This late-July, four-day event has been kicking since the 1930s and showcases professional bull-riders, as well as the crowd favorite "mutton-bustin'"—small children attempting to ride sheep. The Friday night of the rodeo turns into a real hootenanny late at night, with live country music and lots of two-stepping. Belt buckles and pickup trucks also abound. Call (620) 459-4653 or go to www.pprodeo.com.

Cosmosphere's Hall of Space Museum houses the largest collection of space artifacts outside the National Air and Space Museum. It also can boast of the largest collection of space suits in the world and the most complete collection of Russian space artifacts outside Moscow.

The Hall of Space traces the Space Race from Sputnik to the space shuttle. On display are rare 1930s German V-1 and V-2 rockets, artifacts from the Gemini and Mercury programs, the actual Apollo 13 command module *Odyssey*, a 30-ton SR 71 Blackbird spy plane more than 107 feet long (it could fly over Kansas east to west in ten minutes), a Northrop T-38 (the aircraft used to train shuttle astronauts), and a full-scale replica of the space shuttle *Endeavor*. The *Liberty Bell 7,* the Mercury spacecraft that sank after splashing down in 1961, was recovered in 1999 and restored at the Cosmosphere. After a national tour the capsule is on permanent display here.

Also at the Cosmosphere are the Carey IMAX Theatre, with a 44-foot tilted dome screen, and the Justice Planetarium, where a star projector produces simulated views of the night sky and laser light shows. The Cosmosphere is open Mon through Thurs from 9 a.m. to 6 p.m., Fri and Sat 9 a.m. to 9 p.m., Sun noon to 6 p.m. Hall of Space Museum tickets cost $9.50; passes to the entire facility, including IMAX and planetarium shows, are $17 for adults and $15 for seniors and children ages three to twelve. Reservations are recommended. Call (800) 397-0330 or visit the Web site at www.cosmo.org.

Ready to come back to Earth? The **Hutchinson Art Center** at 405 North Washington displays the work of some local artists and many touring exhibits that change every month. The gallery is open Tues through Fri from 9 a.m. to 5 p.m., Sat and Sun from 1 to 5 p.m. Call (620) 663-1081.

trivia

Remember that freckle-faced Little Rascal with the lick of black hair standing up—Carl "Alfalfa" Switzer of *Our Gang* movie fame? He once farmed north of Pretty Prairie after he married a local girl and had a son. The marriage was brief, and he returned to California. At thirty-two, he was killed in a brawl over a $50 debt.

There is a most interesting shop downtown at 22 North Main St. **Ten Thousand Villages** offers handicrafts from Third World countries around the globe. There is a large selection of what they refer to as "fairly traded handicrafts" for you to peruse. Hours are Mon through Thurs from 8:30 a.m. to 3 p.m. Call (620) 669-8932 or visit www.tenthousandvillages.com.

The downtown area has a good-size antiques district featuring high-quality antiques and collectibles. Walk down South Main Street and search through nearly a dozen antiques shops. Wow, that was your workout for the day. Worn out yet? Sylvan Park is nearby for a quiet resting spot. You have earned a good meal, too, with all that walking. Wherever your feet give out along South Main Street, you will find some good eating places.

Deer Creek Inn Bed and Breakfast is at 1114 West Sixty-ninth St. in the center of forty acres of trees and natural grasslands. A screened-in porch is the best spot to take in the fresh air. Hiking on a wilderness trail and soaking in the hot tub on the deck are a good combination, too. Innkeeper Marilyn Darnell will make sure you are comfortable no matter what you choose to do. Rates are $55 to $100 and you can see more at the Web site, www.bbonline .com/ks/deercreek, or call (620) 665-9850.

While you're in Hutchinson, visit the *Dillon Nature Center* at 3002 East Thirtieth Ave. The Discovery Center includes an observation beehive and large aquariums teeming with native fish. Surrounding the center are terraced beds of perennials and some 1,500 annual flowers, planted each spring by dedicated volunteers. There is an abundance of wildlife in the tallgrass prairie area, woodlands, and marsh. You can picnic or canoe, and hikers are welcome on the trail system, which is a National Recreational Trail. Red fox, raccoons, coyotes, deer, and more than 180 species of birds have been seen here. Hours at the Discovery Center vary with the season, so call ahead. The park is open from 8 a.m. to sunset weekdays, 9 a.m. to sunset Sat and Sun. There is no admission charge, but donations are appreciated. For more information, call (620) 663-7411 or visit www.hutchrec.com/dnc.

Five miles west of Hutchinson is the *Dutch Kitchen Restaurant* (620-662-2554), 6803 West Hwy. 61. If you're partial to pies or bonkers over bread, this is the place. They bake them fresh each day, and sweet, spicy cinnamon rolls. Hours are 6 a.m. to 8 p.m. Mon through Sat.

Also west of Hutchinson on Highway 96 at *Nickerson* is the most unusual animal farm/bed-and-breakfast combo you'll ever find in the state. Joe and Sondra Hedrick are hosts at the *Hedrick Exotic Animal Farm and the Hedrick Bed and Breakfast,* at 7910 North Roy L. Smith Rd. A family hobby of raising exotic animals soon became a petting zoo. Now you can watch a small herd of zebras, see a huge white camel move with dignity among the other dozen or more camels, try to count a band of fast-moving kangaroos and wallabies, Sicilian donkeys, giraffes, several llamas, a number of ostriches, and probably a partridge in a pear tree, if you look long enough. A stay at the bed-and-breakfast includes a hands-on tour, as well as petting and feeding the giraffes and zebras. Kenya, one of the farm's half-dozen giraffes, witnessed a marriage proposal here and was invited to a Colorado couple's wedding. (She was unable to attend.) The bed-and-breakfast has seven rooms behind the building's facade, which gives the appearance of a frontier bank, general store, hotel, and saloon, with animal-influenced decor and private baths. Color television and home-cooked, farm-style breakfasts are part of the package. Rooms are $99 to $125 Fri and Sat. Call (888) 489-8039 for reservations or see www.hedricks.com.

Northeast of Hutchinson, you enter lovely, alien lands: the Flint Hills. Here the deep, silty deposits eroded away, leaving the bony outcroppings of flint or chert that girdle the landscape. Lonely prairies remain virtually unchanged here from presettlement days; the stony land didn't lend itself easily to agriculture. These rolling prairie uplands flow in auburn hues.

You can see forever from the tops of some of these hills, perhaps 100 miles in any direction on a clear day; you begin to understand how alone the first settlers must have felt.

Yoder, a small town southeast of Hutchinson on Highway 96, lets you step into the gentle world of the Amish community. A general store, a bakery, and a gift shop here in the quiet Kansas countryside make you feel as if you've tumbled backward into the nineteenth century. You'll find a blacksmith, a harness maker, and a buggy shop among the businesses in Yoder.

Most do not have telephones, and not too many addresses are on the buildings, but once you are in town, just wander around and find what you find. Watch for the **Kansas Station** at Highway 96 and Yoder Road, where you can take a ride around town in an Amish buggy on select Saturdays. There's a buggy inside that you can inspect, too, or you can shop among the goodies—chocolates, wheat straw creations, and gifts—or sit down and enjoy a snack from the deli counter. Call (620) 465-3807 or (800) 952-6328. Open Mon through Sat 8 a.m. to 8 p.m.

Yoder Meats is under the same roof as the Kansas Station. The shop sells hormone-free, fresh-from-the-farm chicken and corn-fed beef. Stock up on sausage, as well as Amish cheeses and beef jerky. Buffalo, elk, and other exotic meats are available, along with lamb, pork, and the best, the very best, hickory-smoked ham and bacon around. Call (800) 952-6328 to order.

The Dutch Mill Bakery, 3518 East Red Rock Rd., is the home of cinnamon rolls like you wish your Grandma made, along with cakes, cookies, pies, and breads—all without preservatives. Hours are Mon 7 a.m. to 1 p.m. and Tues through Fri 7 a.m. to 4 p.m. Call (620) 465-2314. *Yoder Wood Products* at 10409 South Yoder Rd. will also give you a look at quality handcrafted furniture, from china cabinets to gazebos. The showroom takes you back to an era when craftsmen used time as well as tools to fashion heirloom furniture. Call (620) 465-1180. There has been a hardware and lumber store on the corner of Main Street and Lawrence Avenue in Yoder since the late 1890s. *Yoder Hardware and Lumber,* 9816 South Main St., is truly an old-time hardware store with horseshoes, hand tools, crocks, butter churns, hand meat grinders, and sausage stuffers. Rod and Peggy Fry sell nails in bulk, weighing each purchase on an old metal scale. The shop carries a full line of Radio Flyer metal wagons, tricycles, bicycles, and toys, as well as a line of miniatures and collectibles. One of the specialties of the store is a selection of oil lamps and lanterns in many sizes, price ranges, and descriptions, as well as parts to fix up your old lamps and lanterns. Take a look at the Web site, www.yoderkansas .com/yoder_hardware.htm. Call (620) 465-2277 for hours.

Sunflower Inn, at 3307 East Switzer Rd. in Yoder, (620) 465-2200, is where you can slip into this unique little town and become one with the universe. The innkeepers will pamper you and see to your every need. The three serene rooms of this quiet inn have large private baths and queen-sized beds. You will enjoy the warm hospitality in this modernized Amish home. How modern is it? There is free Wi-Fi in the rooms—that's how modern. Rooms are $89. Visit the Web site at www.sunflowerinnofyoder.com for more information.

Carriage Crossing Restaurant at 10002 South Yoder Rd. (620-465–3612) has really good cooking and is open for breakfast, lunch, and supper. There are specials every day and fresh homemade pies for dessert. Order from a huge menu, or try family-style all-you-want-to-eat dinners. There's even a gift shop inside. Restaurant hours are from 6 a.m. to 9 p.m. Mon through Sat, with breakfast served daily until 10:30 a.m. Horse and carriage rides are often offered here on nice Saturday mornings in summer. Most Amish businesses are located on Yoder Road or Red Rock Road, Yoder's main street. Folks at the Carriage Crossing will be glad to give you directions to any place you can't find.

Will wonders never cease? The town, for all its shortage of telephones, automobiles, and modern gewgaws, does indeed have a Web site at www.yoder kansas.com.

Glenn Stark, 1100 Coronado St. in *Kingman,* (620) 532-3043, has been creating art for more than sixty years. His yard and home are filled with both humorous and beautiful sculptures in concrete and wood. You can call and meet Glenn and his wife, Mary, by calling for an appointment, or just drive by and enjoy the yard art. Dozens of life-size statues are on display, and many are shown at the Grassroots Art Center in Lucas. Near the banks of the Chikaskia River you'll find the town of *Argonia.* The *Salter House,* at 220 West Garfield, was the home of Susanna Madora Salter, who was elected the first woman mayor of Argonia (and of the world) in 1887. (Not bad for a presuffragist.) The 1884 house was built from brick fired in a kiln near the site. An adjacent museum in the old Mayfield church holds antiques and artifacts of the area's culture. Call (620) 435-6417.

Gyp Hills

Medicine Lodge lies on a hillside overlooking the Medicine River and its wooded valley. The landscape here is unusual for Kansas. Red bluffs, mesas, and buttes extend from this part of the state into Oklahoma and the Texas Panhandle, and turning south here is like entering another world.

Stormy temperance leader Carry Nation, known for her ax-swinging crusade against demon liquor, lived in Medicine Lodge during her most colorful years. Even though Kansas was, by law, a dry state, Medicine Lodge in the late 1880s had seven saloons. Nation closed the first in 1899 by singing in front of it, the second by praying in front of the door. Before the end of the year, all the saloons in town closed.

Nation traveled to other Kansas towns, using stones and a cane to wreak havoc on saloons there. In 1901 she descended on Wichita, and it was there that she first used her famous hatchet to attack a saloon. In the months following, she was arrested and jailed many times and paid her fines by selling souvenir hatchets.

Carry Nation's Home, now a National Historic Landmark, is a small house at 211 West Fowler in Medicine Lodge. It is furnished with many of her personal belongings and is open daily from 10:30 a.m. to 5 p.m. and 1 to 4 p.m. in the off-season. Call (620) 886-3553 for information.

Every three years, in the fall, Medicine Lodge is the scene of the *Peace Treaty Pageant,* a huge spectacle dating from 1927, when citizens looked for a way to commemorate the Medicine Lodge Peace Treaty, signed at the confluence of Elm Creek and the Medicine River in 1867. The treaty allowed

The First Medicine Lodge

The Kiowa tribe made its home in this beautiful area, where vast herds of buffalo, elk, deer, and antelope grazed in the valleys and bear, turkey, and other game birds inhabited the woods. There were swift-running streams, sweet native grasses, and abundant natural shelter in the bluffs and canyons. The Kiowa believed that the Medicine River was endowed with healing properties. Every year they came to a spot where the river joined a creek. They pitched their tepees, bathed in the river, and drank its mineral waters. They also discovered the healing properties of many of the herbs and plants that grew on the banks of the streams. The Kiowa built a great medicine lodge out of slender tree trunks set on end in a circle, their tops bent toward the center and covered with rushes and earth. They heated large stones, placed healing herbs on them, and poured water on the stones to make clouds of aromatic steam.

settlers to move onto the lands of the Apache, Comanche, Cheyenne, Kiowa, and Arapaho in Kansas, and it moved the Indians to Oklahoma. It takes more than 500 American Indian and military reenactors to re-create the scenes surrounding the treaty. An intertribal powwow and a rodeo take place the same weekend. Call (620) 886-9815 or see www.peactreaty.org for information.

Stop at Medicine Lodge High School on El Dorado Avenue to see the **Equatorial Sun Dial.** This monster of a clock is made of Colorado granite and weighs one ton. It was engineered for this exact location to help students understand the movements of our solar system.

Gypsum Hills Trail Rides takes horseback and horse-drawn-wagon riders out on the trails through the area's spectacular scenery. The red gypsum bluffs overlook canyons richly carpeted with wildflowers. Downy phlox, ragwort, and native cedars tint the canyons. This is one of the country's most colorful sights: stark red bluffs and buttes flecked with white gypsum and capped with deep green cedar trees.

The trail day ends around a campfire, where steaks sizzle to savory perfection, seasoned with the kind of hunger you work up only outdoors. Riders sing cowboy songs, and in the distance you can hear coyotes howl. The trail rides begin at the Gant-Larson Ranch about 9 miles west of Medicine Lodge on US 160. This is strictly a BYOH affair—you must have your own horse to ride; if

Gypsum Hills Scenic Drive

To enjoy a beautiful 29-mile drive to nowhere, travel west of Medicine Lodge on US 160 for a little more than 3 miles. There a scenic-drive sign will point you south. About a mile down the road, you will round a curve and begin to see the beauty of the Gypsum Hills. About 2.5 miles south, just before you reach the crest of the hills, it is worth a long look to the east down one of the most beautiful valleys. Six miles south of US 160, you will turn west onto a dirt road. Just after the turn look to the north, and you will see the back side of Twin Peaks. Look to the northwest and you will see Flowerpot Mound. About 11.5 miles down the dirt road, turn left, or north, at a Y-shaped intersection, and 5 miles later, you will be back at US 160. A turn to the right, or east, will take you back to Medicine Lodge. Within 4 miles you will be at a scenic overlook, which will give you an opportunity to see the valley and hills to the south.

A mile to the east (mile marker 217), a cross sits atop a hill, and for the next mile Twin Peaks will clearly be in view to the south. (Another paved pull-off is on the south side near mile marker 219.) Continue on to cross Cedar Creek and return to Medicine Lodge. Call (620) 886-9815 for information, or get a map at the Stockade Museum.

you don't have a horse, you can ride in one of the horse-drawn wagons. Either way, if you want to see the incredible color of the Gypsum Hills, there is no better way to do it. The combination of cedar trees and the unusual formations of the hills is what the Wild West movies were made of.

Bob and Charlene Larson own the ranch and provide campsites and food; everything else is up to you. Riders bring their own equipment. This is no dude ranch; it is a real working outfit, smack in the middle of some of the most beautiful scenery in the state. Saddle clubs, as well as smaller groups, are welcome. Call the Larsons to make arrangements at least a week in advance at (620) 886-5390.

Group rides occur on the Larson ranch during the first three weekends in May. Make your plans well in advance; there is a 250-rider limit, and they fill up early. Riders come in on Fri night, and the ride begins at 11 a.m. Sat. Dinner on Sat evening, Sun morning breakfast, and lunch at noon are provided for $70 (adults) or $50 (children ages six through twelve). The ride on the first weekend, however, is potluck and therefore just $25.

The **Sagebrush Gallery of Western Art** at 115 East Kansas St. (620-886-5163, www.earlkuhn.com) is also owned by the Kuhn family. Here Earl Kuhn exhibits western paintings and sculptures. Call for hours.

One and a half miles east of Medicine Lodge is the **Pageant Drive-In.** Opened in 1953, it was closed for a while, then restored. It has pole speakers and FM broadcast, too. It is open May through Sept. Visit www.pageantdrivein .com to see what's playing.

Folks around **Zenda** (south of US 54, east of US 281) enjoy the seafood buffet the third Sat of every month at **The Lumber Yard,** 311 North Main St. Yes, it is actually in a lumber yard in this old town, but there's a full menu of steaks, ribs, and chicken, and people travel out of their way to get there. Owners Lisa and Ralph Lilja say that there are the occasional nights when something special is featured. Open Thurs from 11 a.m. to 9 p.m. and Fri and Sat night until 11 p.m. Call (620) 243-6000.

Anthony is southeast of Medicine Lodge at the junction of Highways 2, 44, and 179. If you're here in July, you're in luck because Kansas's oldest race meet is held here at **Anthony Downs** with two weekends of pari-mutuel horse and greyhound races.

Begun in 1904, the meet has grown large enough to attract 5,000 people. An equally enthusiastic crowd comes for the **Sunflower Balloon Fest** on Mother's Day weekend each May. Weather permitting, you can watch a mass launching of twenty-five hot-air balloons Sat morning and evening and Sun morning. Call the chamber of commerce for more information at (620) 842-5456.

South of Medicine Lodge on US 281 in the town of *Hardtner* is Bob and Sue Sterling's restaurant, *Yur Place,* 108 East Central Ave. The food here is typically Kansas—fried chicken, chicken-fried steak, enchiladas–with a lunch special every day.. Yur Place opens daily for breakfast at 5 a.m. (yes, sir, you read that right) and stays open until 8 p.m.Call (620) 296-4477.

North of Medicine Lodge on US 281, in the town of *Pratt,* a covered wagon stands ready to take you back on an imaginary trip to the 1880s at the *Pratt County Historical Museum,* 212 South Ninnescah (Ninnescah and Second Streets, 1 block off either US 54 or US 281). The covered wagon on display tempts children to climb aboard and feel the sodbuster plow settlers carried west.

trivia

Take a look at the twin water towers in Pratt. They were painted Hot and Cold as a practical joke, and now they are a must-see.

Several galleries and an Old Time Main Street show visitors the ingenuity settlers used to survive. Gallery One traces history up to the late 1800s. Gallery Two re-creates a sodbuster's home, right down to the rug beater and cream separator, and a one-room school with McGuffey Readers, slate boards, and desks with inkwells. Gallery Three houses old-time farm implements, while Gallery Four salutes agriculture, the railroad, and the oil industry. Completing the museum's collections is an early Main Street with a drugstore, a tonsorial shop, a photography studio, a bank, a livery stable, a telephone office, and a hotel. A harness maker's horse is hitched to a buggy and stands ready for an imaginary ride. Upstairs is a wedding chapel, still used on occasion.

For genealogy and history buffs, there is a research library with land patents, marriage licenses, census and cemetery records, and newspapers, open by appointment. Visit www.prattkan.com/museum.html.

The museum is open every afternoon from 1 to 4 p.m. Mon through Fri and 1 to 3 p.m. Sat and Sun. Admission is free, but donations are accepted. Call (620) 672-7874 for information or special tours, or visit www.prattcounty museum.org.

Pizza-Taco comes highly recommended by the Pratt locals. Try the great folded taco pizza. Pizza-Taco is at 105 West First St.. Call (620) 672-3649 for hours.

If you're hungry, you might want to head over to *Coldwater.* Known around here as "the eating-out town," Coldwater has about ten sit-down restaurants. Eating out is the social pastime of the town, so if you sit down in any one of these restaurant, you probably won't be alone long.

One-fourth of a mile southwest of Coldwater on US 183 is *Lake Coldwater,* a 250-acre lake in a 930-acre park. Coldwater is the only lake in southwestern Kansas that allows water sports. There are facilities for boating, fishing, and camping. A nine-hole golf course is just east of the lake.

The towns of Coldwater, **Protection,** and **Wilmore** have outdoor artwork created by artist **Stan Herd,** a Protection native. You may have seen aerial photos of Herd's incredible "field art": The artist's immense canvas is the earth itself, and his paints are the various soils and vegetation he plants. Somehow he keeps all this beauty straight in his mind from the back of a tractor. He also creates permanent rock mosaics on the ground. Contact the local chambers of commerce for locations, or the artist at (785) 856 6622. He also has a Web site, www.stanherdart.com.

trivia

Sharon is the birthplace of Martina McBride, who was voted vocalist of the year in 2004 and tied Reba McEntire's record of four Country Music Association awards for Female Vocalist that same year. She was also raised in Sharon (population 210, seven students in her graduating class). Her father, Daryl Schiff, played the guitar and Martina began singing in the family band, called "The Schiffters," at age seven. Her five-year-old brother Marty also played the guitar and still plays in his sister's band. Martina has a pitch-perfect voice and an impressive range. She has sold more than fifteen million records.

Hardesty House, at 712 Main St. in **Ashland,** on US 160/183 west of Coldwater, is a small turn-of-the-twentieth-century hotel. The owner is Les Moore, and his daughter Heather manages the restaurant. Specialties include steak, smoked meats, and seafood. Lunch is served from 11 a.m. to 1:30 p.m. Tues through Fri and dinner from 5 to 8 p.m. Tues through Thurs and until 9 p.m. on Fri and Sat. It is a private restaurant because the county is dry except for social clubs. But if you're from out of town, you can sign in as a guest at the restaurant and enjoy the facilities.

Six rooms and two apartments are available, all with private baths and all decorated with antiques. Call (620) 635-4040.

The **Rolling Hills Bed 'n Breakfast** is in Ashland at 204 East Fourth Ave. (US 160). There are three rooms with shared baths, a spa, and an outdoor pool. This is a "down-home," comfortable, country place that serves up gourmet breakfasts. Call (620) 635-4378 for rates and reservations.

Travel 15 miles north toward **Clark State Fishing Lake,** through Church's Canyon and Horseshoe Bend, where rugged terrain provided hiding places for rustlers when those cattle drives came through. There are photo opportunities aplenty here.

To witness what might be one of the most innovative comeback stories in history, head to **Greensburg,** a small town in Kiowa County. In May 2007, an EF5 tornado (that's the biggest, most dangerous sort, with wind speeds of

"Cannonball" Green and Carry Nation

The town of Greensburg was named for D. R. "Cannonball" Green, a stagecoach driver along the route followed by US 54 (still Cannonball Highway to locals). His nickname was earned from the speed at which he drove. Cannonball was a colorful guy. Carry Nation rode with him often during her temperance crusade. Once, when she was a passenger, Cannonball lit a huge cigar. Nation reached through the window, snatched it from his mouth, and threw it into the dirt. The story goes that Cannonball stopped the coach, lifted her down, and drove off without a word, leaving her miles from town. Temperance is one thing, but "a good cigar is a smoke."

The Greensburg name now has a new significance, however, as the town has made history with its efforts to "go green" with eco-friendly rebuilding efforts following a devastating tornado in 2007.

more than 200 miles per hour) leveled a shocking 95 percent of the town and killed 11 people. The twister was nearly two miles wide and forever changed this rural community. But, instead of giving up on their town, many residents committed to rebuilding Greensburg—with a twist. Their goal? To live up to their name as a truly "green" city. Greensburg's structures are built to the strictest environmental standards, and the town's energy comes from wind turbines. The unique, inspiring story of Greensburg's reconstruction garnered celebrity support and has been the subject of documentaries on networks such as Planet Green, a sister network of Discovery Channel.

The **World's Largest Hand-Dug Well** is at 315 South Sycamore, Greensburg, on US 54 at US 183. The "Big Well" was dug here in 1887 and furnished water for the city and railroad until 1932. It measures 32 feet across and 109 feet deep, a marvel of pioneer engineering. Crews of about a dozen men were hired to dig the well and to quarry and haul stone from the Medicine River, 12 miles away, for the casing of the well. Dirt from the well was hauled away by the same wagons, which had slatted beds. By opening the slats in low spots, roads to the site were "leveled"—these guys were ingenious.

The well itself survived the 2007 tornado, but the Big Well building was destroyed and the viewing canopy was damaged. You can still visit a temporary gift shop, though, from 9 a.m. to 5 p.m. Mon through Sat and 1 to 5 p.m. Sun, or call (620) 723-4102 to find out whether rebuilding efforts are complete—in which case, you can walk the 105 steps to the bottom of the well.

Next to the well, you can see a 1,000-pound pallasite meteorite found east of town years ago—and recovered from the 2007 tornado rubble. It must have created quite an impact when it struck earth, experts think, about the time of Christ.

A few miles southwest of Greensburg is the site of the historical ***Fromme-Birney Round Barn.*** It is just an amazing thing to see. It is not just big, it is huge, and it is not actually, technically, round, it is polygonal—having sixteen sides—but of course, you noticed that right away. It was built in 1912 and took a trainload of shingles to roof. Inside are twenty-eight horse stalls and a circular alleyway big enough to allow a grain wagon to be pulled through. A sixteen-sided granary in the center of the first floor is 16 feet across. The dome covers two haymows. It cost $8,000 to build back then. It is being restored by the Kiowa County Historical Society, which received it as a gift in 1993.

Places to Stay in Southwest Kansas

DODGE CITY

Econo Lodge
1610 West Wyatt
Earp Blvd.
(620) 225-0231

Gunsmoke Trav-L-Park
11070 108 Rd.
(620) 338-8919

GARDEN CITY

AmericInn Lodge & Suites
3020 East Kansas Ave.
(620) 272-9860

Foster's RV Park
4100 East Hwy. 50
(620) 276-8741

GREAT BEND

Best Western Angus Inn
2920 Tenth St.
(620) 792-3541

GREENSBURG

Best Western J-Hawk Motel
515 West Kansas Ave.
(620) 723-2121

HUTCHINSON

Astro Motel
15 East Fourth Ave.
(620) 663-1151

LARNED

Best Western Townsman Inn
123 East 14th St.
(620) 285-3114

LIBERAL

Best Western LaFonda Motel
229 West Pancake Blvd.
(877) 747-8713

Holiday Inn Express Hotel & Suites
1550 North Lincoln Ave.
(620) 624-9700

PRATT

Days Inn
1901 East First St.
(620) 672-9465

SCOTT CITY

Airliner Motel
609 East Fifth St.
(620) 872-2125

Chaparral Inn Motel
401 Hunter Rd.
(620) 872-2181

ULYSSES

Single Tree Inn
2033 West Oklahoma Ave.
(620) 356-1500

YODER

The Hitchin' Post RV
(620) 727-2356

SELECTED CHAMBERS OF COMMERCE AND VISITOR BUREAUS

Dodge City Convention and Visitors Bureau
400 West Wyatt Earp Blvd.
P.O. Box 1474
Dodge City 67801
(620) 225-8186 or (800) OLD–WEST
www.dodgecity.org

Garden City AreaChamber of Commerce
1511 East Fulton Terrace
Garden City 67846
(620) 276-3264 or (800) 879-9803
www.garden-city.org

Great Bend Convention and Visitors Bureau
3007 West Tenth St.
(620) 792-2750 or (877) 427-9299
www.visitgreatbend.com

Hays Convention and Visitors Bureau
2700 Vine St.
(785) 628-8202 or (800) 569-4505
www.haysusa.com

Larned Chamber of Commerce
502 Broadway
Larned 67550
(620) 285-6916
www.larnedks.org

Liberal Tourist Information Center
1 Yellow Brick Rd.
Liberal 67901
(620) 626-0171

Medicine Lodge Chamber of Commerce
215 South Iliff
Medicine Lodge 67104
(620) 886-3417
www.medicinelodge.com

Syracuse Chamber of Commerce
118 North Main
(620) 384-5459
www.syracusekschamber.com

Places to Eat in Southwest Kansas

DODGE CITY

Cowtown Club
503 East Trail St.
(620) 227-5225

HUTCHINSON

Amarillo Mesquite Grill
1401 East Eleventh St.
(620) 669-1211

LARNED

Country Inn
135 East Fourteenth St.
(620) 285-3216

MEDICINE LODGE

Indian Grill
301 West Fowler Ave.
(620) 886-3476

PRATT

Uptown Café & Club D'Est
202 South Main St.
(620) 672-6116
Scott City

NORTH CENTRAL KANSAS →

Part of the Central Lowlands, the landscape here is made up of rolling hills and valleys. The Flint Hills, south of the Kaw River, are in the area known as the Osage Plains. Limestone, chert, shale, and other rock underlie this area; wind and water have carved it into escarpments—long cliffs or bluffs—formed by rocky ledges that eroded more slowly than looser soils and sediments. Between the escarpments are gently undulating plains.

Although most of Kansas has been cultivated, the Flint Hills remain largely in native grass because much of the ground is too rocky for cultivation. Used by ranchers for pasturing cattle, it is one of the last preserves of the tallgrass prairie of bluestem, Indian grass, and switchgrass. Except around rivers, trees are rare in the Flint Hills, partly because ranchers burn off the hills every spring to eliminate weeds and small trees.

In the mid-1800s, the Oregon Trail provided a route to the Northwest; when gold was discovered in California in 1848, traffic became heavy. Part of the trail followed the Kaw River to Topeka, then continued north into Nebraska. Alcove Springs, between Blue Rapids and Marysville, was a well-known stopping place. Watering holes were at a premium, and

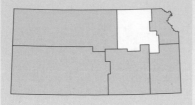

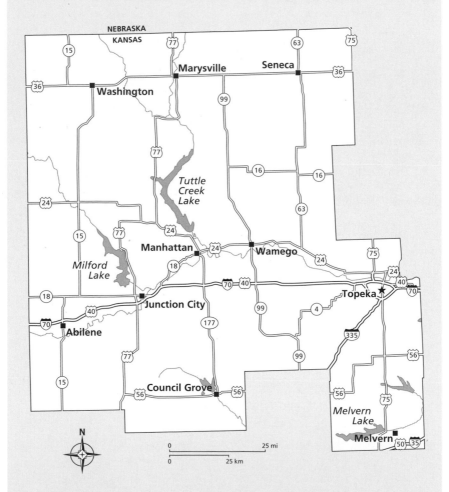

NEBRASKA
KANSAS

Marysville
Seneca
Washington

Tuttle
Creek
Lake

Manhattan
Wamego

Milford
Lake

Junction City

Topeka

Abilene

Council Grove

Melvern
Lake

Melvern

N

0   25 mi
0   25 km

stones in the area contain initials and dates carved by those early travelers. U.S. Highway 36 follows the old Pony Express Route and Oregon Trail.

Lieutenant Zebulon Pike (of Pike's Peak fame) traced the Osage River west and found Pawnee, Osage, and Kansa Indians growing corn, beans, and pumpkins on land called "incapable of cultivation and uninhabitable by people depending on agriculture for their sustenance." Because the land had been seen as worthless, the eastern Indians (Delaware, Shawnee, Wyandot, and Kickapoo) were moved to the "Great American Desert," which has since become the breadbasket of the country.

Tallgrass Prairie

Topeka is the capital of Kansas, so let's start there and take the East Topeka exit (182) off Interstate 70. The city is bisected by the Kansas River and extends across the bowl of the fertile valley; the Oregon Trail crossed the river here.

Topeka has that nice blend of big city/small town; people here are both city-sophisticated and down-home friendly. You won't have a hard time finding a friendly local to point you in the right direction.

The high point on this tour is **Potwin Place,** a quiet, untouched neighborhood established as a separate village in the 1880s. Here brick roadways—designed for buggies, but negotiable by cars—curve among homes set back on cool, shaded lawns. Turreted Queen Annes and handsome Italianate villas give this Victorian neighborhood its charm, but at Christmas it becomes a fairyland of shimmering lights. It's not hard to find; just take Sixth Avenue to Woodlawn and Greenwood Streets.

Nine blocks from the Potwin Place neighborhood stands the city's most famous landmark, the Greek Revival **Ward-Meade Home** at Meade Park, 124

AUTHOR'S FAVORITES

Combat Air Museum	Kirby House
Eisenhower Center	Konza Prairie
Hays House Restaurant	Paxico
John Steuart Curry murals at the Capitol	Seelye Mansion
	The Woodward
Junction City's Kansas Vietnam Veterans Memorial	

Northwest Fillmore St., built in 1870. This beautiful estate also has a recon-structed frontier log cabin, an authentic one-room schoolhouse, a depot dating from the turn of the nineteenth century, a general store, and a drugstore that serves up ice-cream treats from its vintage soda fountain. The grounds contain a splendid botanical garden with more than 500 varieties of trees and shrubs, 9,000 annual flowers, and 5,000 tulips.

Enhance your time traveling: Have a Victorian dinner on fine china and silver in the elegant dining room, a family-style meal at the cabin (hearth-cooked ham, Dutch-oven biscuits), or a picnic-basket dinner in the garden. The family-style meals are served Oct 15 through Mar 15 for groups of at least 12. Call (785) 368-3888 for museum information or for meal reservations, or visit www.topeka.org.

The garden is open daily from 8 a.m. to dusk; the shop buildings, Mon through Sat from 10 a.m. to 4 p.m., Sun noon to 4 p.m. Tours are given year-round at 10 a.m., noon and 2 p.m. weekdays; noon and 2 p.m. weekends. Admission is $4.50 for adults, $4 for seniors, $2 for children ages six to twelve.

The copper-domed *State Capitol Building* at Tenth and Jackson Streets was constructed of native limestone and designed in the French Renaissance style. It is home to the famous *John Steuart Curry Murals,* including one of abolitionist John Brown, and murals by other native Kansans, as well as statues of Dwight D. Eisenhower, Amelia Earhart, and other noted Kansans, each weighing a ton. There's also a hand-operated passenger elevator dating from 1923. The capitol is open year-round Mon through Fri from 8 a.m. to 5 p.m. For tours, call (785) 296-3966.

Capitol Controversy

Construction of Kansas's elaborate state capitol was a thirty-seven-year project—begun in 1866 and finally finished in 1903 at a cost of $3.2 million. The central portion was completed last, so for a time, the east and west wings were connected only by a covered wooden walkway dubbed Cave of the Winds.

With the capitol mired in controversy from the beginning, much of the criticism centered on the art inside, according to the Kansas State Historical Society. Ceres, the mythological goddess of agriculture, was chosen to adorn the dome, then rejected. Twelve-foot-high murals of Grecian women were removed in 1902 after being deemed too risque.

Even the highly prized murals by Kansas native John Steuart Curry were criticized by the public in the 1930s. The mural project came to an end when the executive committee refused to remove eight pieces of marble that the artist felt interrupted the story his murals told, and the artist refused to sign his work.

Across the street from the capitol is the ***First Presbyterian Church,*** 817 Southwest Harrison St., noted for its original Tiffany stained-glass windows. Call (785) 233-9601 to schedule a tour of the century-old church.

One of the country's newer national parks is **Brown v. Board of Education** *National Historic Site.* The site offers exhibits and a film on the landmark school segregation case that went all the way to the U.S. Supreme Court. It's housed in the former Monroe Elementary School at 1515 Southeast Monroe St., where plaintiff Oliver Brown's child attended classes. Although the case also represented plaintiffs from Virginia, South Carolina, Delaware, and Washington, D.C., it retained the Brown name. The site is open from 9 a.m. to 5 p.m. daily, and admission is free. For more information, call (785) 354-4273, or visit the National Park Service's Web site at www.nps.gov/brvb.

trivia

The constitution that was adopted when Kansas became a state in 1861 is still the law. It is one of the oldest state constitutions in use.

Cedar Crest, One Cedar Crest Rd. (I-70 and Fairlawn Road), Topeka, is the governor's residence. The 6,000-square-foot French-style chateau dates from 1928 and is listed on the National Register of Historic Places. A $4 million renovation of the property was completed in 2000. Free tours are offered on Mon from 1 to 4 p.m. Call (785) 296-3636 or go to www.visittopeka.us.

Topeka residents are proud of ***Gage Park,*** and rightly so. The 160-acre city park at Sixth and Gage Avenue is home to the ***Topeka Zoological Park*** (785-368-9131, www.topeka.org/zoo), exhibiting about 400 animals, and the ***Reinisch Rose Garden*** (785-272-5900), where 6,500 plants in 400 varieties bloom from May through Oct. There is no charge to visit the rose gardens. Admission to the zoo is $5.75 for adults, $4.75 for seniors, and $4.25 for children ages three through twelve. Zoo hours are 9 a.m. to 5 p.m. The ticket office closes one hour before the zoo. Also in Gage Park, enjoy a spin on ***The Carousel in the Park,*** a historic carousel built in 1908, with traditional music from a 1909 Wurlitzer organ. Take a mile-long scenic ride through the park on the mini-train and see all the attractions. Hours are seasonal (call ahead), and admission is charged.

In addition to being the headquarters for the Kansas State Historical Society and an excellent source of genealogy material, The ***Kansas History Center,*** 6425 Southwest Sixth Ave., operates the ***Kansas Museum of History.*** Among its features: a full-size Cheyenne tepee, a Wichita tribe grass lodge, a log house, an 1880 Atchison, Topeka, and Santa Fe Railroad locomotive, and exhibits on the Bleeding Kansas and Civil War periods.

TOP ANNUAL EVENTS

APRIL

Tulip Festival
Wamego; third Saturday
(785) 456-7849

Victorian Tea and Historic Homes Tour
Waterville
(785) 363-2515

JUNE

Wah-Shun-Gah Days
(intertribal powwow and festival)
Council Grove
(800) 732-9211; third weekend

AUGUST

Topeka Railroad Festival
(785) 232-5533

SEPTEMBER

Apple Days
Fort Riley
(785) 239-2022

DECEMBER

Home for the Holidays Tour
Abilene; first weekend
(785) 263-2231

Admission is $6 for adults, $4 for students, free for those five and under. It's open from 9 a.m. to 5 p.m. Tues through Sat and 1 to 5 p.m. Sun. Phone (785) 272-8681.

The Junior League of Topeka's major fund-raiser occurs annually in the fall and is called the Merry Market. It includes housewares, arts and crafts, books, antiques, jewelry, electronics, furniture, lawn and garden supplies, hardware, sporting goods, plants, toys, shoes, linens, and clothing for the entire family, at reasonable prices. Photos with Santa, a bell choir and a fashion show are also featured. For more information, call (785) 273-0830.

If you don't have the time to travel to England, the next-best thing is right here in Topeka. *The Woodward,* a bed-and-breakfast at 1272 Southwest Fillmore St., resembles the elegant residences of English nobility. The two-and-one-half-story library was inspired by the great hall of King Henry VIII's Hampton Court Palace in Surrey, England. The home was completed in 1925 and is on the National Register of Historic Places. It contains a premier collection of antique cobalt blue glassware and the original dining room table, which is also listed on the National Register of Historic Places. Owner Elizabeth Taylor's love of this home is obvious in the attention lavished on the decor. A breakfast of oven-puffed pancakes stuffed with fresh fruit and drizzled with orange-maple syrup (chocolate for breakfast is a specialty!) and an evening dessert are served to overnight guests. Prices range from $105 to $245, depending on the size of the bed. Guests have the use of the indoor sauna and outdoor hot tub. Call

(785) 354-7111 or (888) 321-9407. See photos of the rooms at the Web site, www.thewoodward.com.

Another bed-and-breakfast in a unique setting is the ***Brickyard Barn Inn*** at 4020 Northwest Twenty-fifth on the northern edge of Topeka. A 1927 redbrick dairy barn with attached silo houses three guest rooms furnished with English antiques, all with private baths. Owners Scott and Truanna Nickel also have a catering business, so the barn includes a dining room that seats seventy. Breakfast might include such specialties as blueberry-stuffed French toast or Swiss quiche pie. Scott's omelets are great, too. Depending on the season, guests can curl up in front of a crackling fireplace, or cool off in the in-ground pool on the four acres of grounds. Rates are $105 per night, including a full breakfast. Call the Nickels at (785) 235-0057. Their Web site is www.brickyard barninn.com.

If you want to get so far off the beaten track that finding the place is part of the fun, and worth the effort, search out ***Porubsky's Grocery and Deli.*** This is a tiny, family-run store that looks much the way it did in 1947, when Charlie and Lydia Porubsky opened for business. In the deli section an old-fashioned bar stretches down one side; booths line the other.

The food is known all over the capital; autographed photos of governors and senators line the walls. A sign over the bar says GOOD CHILI AIN'T JIST FOR BREAKFAST; the place's loyal following inspired Charlie's grandson Matthew to film a documentary on Porubsky's in 2009. Porubsky's serves thick deli sandwiches with its own homemade tongue-tingling, melt-in-your-mouth pickles. Regulars love to wait for visitors to chomp into them the first time: "We have ignition . . ." The pickles have a little horseradish, a little mustard, a few hot peppers . . . and a lot of secrets. As for the famous chili, the restaurant's "chili season" runs from Oct through Apr, and the tasty stuff isn't served on Fri or Sat. No matter what you order, it will be inexpensive (in the three-to-four-dollar range).

Fleeting Fame

Charles Curtis (1860-1936) was born in North Topeka. In 1907 he was the first native-born Kansan to represent the state in the U.S. Senate. He was elected vice president on the Republican ticket with Herbert Hoover in 1928, becoming the thirty-first person to hold that office. Curtis's home, now the Charles Curtis House Museum at 1101 Southwest Topeka Blvd., is open for tours. The place is open 11 a.m. to 3 p.m. Sat, and admission is $5. Call (785) 357-1371.

Another Topeka resident, Alfred Mossman Landon, served two terms as governor of Kansas. In 1936 he was the Republican nominee for president of the United States. He lost to President Franklin Delano Roosevelt.

Porubsky's is in Little Russia, a Polish-German neighborhood. Now, pay attention and it's easy to find: Cross the Kansas Avenue Bridge into North Topeka, turn right onto Morse (the second street), and north at the top of the Sardou Bridge onto Porubsky Drive. The address is 508 Northeast Sardou, but don't let that confuse you. Porubsky's is open from 11 a.m. to 2 p.m. every day but Sun. Call (785) 234-5788 for more information.

profilesin courage

Edmund Gibson Ross (1826-1907) led a colony of free-state settlers to Kansas. He was appointed to the U.S. Senate and was a political opponent of President Andrew Johnson. But when the House voted to impeach President Johnson in 1868, Ross insisted that Johnson be given a fair trial. He considered the evidence against Johnson to be insufficient, and in the Senate he voted "not guilty." His vote prevented Congress from removing the president from office. It also ruined Ross's own political career. (Adapted from *Profiles in Courage* by John F. Kennedy.)

South of the Kansas River in the neighborhood known as Oakland, in a sleepy-looking residential area, hides a little restaurant that has been snoozing here for more than forty years. People who are looking for real Mexican food search it out by the hundreds. It was one of the first authentic Mexican restaurants in this town. *La Siesta* is at 201 Northeast Woodruff. Owners Connie and Frank Herrera bought the restaurant from Connie's sister Lola Gonzales. They continue to serve basic Mexican food to the tacos-and-enchiladas crowd, but they also serve such items as chiles rellenos (an old family recipe), tamales, sanchos, and sopapillas.

When many customers began looking for low-cholesterol dishes, Lola created chicken enchiladas. New items such as potato Mexicana (a not-so-low-cholesterol baked potato stuffed with meat, chili con queso, guacamole, and sour cream) joined the well-loved chili con queso, made with a sauce so popular that the Herreras began bottling it to sell in grocery stores across Kansas.

The secret to the food here is the real cheddar cheese and the seasoning. Only the freshest ingredients are used. Nothing is microwaved, and everything is made to order—so you might have to wait a bit, but it is worth the wait, and you get to enjoy the Mexican music and appreciate the art on black velvet. Or you can pop back into the kitchen. Connie loves to have the customers come back and visit her there.

La Siesta is open from 10:30 a.m. to 2:30 p.m. Mon through Fri and from 5 to 9 p.m. Fri and Sat. The restaurant seats only fifty-five people, so reservations are suggested; call (785) 354-1325.

The *Combat Air Museum* at Forbes Field Airport on "J" Street (Hangars 602-604), 5 miles south of Topeka, at 6700 Southwest Topeka Blvd., is a must-see for military or aviation history buffs. About two dozen military aircraft from both world wars, Korea, Vietnam, and Desert Storm are on display. Visitors can also watch ongoing restoration of additional aircraft in an on-site workshop. Along with such gems as a Grumman F11F-1 Tiger (the plane flown by the Blue Angels) and a replica of a World War I Curtiss "Jenny" trainer, you'll find military vehicles, missiles, re-creations of a German POW barracks, a field kitchen and chapel, as well as a gallery of military aviation art. Forbes was built for training Air Force pilots. The museum is open Mon through Sat from 9 a.m. to 4:30 p.m., with last admission at 3:30 p.m., and Sun from noon to 4:30 p.m., with last admission at 3:30 p.m. Hours are shorter in the winter; admission is $6 for adults, $4 for children age five to seventeen and active military in uniform. Call (785) 862-3303. Or you may visit the Web site at www .combatairmuseum.org.

Also at Forbes Field, in building 301, is the *Kansas National Guard Museum.* Tours are by appointment and include artifacts from the Kansas Militia and National Guard from 1854 to the present. Several vehicles and aircraft are also displayed. Admission is free. Hours are 10 a.m. to 4 p.m. Tues through Sat. Call (785) 862-1020 for information, or visit www.kansasguardmuseum.org.

trivia

The Kansas Memorial Building in Topeka contains a historic sword. It was picked up on the Kansas plains near Council Grove centuries after it was dropped by one of Francisco Coronado's men, who passed through here in 1541.

Topeka is an arts and antiques center; the *Topeka Art Guild Gallery* (785-273-7646), at 5331 Southwest Twenty-second Place, features handmade jewelry, sculpture, paintings, hand-pulled prints, and pottery, all by Kansas artists. It is open from 11 a.m. to 5 p.m. Wed through Sat. Check out www .topekaartguild.org.

For a list of the many antique shops, including the 8,500-square-foot *Washburn View Antique Mall* (21st and Washburn, 785-233-3733, 10 a.m. to 6 p.m. Mon through Sat, noon to 5 p.m. Sun), visit www.antiquesoftopeka.org.

About 30 miles southwest of Topeka on Highway 31 are the town of *Harveyville* and *Jepson Studios,* where Barry and Jill Jepson make hand-thrown pottery. Barry has his studio and shop just outside town. The pottery barn has everything from cookware to pet dishes, or the perfect item for your home. The Jepsons also have a studio and shop in Paxico off of I-70 (exit 330). Take I-70 to the Auburn exit, then go 10 miles to Auburn. There's a sign directing you to Harveyville, where you'll find the studio at 125 Main St. The

General James Henry Lane, Father of Free Kansas

In 1861, when Kansas joined the Union as a free state, James Henry Lane was elected as one of its first U.S. senators. Arriving in Washington just as the Civil War began, he organized a Frontier Guard to protect the White House. Lane established a firm relationship with President Abraham Lincoln, who named him a brigadier general and sent him home to fight. In the Senate and on the back roads of his home state, he called for total emancipation and the enlistment of black troops. "I would like to see every traitor who has to die, die at the hands of his own slave," he said. In 1862 he began recruiting two regiments of black soldiers. One of those, the First Kansas Colored Infantry, became the first black unit to see combat alongside white troops.

For more information about Lane, visit *Lane's BBQ*, 1306 South Kansas Ave. (785-232-3610), a few blocks from the state capitol, where Harold Lane, one of the general's descendants, will share his story with you.

Jepsons often travel to shows, so call (785) 589-2481 for hours. Visit www
.jepsonstudios.com.

The Kansas Turnpike system today is what the Santa Fe Trail was in its time, a much-beaten path. So we will leave Topeka on U.S. Highway 75, avoiding the southbound Kansas Turnpike, and head for Tecumseh and *Pomona Lake,* created by the Marais des Cygnes River.

Chuck and Shirley Linn had a summer place near Tecumseh, east of Topeka, an 1850s tin-roofed, limestone house with walls so thick and aircirculation so good that no air-conditioning was needed in the hot summer months. A few years ago they decided to renovate the place and move to the forty-acre spread permanently.

Now, colored Angora goats roam the pasture and twenty English Angora rabbits live in the seventy-five-year-old barn cooled by an attic fan and ceiling fans. *Shirley Linn's Studio* is in the granary, where she spins, weaves, and creates garments of the soft natural angora. Shirley invites other area artisans to join her at the farm each fall for a show and sale. Call for dates. The granary/ studio (785-379-0421) is located at 7541 Southeast Sixty-first St. From Topeka, head east on Forty-fifth Street to Stubbs Road. Follow it south to Sixty-first Street. It's at the southwest corner

trivia

Looking for a canoe route? The Section 3 Kaw River access ramp is near I-70 at Topeka. This stretch ends 34 miles later at Burcham Park in Lawrence. It's about a twelve- to fourteen-hour trip.

of Sixty-first Street and Stubbs Road. Visit the Web site at www.rockbottom farm.com.

Old Stone House and Breakfast along the Oregon Trail, in Tecumseh at 6033 Southeast Hwy. 40 will please whether you are a history buff or just relish the peacefulness of the country.At this 1850 native limestone farmhouse, if you are interested, hosts Alan and Sabra Shirrell will tell you tales of Indians, slavery, and Kansas's struggle to become a free state. They cater to vegetarians, so you can expect a fine meal if that is your inclination. Rooms are $85. Call (785) 379-5568 for reservations.

South of Topeka on US 75 and east on US 56 is the town of *Overbrook,* which makes a good day trip from the capital city. Fieldstone *Orchards, Vineyard and Country Store* at 7049 East 149th, is 2 miles east of US 56 and Maple and 1 mile north. Fieldstone is situated on 180 acres of working farm with 8½ acres of vineyards, 1,000 apple trees, and (are you ready for this?) 2½ acres of asparagus. Asparagus season is from Apr 15 to May 30. Blackberries and cherries are available about June 15. Or perhaps apples or apple cider sound good. Currants and peaches also abound. If the month is right, you can traverse the grounds in a Fieldstone electric cart and pick your own fruit. The nearby vineyard is limited by the Kansas weather but results in a great white wine. The country store, open 10 a.m. to 6 p.m. Tues to Sat and noon to 6 p.m. Sun, sells cookbooks, cider, apple peelers, asparagus steamers and other goodies.

trivia

During the Civil War, the proslavery guerrilla fighter William Quantrill planned to attack Burlingame, west of Overbrook, just as he had Lawrence. With the men away fighting for the Union, the women got together and built a fort of rocks. They managed to hold off Quantrill and his raiders for six weeks, when the Union army came to their aid.

Call (785) 665-7643 for more information, or check the Web site at www .fieldstonee.com.

While in Overbrook shop at *From the Heart Gift Shop* at 401 Walnut in a cute Victorian house. The shop carries Boyd's Bears for collectors, along with baskets, birdhouses, and other country gifts. It is always Christmas in the little shop on the second floor. The shop is open Fri from 10 a.m. to 5 p.m., Sat from 10 a.m. to 4 p.m. Call (785) 665-7512.

The *Overbrook Quilt Connection* at 500 Maple St. showcases a display of large quilts and more than 1,000 bolts of fabric. Carolyn Meerian and Roxanne Fawl have quilting classes on Sat. Open Tues through Sat from 10 a.m. to 5 p.m. Call (785) 665-7841 or visit www.overbrookquilts.com for a class schedule.

Tucked between US 50 and US 56, **Americus** (just seven minutes north-west of Emporia), founded in 1857, is the home of **Marlow Woodcuts** at 402 First St. It's a family business; Wanda Douglas, her son Brad, daughters Pamela and Rita, and Rita's husband, Steve, make more than 8,000 original woodcuts each year. They have had visitors from more than fifty-five countries since 1985.

The woodcutsare priced from a few bucks for a small trinket to more than $200 for a nativity scene.. To stop by and see the Marsh family at work, call (620) 443-5678. You can also see their current stock by visiting www.marlow woodcuts.com.

Americus is also home to **Mel's Country Brass,** at 558 Mulberry, where Melba Rhudy will engrave metal or glass or "anything that stands still long enough." She has made some unique gifts for the people-who-have-everything types. Want to engrave a photo of the old homestead on Grandpa's old saw? Or maybe something more romantic, such as champagne glasses for a wedding? Coffee mugs with funny sayings, vases, gun stocks, knives—just about anything you can think of, she can engrave. She can draw from a photograph or freehand. The brass engravings are her favorite because they make such special gift items. "I'm just country through and through," she says, and she obviously loves her work. Hours are by appointment. Call (620) 443-5828.

trivia

The Osage chiefs opened the Santa Fe Trail in 1825 when they sold the right-of-way through their land for $800.

If you have never experienced the Kansas Turnpike, now's your chance, but take it only as far as the scenic route, US 56, where you will turn west to **Council Grove.**

On the edge of the Flint Hills in the fertile Neosho River Valley, Council Grove was the last outfitting post between the Missouri River and Santa Fe and a natural stopover on the Santa Fe Trail. Because of its abundant grass and timber, Native Americans had used it for centuries. The U.S. government negotiated with the Osage for a passage across their lands in 1825; this became the Santa Fe Trail. The city was named after that council with the Osage. The stump of Council Oak remains where the treaty was signed, east of the present-day Neosho River bridge. In 1846 a new treaty with the Kansa, or Kaw, Indians gave them a 20-square-mile reservation where the city now stands (some treaty).

There are eighteen historic sites in the Grove, as locals call it, and you can pick up a tour guide at the visitor bureau at 200 East Main St., or call (620) 767-5882.

In a grove of trees along the Neosho River is the stately ***Kaw Mission State Historic Site,*** built in 1850 as a Methodist mission school for Native American children of the Kansa tribe. Now a museum and state historic site, the two-story limestone building at 500 North Mission houses Native American artifacts and items related to Council Grove history. From Mar to Nov, hours are 9:30 a.m. to 5 p.m. Wed to Sat; the rest of the year, hours are the same, but only Thurs to Sat. Admission is $2, or $1 for students and seniors. A tour of Council Grove's historic sites and the Neosho Riverwalk also begins here. Call (620) 767-5410.

trivia

The William Young Archeological Site is an occupational site of an Archaic culture (which dates from 6000 B.C. to 81 B.C.). The group, which inhabited the area about 3000 B.C., is known as the Munker Creek Culture. They lived on the floodplain of Council Grove Lake about a mile north of Council Grove on Highway 177/57. Most of the site is underwater, but there are artifacts at the project office by the dam.

At the east entrance to the Riverwalk, you'll see the **Guardian of the Grove,** a 10-foot-tall statue of a Native American warrior, honoring the Kaw tribe. It is by local artist Mark Sampsel.

Another historically significant figure is represented at the corner of Union and Main Streets. **Madonna of the Trail,** a 10-foot-tall statue of pink algonite stone, depicts a pioneer woman with two children and pays tribute to the courage of women who moved westward. It is one of eleven erected along the Santa Fe and Oregon Trails by the Daughters of the American Revolution in 1928.

You can't miss the ***Farmers and Drovers Bank*** at 201 West Main St. The ornate two-story redbrick building with the limestone trim, stained-glass windows, Romanesque arches, and Byzantine dome dates from 1892 and is listed on the National Register of Historic Places. The bank continues to operate at this site.

The Last Chance Store, West Main and Chautauqua Streets, was built in 1857; it was the last supply stop on the Santa Fe Trail. It is not open for tours. One block east of the bridge on Main Street is the trunk of a 300-year-old bur oak known as the Post Office Oak. Letters for passing wagon trains and pack trains on the Santa Fe Trail were left from 1825 to 1847 at the base of this ancient oak tree. A stone building dating from 1864 stands next to the tree and houses a museum, open Sunday afternoons in the summer and by appointment.

Hays House Restaurant at 112 West Main St. (620-767-5911) is the oldest continuously operated restaurant west of the Mississippi River, in business since Seth Hays built it in 1857. It is considered one of the finest in the state.

A lot of history could be whispered by these walls: Hays was the great-grandson of Daniel Boone; Kit Carson was his cousin. But old family reci-pes are the only history being spoken here—Beulah's ham, marinated brisket of beef, and crispy fried chicken. The current owners are Rick and Alisa Paul; Rick's also the chef. The restaurant is open from 11 a.m. to 8 p.m. Tues to Thurs, 11 a.m. to 9 p.m. Fri, 6 a.m. to 9 p.m. Sat and 6 a.m. to 8 p.m. Sun. If you like buffets, you're in luck; Hays House offers a breakfast spread from 7 to 11 a.m. directly followed by a lunch smorgasbord until 3 p.m. Go to www.hayshouse.com.

trivia

The waving sea of prairie grass is called the Grassland Sea. This fragile ecosystem is home to forty species of grasses and ten million insects per acre.

The Cottage House Hotel at 25 North Neosho began as a three-room cottage and blacksmith shop in 1867. In 1871 a two-story brick house engulfed the cottage, and it became a boardinghouse. In 1879, with a 5,000-square-foot, two-story Queen Anne addition, the boardinghouse became a hotel. Conti-nental breakfast is served in your room or in the coffee room. Prices range from $50 to $165 for rooms and suites; all have private baths. There are two honeymoon cottages with bed, whirlpool bath, and a kitchenette/sitting room. Many rooms have more than one bed, and several are adjoining, family-style. Call (620) 767-6828 or (800) 727-7903 (reservations only). You can visit online at www.cottagehousehotel.com.

A monument 2 miles south of Council Grove marks the vicinity where Father Juan Padilla, a Franciscan priest who accompanied Coronado, returned in 1542 to convert the Indians. He was killed that same year and became the first Christian martyr in the United States.

Junction City, at the confluence of the Republican and Smoky Hill Rivers, is in the heart of the gently rolling Flint Hills. It was developed as a trading point for soldiers from the Fort Riley Reservation.

Stop at Heritage Park, at Sixth and Washington Streets, near Junction City's downtown. Over the northeast entrance to the park is the *Civil War Memorial Arch.* It was erected in 1898 by veterans of the Grand Army of the Republic. Inside the park, the *Kansas Vietnam Veterans Memorial* is similar to the memorial in Washington, D.C., honoring veterans of the same war. Thirteen feet high and 46 feet long, the ebony-colored granite stone lists the names of the 797 Kansans killed or still missing in action during the Viet-nam War. When the remains of any of them are recovered, a star is added by the name. Life-size statues of soldiers of the Vietnam era stand beside a large replica of a Purple Heart Medal.

The **Buffalo Soldier Memorial Statue** can be seen at Eighteenth and Buffalo Soldier Drive. A 9-foot-tall bronzed statue of a soldier and his horse honors the African-American men, or Buffalo Soldiers, who made up the Ninth and Tenth Cavalry Regiments. The soldiers, many of them Civil War veterans, served on the frontier in Kansas and other western states through the 1880s, building forts and protecting stage, mail, and rail routes from outlaws and marauding bands of Indians. For more information call (800) 528-2489.

Fort Riley is located just north of I-70 and Junction City. Home of "America's Army," the post was originally built for defense of the Santa Fe and Oregon Trails. The fort is one of the largest inland military reservations in the country.

Fort Riley has excellent historical sites and museums. And why not, since some of the most famous names in army history were here: Buffalo Bill Cody, George Custer, and George S. Patton.

The *U.S. Cavalry Museum* at the corner of Custer and Henry Streets was built in 1854 as a post hospital, later becoming post and Cavalry School headquarters. The museum contains artifacts emphasizing the role of the U.S. Cavalry in the expansion of the West and the integral part the fort has played in U.S. history, producing leaders in every war. During peacetime, the fort fields Olympic equestrian teams. The museum features murals and dioramas, as well as a picture and sculpture gallery. It also carries an excellent selection of cavalry and military history books and limited-edition fine-art prints. It is open year-round Mon through Sat from 9 a.m. to 4 p.m., Sun from noon to 4 p.m. For information call (785) 239-2737, or go to www .uscavalry.org.

Adjacent to the U.S. Cavalry Museum is the Fort *Riley Regimental Museum,* where you can trace the exploits of the Big Red One, as the division is known, from World War I through Desert Storm. The division's First Brigade still trains at Fort Riley. Museum hours are 10 a.m. to 4 p.m. Mon through Sat, noon to 4 p.m. Sun. Closed Thanksgiving Day, Christmas Day, and New Year's Day. Call (785) 784-5797.

Also at Fort Riley, in the Camp Whitside portion of the post (once a pioneer settlement called Pawnee City), is the *First Territorial Capitol of Kansas.* This two-story native limestone building served briefly as the territory's capitol in 1855. The first territorial legislature met here in July of that year; the slavery issue was hotly discussed, with division over the issue leading to the Bleeding Kansas era and Civil War. The museum is open 1 to 5 p.m. Fri to Sun from Mar to Oct, or by appointment from Nov to Feb. Tours can be arranged by calling (785) 784-5535 or (785) 238-1666. The adjoining *Kaw River Nature Trail* is open from dawn to dusk every day.

The Custer House at 24 Sheridan Ave. was constructed in 1855 of native limestone. It is the only surviving set of quarters from the fort's earliest history. It depicts military life on the western frontier during the Indian wars period. (General Custer was at the fort in 1866.) From mid-May through Sept, hours are 9 a.m. to 4:30 p.m. Sat, and noon to 4:30 p.m. Sun. The rest of the year, tours can be arranged by calling (785) 239-6727.

trivia

The Episcopal Church (785-238-2897) at 314 North Adams, Junction City, is the oldest Episcopal church in continuous use in the state, dating from 1859. Services are on Sun at 8 and 10 a.m.

Across the street is the statue of **The Old Trooper,** known here as Old Bill. The soldier and his mount have become the symbol of the proud heritage of the horse cavalry. It was designed and constructed by two soldiers in 1960, and marks the grave site of Chief, the last cavalry horse registered on the government payroll.

The first nine holes of the *Custer Hill Golf Course* on Fort Riley are a Robert Trent Jones design. It is a pleasantly demanding course, with tree-lined fairways and two ponds strategically located with bunkers and fairly small greens. The course is open to the public, but members of the military have priority. Call (785) 784-6000 for tee times.

You can take I-70 from Junction City about 10 miles west to *Chapman* and search out the *Windmill Inn,* 1787 Rain Rd., 9 miles south of exit 286, for an intimate weekend in the country. Surrounded by acres of farmland, this carefully restored Prairie-style four-square farmhouse and a 45-foot-tall windmill re-create the charm of a bygone era. The inn features beautiful oak woodwork, brilliant stained glass and beveled glass in the common areas, and a wraparound front porch that lures you to come out and relax in a swing or rocking chair and watch the courtship dances of the greater prairie chicken—a rare sight worth bringing a camera to capture. Hosts Tim and Deb Sanders are fine cooks, too. In the morning you'll awaken to the aroma of home cooking, and a full country breakfast will be served in the large, sunlit dining room. You can sip coffee and eat a homemade muffin on the front porch and enjoy the tranquil gardens.

In fact, with some advance notice, you are invited to enjoy dinner with the Sanderses, too. Groups of eight or more can influence the chef's choice for the evening meal. Since the inn caters receptions and meetings, the menu contains everything from beef to seafood: thick pork chops with maple pan gravy, grilled lamb chops with herbs, Chicken a la Windmill simmered with herbs and pearl onions, and what they call the Ultimate Meat Loaf (not like Mom used to make).

The home has three guest rooms, all with private baths. Room rates range from $99 to $125. Call (785) 263-8755, or visit www.bbonline.com/ks/windmill.

A scenic route to Salina is the road along wooded Smoky Hill River on Old Highway 40.

This route will also take you through Chapman, home of Joe Engle, one of three Kansas astronauts, and the site of one of the area's beautiful post-rock churches, **St. Michael's Catholic Church** on East Sixth Street. Other post-rock buildings and homes are all along Old 40, many with towers and balconies.

Old 40 continues across Mill Creek to **Abilene.** It is an excellent road paralleling the interstate (without the traffic), with fields of hay and milo nestled in rocky hills. Short stacked-stone walls line the fields along the roadway, creating the feel of the New England countryside rather than Kansas—except for the occasional oil well.

Abilene bears one of the most famous names of the Old West. It was the first cattle boomtown and the end of the famous Chisholm Cattle Trail, the western terminus of the railroad in the days of the cattle drives. In the five years from 1867 to 1872, nearly three million head of cattle were moved to Abilene and shipped to eastern markets on the Kansas Pacific Railroad.

Founded in 1857 as a stagecoach stop, the crude little village was inundated with cattle traders. It grew almost overnight from a population of 300 to 3,000, with the largest stockyards west of Kansas City, several hotels, a dozen saloons, gambling houses, and bawdy houses. Texas Street was the Broadway of the Plains.

Marshal Tom Smith became a hero here. Sadly, after bringing law and order to the town, he became the first U.S. marshal killed in the line of duty. He was succeeded by Marshal Wild Bill (James Butler) Hickok, the best-known gunman in the Old West. The six-gun was the law in this tough town, known as the roughest in the West.

Abilene's most famous citizen wasn't a lawman, but the thirty-fourth president of the United States. Dwight D. Eisenhower lived in Abilene from 1898 (when he was eight years old) until leaving for West Point in 1911. "The

The First Great Cattle Town

Abilene was the first of the great cattle towns on the Chisholm Trail. In 1867 about 35,000 head of cattle were brought to town. The number soon rose to 600,000 head of Texas cattle, which were shipped by rail to eastern markets. Like other cattle towns, Abilene was rowdy and lawless until 1870, when Tom Smith was hired as city marshal and peace was restored.

proudest thing I can claim is that I am from Abilene," Eisenhower said. Abilene is proud of him as well.

The *Eisenhower Presidential Library and Museum,* at 200 Southeast Fourth St., honors his contributions to his country while serving as commander of the Allied Forces in World War II and during two terms in the White House. Included in the complex are five structures. The visitor center houses an auditorium, where a short film on Eisenhower's life is shown. The *Eisenhower family home,* located on its original site, contains furniture and other items belonging to the family. The *Eisenhower Museum* is built of Kansas limestone and was dedicated on Veterans Day 1954 during Eisenhower's first term in office. Exhibits include military and World War II memorabilia; a timeline of his presidency including the cold war, Civil Rights, and the space race; gifts given to Ike by other world leaders; and a tribute to Mamie Eisenhower's role as First Lady. The *Presidential Library* contains some three million documents related to Eisenhower's public life. Dwight D. Eisenhower, his wife, Mamie, and their firstborn son, Doud Dwight Eisenhower, who died during childhood, are buried at the *Place of Meditation,* which includes a chapel designed by Eisenhower.

The Eisenhower Presidential Center is open from 9 a.m. to 4:45 p.m. every day except Thanksgiving Day, Christmas Day, and New Year's Day. Admission is $8 for adults, $6 for seniors and retired military, $1 for ages eight to fifteen and free for active military. For information call (877) RINGIKE (746-4453), or visit www.eisenhower.archives.gov.

Abilene is also known for the *Greyhound Hall of Fame Library.* It is across the street from the Eisenhower Center, at 407 South Buckeye Ave. Honoring this magnificent racing dog that has lineage dating from 5000 B.C., the

Kids Like Ike, Too

At the Eisenhower Presidential Center, you'll see an 11-foot-tall bronze statue of Abilene's most famous son as an adult. But local schoolchildren wanted to honor their hometown hero as a boy.

So the Abilene Kids Council, a fifteen-member board of elementary and middle school children who act as an advisory group to the local city council, led local kids in raising almost $21,000 for a likeness of Eisenhower as a boy.

The Little Ike statue was erected in 1999. It stands in a downtown park at East First Street and Buckeye Avenue, near Abilene's Civic Center.

Although Eisenhower's birthday, Oct 14, is not an official state holiday, the Kansas legislature did declare it a state commemorative day. Children in schools all over Kansas study about and honor Eisenhower—the boy and the man—on that day each year.

Cinnamon, the Canine American

We went to Abilene to visit the Eisenhower Library, to search out great places to eat and shop, and to find interesting things to do. What we had not counted on was bringing home a new member of our family. We stayed at a bed-and-breakfast just outside of town. The innkeepers invited us to join them for coffee early in the morning on the patio to see the sun rise over the wheat field behind the house—a magnificent sight that rivals an East Coast sunrise over the sea. We were chatting about things and I mentioned that I was going to the Greyhound Hall of Fame that day. One of the innkeepers asked me if I wanted to see a breeding farm, and the next thing I knew, we were fondling puppies and being licked to death by future racers.

When we went to the Hall of Fame, we met the resident greyhounds and found ourselves signing up for adoption of the puppies and dogs who, for whatever reason, couldn't make it in racing. Cinnamon had another name when she came to us, but she was happy to accept the new name, which matched her color. She was no loser even if she didn't score well in races. She was fast, and she was housebroken and leash trained, thank goodness, because letting her out without a leash was asking for a very long, hard run to catch her again. I also learned that greyhounds don't do steps. When confronted with a staircase, Cindy would freeze. I became her "step-mother" and took her to our local grade school, which had a huge, wide staircase outdoors leading to the front door, and much to the amusement of the children on the playground, we went up and down the steps, Rocky-like, every day.

Greyhounds must be dressed, just as humans, for the weather, since they have virtually no fat and very little fur. We went out in our matching raincoats, then jackets, and finally parkas, all winter, with the children cheering us on and lining up for petting and kissing. The Humane Society recently suggested pets be called "canine Americans" instead of "dogs," but the kids just called her Cindy.

exhibit traces the greyhound's history in a short movie. Resident greyhounds demonstrate the breed's lovable nature by enjoying hundreds of pats and hugs every day. The hours are from 9 a.m. to 5 p.m. seven days a week, and admission is free. Call (785) 263-3000 or (800) 932-7881.

There is now an organization called Greyhound Pets of America, which places dogs past their racing prime (from four to five years old) and young dogs who haven't been successful at the track in homes across the country. The local chapter, called T.L.C. Greyhound Adoption, can be reached at (785) 655-2208, or see www.tlcgreyhoundadoption.com. There are chapters in every state.

Also in town is a wonderful antique railroad—the *Abilene and Smoky Valley Railroad*—that leaves from the depot at the Greyhound Hall of Fame for a one-and-a-half-hour round-trip through the Smoky River Valley to Enterprise. Ride in a restored coach or diner car, pulled by a diesel-electric locomotive dating from 1945. The railroad uses a restored 1919 steam locomotive. Dinner excursions are also available. Fares are $7 to $14, or more for a dinner ticket. Trains run at 10 a.m. and 2 p.m. Sat and at 2 p.m. Sun, May through Oct; from Memorial Day through Labor Day, you can also catch 10 a.m. and 2 p.m. trains on Wed, Thurs and Fri. Call (888) 426-6687 or (758) 263-1077 for schedule information, or visit on the Web at www.asvrr.org.

The *Heritage Center,* east of the Eisenhower Center at 412 South Campbell, houses two Abilene museums. The *Museum of Independent Telephony* honors Clayson Brown, a local man who started an independent telephone company here, then purchased others across the state and country. Today we know his company as Sprint. The museum has an extensive collection of antique telephones.

The *Dickinson County Historical Museum* is famous nationwide for its circa 1900 *C. W. Parker Carousel,* a National Historic Landmark. It's restored and operating; you can ride it for $2. It's outdoors, along with an 1867 log cabin, a barn dating from 1915, a 1920s corner store, a blacksmith shop, and other pieces of local history.

Both museums can be reached at the same number, (785) 263-2681, or visit www.heritagecenterdk.com. A single ticket is good for admission to both. Admission is $4 adults, $3 seniors, and $2 children (it includes the carousel). Hours are Mon through Fri 9 a.m. to 4 p.m., Sat 10 a.m. to 8 p.m., Sun 1 to 5 p.m. during the summer; during the winter, the museums close an hour early during the week and at 5 p.m. on Sat.

Tour the *Seelye Mansion,* a twenty-five-room Georgian mansion at 1105 North Buckeye Ave., dating from 1905. Along with eleven bedrooms, the home includes its own bowling alley, a ballroom, and a Tiffany-designed fireplace. The original Edison light fixtures and most of the family's furniture are there, too. The period gardens have also been restored. Dr. A. B. Seelye, for whom the home was built, owned a successful patent medicine company, and many artifacts from the business are displayed in the *Patent Medicine Museum* here. Tours are at 10 a.m. Mon through Sat and at 1 p.m. Sun. During the month of Dec, the home is decorated for the holidays. (Closed Christmas Day.) Admission is $10 for adults, $5 for children ages six to sixteen. Group rates are available. Call (785) 263-1084 or visit www.seelyemansion.org for information.

Also open, by appointment, is the *LeBold Vahsholtz Mansion* at 106 North Vine. The twenty-three-room Italianate mansion was built in 1880 by banker and Abilene mayor C. H. Lebold and served as an orphanage and home for single female telephone operators before being restored. It is listed on the National Register of Historic Places. Hours are Sat and Sun 10 a.m. to 4 p.m. Call (785) 263-4356 for admission fees and to arrange a tour.

Many other privately owned mansions are open for tours the first weekend in Dec, when Abilene hosts an annual *Christmas homes tour.* The rest of the year you'll have to be content with driving or walking streets such as Buckeye, Cedar, and Third and viewing the exteriors.

At 300 North Mulberry St. is an old limestone church that looks like a medieval castle. Wild Bill Hickok and Dwight Eisenhower both worshipped here. Terry Tietjens left the enormous stained-glass windows intact and transformed the building's interior into a performing arts center, now called the *Great Plains Theatre.* Theater performances featuring professional actors from all over the United States are staged here. It seats almost 200 people and is wheelchair accessible. Each season, the theater offers a number of plays, with multiple performances of each, plus a children's theater production. Season tickets are available. Call (785) 263-4574 or (888) 222-4574 for information on what's currently playing.

See and shop for fine Native American arts and crafts at the *American Indian Art Center* at 206 South Buckeye. You'll find dolls, pottery, paintings, jewelry, and carvings by one hundred artists from thirty tribes in the region. Hours are 9:30 a.m. to 5 p.m. Mon through Sat and 11 a.m. to 4 p.m. Sun. Call (785) 263-0090 for extended summer hours. Admission is free.

Bow Studio and Gallery, 921 South Buckeye (785-263-7166, www.bowsart.com), is on the western edge of the Flint Hills just off I-70. Inga and Bob Bow established the studio to display unique designs in clay tiles and plates handmade from local clays. The soft clay is rolled into large slabs, and Kansas wheat and wildflowers are impressed into it; the tiles are then cut, glazed, and fired. Terra-cotta sculptures, fountains, and lavabos are also available. Hours are 10 a.m. to 7 p.m. every day, but it's recommended to call ahead.

If you're a doll collector, stop by the public library at 209 Northwest Fourth St. to see the *Abilene Library Doll Collection.* The collection includes dolls owned by Mamie Eisenhower, WPA dolls, and foreign dolls. They can be viewed at no charge during regular hours. Call (785) 263-3082 for information.

Also of interest in Abilene is the *Vintage Fashion Museum* (785-263-7997) at 212 North Broadway. It features clothing dating from 1860 to the 1970s. Hours are 10 a.m. to 4 p.m. Thurs through Sat. Admission is $5, and children age twelve and under are free.

The Kirby House, now a restaurant, is located at 205 Northeast Third St., 1 block east of Buckeye Avenue (785-263-7336, www.kirby-house.com). It was built in 1885 and has been restored to its original Italianate appearance, complete with a tower and a new front porch.

A picket fence surrounds the stately home. The foyer has a parquet floor and walnut staircase. The front parlor has lead-glass and bay windows and a maple fireplace. Guests are seated in nine dining rooms on all levels of the mansion—even the tower, where there is a secluded table for two. It's a long climb, so there is a $25 extra charge for the waitress, but it's so romantic, it's worth it.

Now, let's talk about food. The specialty of the house is a spicy country-fried steak (with cream gravy), so big it hangs over the edges of the plate, barely leaving room for the baked potato and vegetables. There is also perfect prime rib, as well as chicken, seafood and vegetarian entrees. Kirby House is open daily for lunch from 11 a.m. to 2 p.m. and for dinner from 5 to 8 p.m.; closed Sun except for Easter, Mother's Day and Father's Day.

Another Abilene restaurant with an interesting history is the **Brookville Hotel Restaurant,** at 105 East Lafayette, just off I-70. Four generations of the Martin family ran the hotel-turned-restaurant in neighboring Brookville, but lack of a city sewer system there led them to relocate the business. Rather than attempt moving the 1870 structure, the Martins chose to replicate it, from the tin ceilings and vintage wallpaper to the old oak tellers' cages from the Brookville bank that became an additional dining room for the restaurant during its years there.

The menu didn't change; there's still just one item on it—fried chicken. Platters of it are served with mashed potatoes, gravy, biscuits, corn, coleslaw, cottage cheese and an ice-cream dessert. Adults pay $13.95; children age three to eleven are $7.95. Hours are 5 to 7:30 p.m. Wed through Fri, 11:30 a.m. to 2 p.m. and 4:30 to 7:30 p.m. Sat, and 11:30 a.m. to 2 p.m. and 5 to 7 p.m. Sun. Closed Mon and Tues. Reservations are a very good idea on weekends; call (785) 263-2244, or visit www.brookvillehotel.com.

Abilene's Victorian Inn Bed and Breakfast (785-263-7774 or 888-807-7774, www.abilenesvictorianinn.com) at 820 Northwest Third St. is in one of Abilene's fine historic homes. Third Street is lined with lovely old homes with an early 1900s feel, but this one is Abilene's longest established bed and breakfast. This "painted lady" offers four guest rooms and two suites, all with private baths, and is filled with antiques; each room reflects comfortable elegance. Owners Adrian and Joy Potter serve a gourmet breakfast daily. Rooms are $79 to $129 for two guests.

God's Garden is in Abilene, so if you want a private, quiet moment, find this six-acre spot at 1774 Camp Rd. There is night lighting in the garden until 10:30 p.m., but a daylight stroll will show you eighty varieties of roses. The garden is open 7 a.m. to 10 p.m. from late spring to early fall, and there is no admission charge; it is supported by donations only. Phone (785) 479-5901.

Abilene's historic downtown area has quite a few specialty shops filled with antiques, gifts, toys, quilts, and more.

Cypress Bridge at 110 Northwest Third St. (785-263-1963) is a family-owned candle and home-décor shop in Abilene's charming downtown. Owners Sharon Petersen and Angela Adams create hand-poured candles right in the store. A visit to the store is a tour of pleasant aromas. Hours are 9 a.m. to 6 p.m. Mon through Wed, 9 a.m. to 7 p.m. Thurs, 9 a.m. to 4 p.m. Fri and noon to 5 p.m. Sun (closed Sat). Call (785) 263-1963.

Mr. K's Farmhouse (407 South Van Buren; 785-263-7995) is a farmhouse restaurant on top of a hill off Old Highway 40 just west of Abilene. The family-style dinners include generous portions of steak, chicken, and seafood. A paddle hanging on the wall supposedly was used on President Eisenhower on one of his visits home. No, it is not the Kansas way of telling the chief of staff we don't agree with his politics; it was done when he had been out of office for a while. Or so they say. See, good food and history, too! Hours are 11 a.m. to 2 p.m. every day but Mon, plus 5 to 9 p.m. Tues through Sat. See www.mrksfarmhouse.com.

The last stop before leaving Abilene must be the *Russell Stover Candy Factory Outlet,* near the edge of town on the south side of I-70 exit 272 at 1993 (on the appropriately named) Caramel Blvd. Even if you don't plan to buy any of the famous Midwestern chocolate-covered nuts and creams, stop by for a taste. It's free and the people here know if you taste one, you will just have to buy enough to last you the rest of the year. Hours are Mon through Sat from 9 a.m. to 6 p.m., Sun from 10 a.m. to 5 p.m. There is a demonstration kitchen; call ahead to see if they're making candy, if you'd like to watch (785-263-0463).

The view to the west is vast. Soft green hills touched with blue are spotted with the occasional oil well. The towns and cities of western Kansas have wide streets—wide enough for a herd of cattle to traverse—some of them the original brick; homes are set back on large lawns. Nothing is crowded or cramped here.

Pony Express Country

Wakefield, on Highway 82 East off Highway 15 North, is a quiet little community of only 800 souls, a great place to get away from it all. Enjoy some solitude at the *Kansas Landscape Arboretum,* on Highway 82 near Wakefield. If you've ever wondered what a bald cypress or golden rain tree looks like, and whether it would grow in Kansas, you'll find your answer here. There are 328 trees in 140 varieties planted as memorials. Walk one of the mulched paths through the woods, or drive the winding road near Milford Lake. Visit sunrise to sunset; there is no admission fee but donations are welcome. For information call (785) 461-5760.

Also along Milford Lake are a state park, a nature center, and a wildlife management area. *Milford State Park* offers trails for hiking and horseback riding, picnic shelters, campsites, and a boat ramp. The park entrance is off Highway 57. A vehicle sticker is must be purchased to enter the park; camping is additional. Call (785) 238-3014 for more information. The *Milford Nature Center* has exhibits and live animals and in winter offers a popular program on eagles. You can visit the outdoor portions of the nearby fish hatchery anytime, but the nature center can arrange indoor tours in Apr when the fish are hatching. The nature center and hatchery are below the dam. Admission is free. Call (785) 238-5323 for nature center hours. The wildlife management area provides habitat for pheasant, quail, whitetail deer, and other animals. Hunting is permitted in season. The rest of the year, hikers will find signposts and map boxes throughout the area.

trivia

In this region tall grass stretches as far as you can see, and winds play across the nearly treeless landscape, creating swirling patterns of wheat and grass. Native Americans learned to survive in this unsheltered country, and ranchers still follow their ancient custom of burning off pastures to encourage new growth. Flames often cast an orange glow in the skies here. In the spring, rain transforms the blackened landscape into vibrant shades of green.

Turn your attention northwest of Wakefield on Highway 9. When the road changes from asphalt to gravel, look for *Tailgaters Steakhouse* on Parallel Street in Vining where Judd Sorell serves the best steak around. Call (785) 455-3438. Hours are Mon through Fri 4 p.m. to 2 a.m. (grill stops at 9 p.m. Mon through Thurs and at 10 p.m. Fri), Sat from 2 p.m. to 2 a.m. (grill stops at 10 p.m.).

The town of *Clyde,* west of Highway 15, is home to about 800 people. There is a museum with an old jail and a completely furnished one-room schoolhouse. If you get hungry there is a friendly place at 325 Washington named *Rosie's* (785-446-2850). The grill is on from 11 a.m. to 1:30 p.m. and 5 to 8 p.m. daily. Good burgers any time. Within walking distance of Clyde's attractions is *Clyde Hotel* at 422 Washington, the project of Jerry and Laura Lee Stenberg. This 1870 inn has been remodeled for comfort, yet it retains the charm of days gone by. The inn has a stained-glass window from an old Methodist church that filters the summer sunlight. In spring and summer guests enjoy a walk in the beautifully landscaped courtyard and admire the gazebo, fountain, and flowers. There are seven rooms, each with a private bath. The rooms have king- and queen-size beds. Rates are $52 to $62. Reservations are required for the continental breakfast. Call (785) 446-2231.

Head east on US 36 to *Washington's* rich river valleys. While you're there, please visit *Kansas Specialty Dog Service,* where guide and social dogs are trained for the blind, the disabled, and nursing homes. They use golden retrievers, black and yellow Labradors, German shepherds, and boxers. A puppy raiser takes an eight-to-ten-week-old puppy and houses it for twelve to eighteen months. When the pup returns to the facility, it will learn about forty commands. An additional six months is required to complete this cycle of training. A disabled individual will spend two to four weeks training with a dog that is matched to him or her. A tour of the facility is encouraged unless a class is in the process of receiving dogs. Call (785) 325-2256 or visit www.ksds.org.

Connie Allen and Marilyn Hanshaw turned their awe-inspiring pies into a business, *Marcon Pies* at 124 West Eighth, Washington, where pies are baked daily and delivered to area stores and restaurants. Connie and Marilyn no longer own the place but "haven't hung up their rolling pins yet"—they still stop by to help with the baking. The aroma of freshly baked pies is sure to interest you in sampling the product and purchasing one or two to take home. Marcon Pies is 1 block south of US 36 at D Street, and ⅓ block east. Tour hours are 8 a.m. to 5 p.m. Mon through Fri. Call (785) 325-2439 or log on to www.marcon pies.com. Call ahead for tour reservations.

South of US 36 is the town of *Greenleaf.* Just past Greenleaf, Kathy Dawson and Fred Cairns have *Lynes Unlimited* at 172 Upland Rd. (785-747-2612), a small shop where their award-winning, handcrafted wooden toys are made.

Kathy says they make playthings for children, but they also make very specialized and detailed adult toys from pine and hardwoods—sleds and sleighs, for example. Prices range from a few bucks for a toy car or truck to more than a thousand dollars for a 6-foot-long scale-model train. The shop is 9 miles south of Greenleaf on a paved road (the last mile is gravel) and is easy to find. Hours are by appointment.

Slightly north of US 36 on Highway 148 is *Hanover.* The *Hollenberg Pony Express Station* is 2 miles northeast of Hanover, just a mile east of Highway 243, and is the only remaining original, unaltered Pony Express station in its original location in the United States. It was built in 1857, the most westerly station in Kansas (123 miles from St. Joseph, Missouri), and in 1859 was the western terminus of railroad and telegraph lines. From that point, travel by wagon or stagecoach was slow. The Butterfield Overland Mail Company covered the distance in twenty-two days.

In 1860 the Pony Express was inaugurated by the firm of Russell, Majors & Waddell, proving that mail could be delivered faster. Charges were set at $5 a letter; it makes our present-day stamps look pretty good. The visitor center includes a mural depicting the Oregon Trail and exhibits about the Hollenberg family who lived at and ran the station. It is a state historic site. There is no admission, but donations are welcome. Hours are 10 a.m. to 5 p.m. Wed through Sat. Admission is $3 for adults and $1 for students. Call (785) 337-2635, or visit the Web site at www.kshs.org.

Grace Riepen and her daughter Kathy Gastmann are co-owners of *A Season's Harvest* at their home at 411 East Elm St. in Hanover. The home is surrounded by herb gardens, and the women offer wreaths and arrangements created from the flowers and herbs grown here. But they don't stop with sweet-smelling wreaths; they also offer garden tours—June is the most fragrant time—and herbal dinners.

What's an herbal dinner, you ask? It is meat, potatoes, vegetables, and dessert all flavored with herbs; it also includes herbal legend and lore. The dinners, $16 per person, are scheduled for groups. They have recently opened a tearoom in the shop, so you can stop in and have a bite to eat. Call Kathy at (785) 337-2553 to schedule a dinner. She also does herbal bridal showers, weddings, and Victorian tea parties for groups by reservation, and she offers a Christmas open house featuring a program about Christmas herbs. The shop visits and garden tour are by appointment only, but do go; the fragrance in your vehicle will be improved tremendously for the rest of your trip. *Gloria's Coffee & Quilts Bed and Breakfast,* 205 North Main St., on West Highway 9 in *Barnes,* is in the nineteenth-century home of Gloria Moore. Guests choose from three rooms with a queen-size bed and private bath. Rooms are $65 to $85, including a full breakfast (pecan waffles are the favored choice). Call (785) 763-4569 or (888) 511-4569.

Oregon Trail

You see them in the city parks and anywhere else you look in *Marysville.* The unusual black squirrel is the city mascot that appears on the city flag and is protected by city ordinance.

Legend has it that a boy who didn't like to see animals in cages turned a batch of them loose at a carnival in 1912. Others say the black squirrels were seen in the area as early as the late 1800s.

The Pony Express came though Marysville in the 1860s. The *Pony Express Barn-Museum* is the oldest building in Marshall County. A bronze Pony Express horse and rider still appear to thunder across the prairie at the west edge of town at Pony Express Park. A perfect replica of a rope ferry used to pull wagons and livestock across the Big Blue River is at Historic Trails Park. The original ferry was very near this location from 1851 until 1864, when a bridge was built. Thousands of pioneers and hundreds of wagons camped for days waiting for a turn to cross. There were many graves near the crossing as settlers fell to illnesses during these long waits. A rope crossed the river above the ferry, which rode a pulley back and forth. A wheel guided another rope to shift the ferry away from swift river currents. For more information about any of these, call Marysville Chamber of Commerce at (800) 752-3965.

The magnificent **Koester Block** of Marysville, on US 36, has been restored to its late-nineteenth-century splendor. Two stone lions guard the walkway, and a brick wall surrounds the two Koester homes, one now a museum.

The white-clapboard, 1876 **Koester House Museum** at 919 Broadway still has the original furnishings. It was donated to the city by fourth-generation heirs in 1972 and is open May to Nov from 10 a.m. to noon and 1 to 4:30 p.m. Call the museum at (785) 562-2417 for hours or, in the off-season, call John Howard at (785) 562-3637 to arrange a visit.

Take U.S. Highway 77 from Marysville, and follow it south and west to the town of **Waterville.** On **Banker's Row** nineteenth-century Victorian mansions stand behind rolling lawns along East Hazelwood Street. There are theater productions at the old opera house in town, which also houses City Hall.

North on Highway 178 just before you reach Seneca is the town of **St. Benedict,** formerly known as Wild Cat before the post office officially named it. Anyway, in St. Benedict is **St. Mary's Church,** circa 1881–1894, a remarkable example of preservation and restoration that is on the National Register of Historic Places. Parishioners quarried the limestone for the late Roman–style exterior about 3 miles north of town, then aided masons in the construction. That kind of devotion is still apparent today —the one hundred families who make up the parish donated a great deal of both time and money to accomplish this amazing restoration. Even the pipe organ, circa 1916, was restored after sitting unused for more than twenty-five years. The paintings, ceilings, and wall decorations were carefully photographed and documented and faithfully restored. The six Bavarian-made transept windows, dominated by hues of ocher, amber, azure, and crimson leaded glass, are in paired arch sections. A saint is depicted in hand-painted glass within each section. This is truly worth the drive to see, especially on a Sunday morning.

trivia

When the town of Haddam, west of Marysville, held a municipal election in 1901, women won the offices of mayor, city clerk, police judge, and the entire city council—even though women were not given the right to vote until 1920. The women decided a jail needed to be built and had a stone one built within five months. The jail, on its original site, is ½ block south of Haddam's main street.

In the town of **Seneca,** farther east on US 36, is **Stein House Bed and Breakfast** (314 North Seventh), built in the early 1900s. Enjoy the quiet, or visit one of the nearby casinos. There are three rooms with shared baths; rates are $65 to $70 with a full breakfast. For reservations call (785) 336-3790.

trivia

Alcove Spring, between Blue Rapids and Marysville, was a well-known stopping place on the Oregon Trail. Stones in the area contain initials and dates carved by a number of travelers.

Just off Highway 63 North on Highway 71 East is the town of **Bern.** A warm country welcome awaits you at **Lear Acres** (785-336-3903), a livestock and grain farm. The large two-story farmhouse is owned by Byron and Toby Lear; it was built by Byron's father in 1918, and Byron was born there. It offers space to move about, a peaceful atmosphere, and, because it sits on a hill, a panoramic view. Breakfast is farm-raised, from the fruits and breads to the meat and eggs.

Toby fixes a country breakfast of eggs (go get your own, if you want to), bacon or sausage, muffins or rolls made with flour from local wheat, and homemade wild plum jelly. The place offers double rooms with shared baths and air-conditioning. Toby can direct you to some small antiques shops nearby as well as interesting old graveyards, churches on the historic register, and hunting and fishing opportunities. Call for rates.

Head southwest toward Tuttle Creek Lake and Highway 16. At 429 East Hwy. 16 in **Olsburg,** you'll find a roadside steakhouse known simply as **Bricks.** You can get a buffalo steak done to perfection Wed through Sun starting at 5 p.m. Call for specific hours. The phone number is (785) 468-3517.

From Olsburg head east on Highway 16 until it turns into a winding road that leads southeast to **Westmoreland** on Highway 99. About 1 mile south of Westmoreland on Highway 99, stop to see the life-size covered wagon pulled by a yoke of bronzed oxen—a tribute to the travelers of the Oregon Trail.

Manhattan (known hereabouts as the Little Apple) is home to Kansas State University. As in most college towns, there is a lot going on—plenty of places to eat, an abundance of motel rooms, and some interesting bed-and-breakfast inns, too.

Anyone with an appreciation for plants must see the **Kansas State University Gardens.** A living laboratory for students enrolled in the college's horticulture program, the gardens are student-designed and -installed. When completed, the gardens will cover nineteen acres.

Near a historic conservatory dating from 1909, where butterflies fly freely among tropical plants, a native plant garden, a butterfly garden, a cottage garden filled with old-fashioned varieties of flowers, and a day lily garden are already planted. A fountain sets off the rose garden, which will be enlarged and complemented by an iris garden. In the next few years, two ponds, a waterfall, a children's garden, a woodland garden, a sensory garden for the physically challenged, and a commons with a gazebo for weddings and other events will be added. The gardens are off Denison; park by the old dairy barn or the conservatory. Call (785) 532-6170 for more information.

Also on the K-State campus is the **Marianna Kistler Beach Museum of Art,** near Fourteenth and Anderson Avenue. The museum specializes in twentieth-century American art, with an emphasis on Midwestern artists. Hours are Tues through Sat from 10 a.m. to 5 p.m., and Sun from noon to 5 p.m. Admission is free. Call (785) 532-7718 for information, or visit the Web site at http://beach.k-state.edu.

For those of you who just can't pass up a museum about food, the **American Museum of Baking** is tucked away in its own room at the Emerson Library at 1213 Bakers Way (785-537-4750). There are priceless samples of Egyptian bread and cake more than 3,800 years old, Roman bread, and grain from the colonies in North Africa. Wooden and pottery bread–stamping tools from Roman Byzantium and many other artifacts, along with a collection of cookbooks more than 200 years old, can be seen here. The display follows the development of commercial baking in North America leading to sliced white bread, the all-American favorite. This is considered to be one of the most important collections on the history of baking in the world. Tours are available from 1 to 4 p.m. Tues and Thurs.

trivia

The town of Irving was near Frankfort, just off Highway 9 between Highway 99 and US 77. But it doesn't exist anymore; it's a ghost town. Many of the people who used to live in Irving are still alive, however, and the town site has a marker and a mailbox so that folks can leave messages for one another when they are passing through. There is even an Irving reunion and picnic every summer.

Near Manhattan is the **Konza Prairie,** a stretch of 8,616 acres of untouched native tallgrass prairie. Named for the Konza Indians who once lived in the region, it is owned by The Nature Conservancy and used for study by Kansas State University. Along with grass that can exceed 8 feet in height, the prairie is home to 600-plus species of plants. More than 200 species of resident and migratory birds have been recorded here. A bison herd of about 200 animals grazes about a quarter of the preserve so scientists can study the effects of grazing on the prairie. Sections of the prairie are also burned each spring, and its effects are studied.

Fourteen miles of hiking trails are open to the public daily from dawn until dusk, weather and trail conditions permitting. A self-guided tour brochure is available at the entrance. Group tours are available by appointment. Other facilities at Konza Prairie, including the 1900s limestone ranch house, are for the use of researchers only. To get to Konza Prairie, take I-70 exit 307 and head northeast on McDowell Creek Road about 6 miles. For more information, call (785) 587-0441, or visit the Web site at http://kpbs.konza.ksu.edu.

trivia

The incredible number of ghost towns in Kansas is like a good news/bad news joke. The bad news is that Kansas has more ghost towns than you can count— towns that for one reason or another have disappeared. The good news is that if they all had survived, there would be a town every 7 miles all over the state— making it too crowded to farm.

Manhattan has plenty of history, too. At 2309 Claflin Rd. are three historic attractions, the Goodnow House, the Riley County Historical Museum, and the Hartford House. For tours of these properties, the Pioneer Log Cabin in City Park, a one-room schoolhouse near Tuttle Creek Boulevard and Barnes Road, or the Wolf House Museum, an 1868 boardinghouse at 630 Fremont St., call the Riley County Historical Museum at (785) 565-6490.

The *Goodnow House* dates from 1861 and belonged to Issac Tichenor Goodnow and his wife, Ellen, who came to Kansas to help in the free-state efforts. The house has some unusual features. Ellen insisted on having a window centered in her bedroom wall, so the chimney detours around it. Worried that a horse might be injured jumping a fence with pointed pickets, she had the house surrounded by a stone wall topped with curved iron rods. Many of the period furnishings are from the Goodnow family. Hours are 9 a.m. to 5 p.m. Tues through Fri (subject to staff availability) and 2 to 5 p.m. Sat and Sun, or by appointment. Admission is free, but donations are welcome. Information is available at the Kansas State Historical Society's Web site at www.kshs.org/places/goodnow, or call (785) 565-6490.

The *Riley County Historical Society Modern Museum Building* houses changing exhibits on Riley County history and the Seaton Research Library, a wealth of archival material for history buffs and genealogists. The library is open by appointment only.

The *Hartford House* is a prefabricated house (perfect for the nearly treeless prairie) brought by steamboat in 1855, along with more than one hundred folks from Ohio determined to populate the state with abolitionists. The steamboat was headed farther west but stopped here when it ran aground due to low water. One eastern name was traded for another when the existing settlement, Boston, became Manhattan.

Voted to serve the best steak in Manhattan, the *Little Apple Brewing Company* at 1110 Westloop lives up to its reputation. Little Apple's brews are made right here on the premises and are of the best malts, hops, and yeast. Brewer John Briden creates hand-crafted beers. His favorite is Riley's Red Ale, a full-flavored, amber-colored beer. But there are other choices depending on your taste. The most popular beer is Wildcat Wheat, a light American-style ale, served with a slice of lemon. Prairie Pale Ale is high in alcohol, based on the ale from India, and it constitutes the tan half of a favorite drink, the Black and Tan. Lower in alcohol is Bison Brown Ale, although its deep, rich color and malty caramel flavor belie the easy drinking. If you like a stout, try the XX Black Angus Stout. Hours are 11 a.m. to 11 p.m. Mon to Thurs, 11 a.m. to midnight Fri and Sat and 11 a.m. to 9:30 p.m. Sun. Note that the kitchen shuts down an hour before closing every day but Sun. Call (785) 539-5500 for hours or to make a reservation if there are six or more in your party, or visit www .littleapplebrewery.com.

If you're looking for conveniently located lodging, try the 1908 Prairie-style *Morning Star Bed and Breakfast on the Park* at 617 Houston St. The three-story Queen Anne, circa 1902, is in a historic district near K-State; you may be sharing the house with a visiting faculty member. Three rooms have down pillows and comforters; one has a private bath, and two are available with a private or shared bath. All rooms have queen- or king-size beds, a two-person Jacuzzi, and phone and data ports. A full breakfast featuring such specialties as blueberry French toast, granola pancakes or Greek omelettes is served in the dining room, or outside on the porch when weather permits. Rates are $89 to $179. Call (785) 587-9703 or visit the Web site at www.morningstaronthepark.com.

The *Guest Haus Bed and Breakfast,* 1724 Sheffield Circle, offers two rooms with shared baths. A continental breakfast is provided. Call the hosts, Mike and Gloria Heiberger, at (785) 776-6543, for rates. Be prepared for a two-night minimum stay if the Kansas State University Wildcats football team is playing at home that weekend (fans flood the town, most wearing purple sweatshirts). Visit the Web site at www.guesthaus.com.

The *Old Dutch Mill* at the city park on Fourth Street in *Wamego* is a town landmark. Built of native limestone in 1879—an authentic Dutch mill in Kansas—it is listed on the National Register of Historic Places. Look for the sculpted bust of Ceres, the Roman goddess of grain, above the window.

The mill, originally located 12 miles north of Wamego, was donated to the city in 1924. It was dismantled, each stone numbered, and hauled into town by horse-drawn wagons; here it was rebuilt by volunteers. This is a working mill, grinding local wheat to stone-ground flour, which is for sale. You won't see the wheat being ground (the apparatus is all enclosed), but you can visit the mill during select hours. Call (785) 456-2040 for more information or to schedule a visit.

Try to plan your visit during the Tulip Festival, when thousands of Holland tulips are in bloom, or over the Fourth of July. These are two of the biggest small-town celebrations and parades in the state. Wamego's nighttime Christmas parade has spectators lining the streets awaiting the arrival of Santa in his lighted sleigh. At the **Oregon Trail Nature Park** east of town is a huge silo mural done by local artist Cindy Martin. The park has several walking trails and a shelter house for picnics.

detourina canoe

It's possible to canoe on the Kansas River and its tributaries all the way from Junction City to Kansas City. One of the most scenic sections is a 15-mile stretch through the Flint Hills from Ogden to Manhattan. For information on access points, water levels, and difficulty ratings, check the Kansas Canoe and Kayak Association's Web site, www.kansascanoe.org.

Stop in Wamego and get a room at the **Eagle View Inn Bed and Breakfast** (785-456-9053) in the William Boyd building at 520 Lincoln Ave. It was originally the Boyd Blacksmith Shop, built in 1885. The upstairs was a boardinghouse. Now innkeepers John and Martha Powers welcome you to their B&B. Four rooms are available with queen- and king-size beds. They range in price from $65 to $75. Breakfast is served in **The Friendly Cooker Restaurant** (785-456-9053, www.inntravels.com), located on the first floor of the building. It is famous for its down-home cooking, and inn guests enjoy a breakfast of homemade buttermilk pancakes, with hosts John and Martha picking up the tab. The **Columbian Theatre Museum and Art Center** is the locale for cultural and civic activity. It has been elegantly restored in a $1.8 million renovation project. Its murals are a wonder; they date from the 1893 Columbian Exposition in Chicago. The 250-seat theater hosts dramatic and musical performances. For show and ticket information, call (800) 899-1893 and visit www.columbian theatre.com.

If you have never ventured off the interstate before and have any kind of phobia about it, **Paxico** is a good place to begin your therapy. Get off at the Paxico (334) exit to experience this antiques-happy little burg, leaving I-70 at one exit and returning to it at the next interchange. Paxico is remarkable because it has a series of historic buildings in near-original turn-of-the-twentieth-century condition.

ALSO WORTH SEEING

Council Grove Lake

Marion Lake
Marion

Melvern Lake
Melvern

Milford Lake,
Junction City

**Osage State Fishing Lake
and Wildlife Area,**
Reading

Paxico boasts a retail pottery outlet, art gallery, flea market, winery, and lots of antiques. Steve "Bud" Hund, owner of *Mill Creek Antiques,* 109 Newberry Ave., is the drive behind the comeback of Paxico; he also happens to be a descendant of the town's German founders. Bud started with a two-story building and a part-time antiques business. Today the buildings are full, and people drive from Lawrence, Topeka, and Kansas City to shop for the bargains to be found here.

Mill Creek sells American furniture and old lamps, but Bud's specialty is stoves. He has a regular museum of heating and cooking stoves that burn coal, wood, or gas. Big stoves and little stoves of cast iron are all here. He buys rusty and snaggle-toothed specimens at farm auctions, sands them, repairs them, and lines them up in his shop to await new homes. Call (785) 636-5520 for hours or see www.millcreekantiques.com.

Paxico is a fun little town, and many of the shops are just stepping distance apart. Start with *Hidden Treasures* at 216 Main St. Owners Rex and Kay Fiedler have traveled throughout Kansas to gather antiques, collectibles, glassware, and vintage home decor. Their shop is open 10 a.m. to 5 p.m. Sat and noon to 4:30 p.m. Sun. Call (785) 636-8933 or visit www.hiddentreasurespaxico.com.

Wyldewood Cellars, 22936 Grapevine Rd., is known as the "Heartland's Premier Winery" and is family-owned and -operated—in the tradition of Kansas farm families for generations. Having won more than 130 national and international wine awards, it is the most awarded winery in the state. (785) 636-8446 or see www.wyldewoodcellars.com.

Sisters & Co. at 105 Newbury Ave. in the heart of Paxico's historic district offers a wide selection of antiques, unusual gifts, and collectibles. Be sure to enjoy a tasty old-fashioned ice cream cone while you're taking a look around. Hours are 10 a.m. to 5 p.m. Mon through Sat and noon to 4:30 p.m. Sun. Phone (785) 636-8400 or visit www.paxicomerchants.com/sisters.

Jepson Pottery has been in business since 1974. The potter, Barry Jepson, has another studio in Harveyville. His stoneware pottery is hand-thrown, which makes each piece unique. Call (785) 636-5486 for hours, or visit the Web site, www.jepsonstudio.com.

Paxico Antiques at 103 Main St. invites you to sort about in kitchen collectibles, vintage jewelry, glassware, ceramic pottery, and of course, antiques. Call Vicki Jacobson at (785) 636-5426 for hours. You can also visit www.paxico antiques.com.

WB Antiques at 103 Newbury Ave. is also open seven days a week from 10 a.m. to 5 p.m. Step back in time to the age of fancy hats, colorful jewelry, fascinating books, and lovely linens. Phone (785) 636-5122 or see www.paxico merchants.com/wb.

If you are pulling a trailer or driving a motor home, *Mill Creek Campground* (22450 Campground Rd.; 785-636-5321) is a natural. As the name suggests, the wide, rocky Mill Creek flows through the campground. Beautiful cliffs rise to one side, and you can swim, fish, canoe, or picnic. Owners Dan and Judy Meinhardt have tried to restore the Old West feeling of the campground, but it has 100-foot, level, pull-through parking sites and can accommodate everything from a tent to an Airstream. See www.millcreek campground.com.

Get off I-70 onto the Skyline Mill Creek Scenic Drive and wander over this scenic byway for breathtaking vistas of the Flint Hills. You'll encounter a variety of native stone buildings and, of course, good eating places. This road-less-traveled goes through *Alma,* where maps are available at the *Wabaunsee County Historical Museum* at Third and Missouri from Mar 1 to Nov 30, between the hours of 10 a.m. and noon and 1 to 4 p.m. Tues through Sat, and 1 to 4 p.m. on Sun; from Dec 1 to Feb 28 Tues and Wed 10 a.m. to noon and 1 to 4 p.m. There is no charge, but a $2 donation is suggested. Call (785) 765-2200 or visit new.wabaunsee.org.

This City of Stone is built of locally quarried limestone, and the unique architectural features of many of the buildings draw architects from around the country. The *Alma Bakery and Sweet Shoppe* is at 118 West Third St. The sweet scent of freshly baking breads, cinnamon rolls, and cookies will lure you in. Baker Jeanette Rohleder-Supernaw fills shelves with turnovers and puff pastries to tempt you, and assorted sweets such as fudge, brittle, and toffee will beg to go home with you. Try the popular Bierock, a meat-and-cabbage-filled meal baked in a roll. The bakery has no set hours, really, but Jeanette says, "I'm here every day Monday through Saturday." So call first if in doubt, (785) 765-2235. Also see www.almabakeryandsweetshoppe.com. *Deb's Restaurant* nearby at 327 Missouri, offers down-home cooking with a special every day that includes dessert. It is open Mon through Thurs from 7 a.m. to 7:30 p.m., Fri and Sat from 7 a.m. to 8 p.m., and Sun from 11 a.m. to 2 p.m. Call (785) 765-2527.

Travelers at the north edge of Third Street should bear left where the gravel road forks. This road runs parallel to Mill Creek and continues to *Alta Vista.* Watch for impressive stone houses and barns along the way as well as two old stone schoolhouses. Alta Vista is about 12 miles along this road.

North out of Alta Vista, take Highway 177, which winds through some of the area's most enchanting hill country, or even better, follow the Skyline Drive signs leading out of town. Narrow lanes of blacktop or gravel parallel the highway, and waist-high stone fences extend to the horizon. These fences were built by hand by the region's early settlers.

Surrounded by bluestem prairie and secluded, wooded valleys, the area is home to many varieties of wildlife and wildflowers. It is one of the best places to see the "sea of grass" as it once was. Year-round beauty marks this area. In the spring young prairie grasses form a backdrop for the explosion of wildflower colors. In late summer and autumn, bluestem grass ripens into tall, golden plumes, and giant sunflowers dot the prairie.

Places to Stay in North Central Kansas

ABILENE

Diamond Motel
1407 Northwest Third St.
(785) 263-2360

Holiday Inn Express Hotel and Suites
110 East Lafayette Ave.
(785) 263-4049

COUNCIL GROVE

Cottage House Hotel & Motel
25 North Neosho St.
(620) 767-6828

JUNCTION CITY

Econo Lodge
211 West Flint Hills Blvd.
(785) 238-8181

Thunderbird Marina RV
on Milford Lake
4725 West Rolling Hills Rd.
(785) 238-5864

TOPEKA

Candlelight Inn
2831 Southwest Fairlawn Rd.
(I-70, exit 357)
(785) 272-9550

Comfort Inn
1518 Southwest Wanamaker Rd.
(785) 273-5365

Ramada Inn
420 Southeast Sixth Ave.
(off I-70)
(785) 234-5400

WASHINGTON

Washington Motel
310 West Seventh St.
(785) 325-2281

Places to Eat in North Central Kansas

COUNCIL GROVE

Hays House
112 West Main St.
(620) 767-5911

HANOVER

Pony Express café
1898 All American Rd.
(Junction of US 36 and Highway 148)
(785) 337-2270

JUNCTION CITY

Pusan Diner
1634 North Washington St.
(785) 238-8848

Stacy's Restaurant
118 West Flint Hills Blvd.
(785) 238-3039

MANHATTAN

Little Apple Brewing Co.
1110 West Loop Place
Shopping Center
(off I-70)
(785) 539-5500

Little Grill
6625 Dyer Rd.
(785) 323-0112

SENECA

Spanky's
405 Main St.
(785) 336-6031

Valentino's Grand Italian Buffet of Seneca
604 North Eleventh St.
(785) 336-3575

TOPEKA

Bobo's Drive In
2300 Southwest Tenth Ave.
(785) 234-4511

Paisano's Ristorante II
4043 Southwest Tenth St.
(785) 273-0100

WASHINGTON

Itty Bitty Deli
225 C St.
(785) 325-3223

SELECTED CHAMBERS OF COMMERCE AND VISITOR BUREAUS

Abilene Convention and Visitors Bureau
201 Northwest Second St.
(785) 263-2231 or (800) 569-5915
www.abilenekansas.org

Council Grove and Morris County Chamber of Commerce
212 West Main St.
(620) 767-5413
www.councilgrove.com

Junction City/Geary County Convention and Visitors Bureau
823 North Washington St.
(785) 238-2885
www.junctioncity.org

Manhattan Convention and Visitors Bureau
501 Poyntz Ave.
(785) 776-8829
www.manhattancvb.org

Topeka Convention and Visitors Bureau
1275 Southwest Topeka Blvd.
(785) 234-1030 or (800) 235-1030
www.visittopeka.us

NORTHWEST KANSAS →

You are about to enter the **Smoky Hills,** tucked between the Flint Hills and the High Plains. The landscape is grand in scale, sculpted and folded by the many creeks and rivers flowing through it. In the northwest corner, numerous dry draws run into branch lines of the two main waterways, the Beaver and Sappa Creeks, which then join the Republican River. The resulting landscape is one of high plains and rolling countryside tilting gently toward the creek bottoms.

Millions of buffalo roamed here, along with deer and antelope, as you know, from singing "Home on the Range" (the Kansas state song, by the way) in day camp. The Cheyenne and Pawnee lived here and met Coronado in 1541.

The Dakota Sandstone hills on the east, Post Rock Country in the middle, and the Blue Hills along the western edge define the area. Although this territory is larger than Vermont, New Hampshire, or New Jersey, the population is spread thin; the sky reaches all the way to the horizon, with little to clutter the view.

At one time dust storms darkened the sky. From as early as 1883, there is a record of the Sioux Indians telling a man named John Christiansen that the sodbusters had the earth

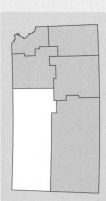

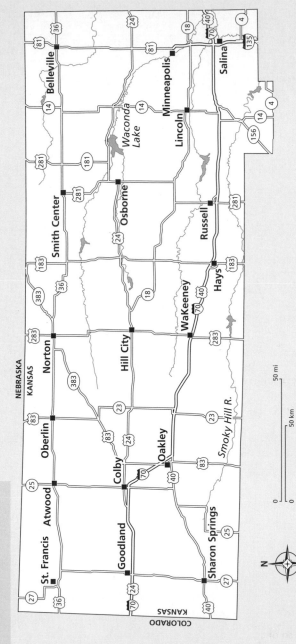

"wrong side up"—the Indians only split the sod to plant corn. Years later, in the time of the Dust Bowl, thousands of tons of topsoil were blown away, and the settlers learned the lesson the Native Americans had tried to teach them.

It's a long way between cities here, with a lot of land in between. Prairies are not flat but have easy slopes, graceful rolls that resemble the heavy swell of the ocean after a storm. Roads weave through fields of wheat, corn, milo, and remnants of virgin short-grass grazing lands. Prehistoric inland seas helped sculpt the land, laying down hundreds of feet of sedimentary rocks; it is a fossil hunter's paradise.

Interstate 70 parallels the Old Smoky Hill Trail that led to the goldfields of Denver in 1859. (There is an excellent chance that you are already on I-70; it is called the Main Street of Kansas and shoots like a tunnel through the state at a posted 70 miles per hour.) But off this freeway lie some of the most fascinating towns in the state. The choice of motels is endless, but there are also more than fifteen bed-and-breakfasts and restored old hotels tucked in unexpected places and waiting for you.

Main Street U.S.A.

We begin in *Salina.* The town lies in a basin near the confluence of the Saline and Smoky Hill Rivers. The scenic Smoky Hills gently rise and fall all around the city.

Post Rock Tours start in Salina and travel along Highway 18; it's an easy way to see many of the massive buildings constructed from post rock, a layer of particularly fine quarrying limestone that extends from Nebraska to WaKeeney. The stone, plentiful in this part of the country, was used extensively as fence-post and building material by the clever pioneers, who found a chronic

AUTHOR'S FAVORITES

Cathedral of the Plains	LandMark Inn and Teller Room
Dane G. Hansen Memorial Museum and Plaza	Monument Rocks
	Mushroom Rocks State Park
Drover's Mercantile	Smoky Hill Vineyards and Winery
Garden of Eden	Sternberg Museum of Natural History
Kansas Originals Market	

TOP ANNUAL EVENTS

APRIL

Storytelling Festival
Downs; last weekend
(785) 454-3421

JUNE

Czech Fest
Wilson
(785) 658-2211

Prairie Heritage Day
Colby
(785) 460-4400

Smoky Hill River Festival
Salina; second weekend
(785) 309-5570

Stearman Fly-In
St. Francis; vintage planes, parachutists,
hot air balloons; second weekend
(785) 332-2961

JULY

Pickin' on the Plains Bluegrass Festival
Colby; third weekend
(785) 460-7643 or (800) 611-8835

Tri-State Antique Engine and Threshers Show
Bird City; last weekend
(785) 734-2504

Wild West Festival
Hays; July 4 weekend
(785) 623-4476

SEPTEMBER

Land Institute's Prairie Festival
Salina
(785) 823-5376

Smoky Hill Museum Street Fair
Salina
(785) 309-5776

shortage of wood in this nearly treeless land and recognized the impermanence of sod for building. Contact Duane Vonada (785-526-7391 or 785-526-7369) or visit www.vonadastone.com for more information.

If you didn't stay at a bed-and-breakfast and are looking for breakfast (or lunch or dinner), folks will direct you to a place called ***Russell's Restaurant and Sweet Shoppe*** at 649 Westport Blvd. (corner of Crawford Street and U.S. Highway 81 in Salina). It is always open, 24/7. You know the old maxim about asking a trucker where the best food is to be found? Russell's is that place. The restaurant is famous for its anytime breakfast menu (Mexican omelet, Belgian waffles) and hickory-smoked dinners (Thurs is all-you-can-eat chicken night). The bakery is a wonderland of strawberry chiffon pies and other desserts. Call (785) 825-5733 or go to www.russellsrestaurant.com. It is simply the best food in town.

The ***Central Kansas Flywheels Yesteryear Museum*** at 1100 West Diamond Dr., Salina (785-825-8473; www.yesteryearmuseum.com), is made up of families who are interested in preserving the heritage of the state. The group started collecting antique tractors and named itself for one of the engine parts.

An unlikely looking metal building off I-70 (exit 252) houses an 1880s print shop, and so many pieces of old machinery are lovingly displayed that it is well worth the donation at the door to the all-volunteer organization. CKFI holds an annual Antique Engine and Threshing Show in October. Open year-round, Tues through Sat 9 a.m. to 5 p.m. They ask for a $4 donation for adults; children age twelve and younger are free.

If you're shopping for antiques, there are numerous shops downtown, including *Auld Lang Syne Antiques and Collectibles* (785-825-0020) in the former First National Bank building at Santa Fe and Iron Avenues (101 North Santa Fe Ave.). A map of the antiques and specialty shops is available from the chamber of commerce at 120 West Ash (785-827-9301). Hours are 10 a.m. to 5:30 p.m. Mon through Sat, 1 to 5:30 p.m. Sun. See http://auldlangsyne antiquesandcollectibles.com.

The *Smoky Hill Museum* at 211 West Iron Ave. features local history, a country store, and period rooms. You can enter a full-scale replica of Salina's first home, learn about Salina's role as a business crossroads of the Heartland or even hear about local ghost lore. It is open Tues through Fri from noon to 5 p.m., Sat from 10 a.m. to 5 p.m., and Sun from 1 to 5 p.m. Call (785) 309-5776 or visit www.smokyhillmuseum.org.

> ## trivia
>
> If you have a canoe atop your van, the Smoky Hill River has a public canoe trail that begins 20 miles west of and ends 4 miles southeast of Kanopolis. It is 10.5 miles long and takes about four or five hours to complete. Call the Army Corps of Engineers office in Marquette (785-546-2294) for the entry location.

The *Salina Art Center,* at 242 South Santa Fe Ave., has been called the best contemporary art institution in the state. Visitors can find everything from photographs to sculpture in a 1920s Spanish Revival building. This art center hosts continually changing exhibitions by talented regional artists as well as recognized masters. It offers programs for adults and children that are related to the exhibitions. The ARTery is a hands-on laboratory where children can touch, weave, draw, design, and go on scavenger hunts. Hours are noon to 5 p.m. Wed through Sat, 1 to 5 p.m. Sun. Call (785) 827-1431 or log on to www.salinaartcenter.org.

Just 1 block north of the center, the *Salina Art Center Cinema* (150 South Santa Fe Ave.) is in a renovated storefront in the downtown historic district. This is the place for offbeat, imaginative, and thought-provoking films that you might not find in a conventional theater. There is an $8 admission fee. Call (785) 452-9868 for showtimes.

Popular with the locals is the *Hickory Hut* at 1617 West Crawford St. (785-825-1588), for barbecue, of course, with drive-up and takeout for a picnic.

Or there's the **Cozy Inn,** 108 North Seventh St., a six-stool eatery serving tiny hamburgers with fried onions, just the way it has for eighty years. Call (785) 825-2699. Or try **Scheme,** at 123 North Seventh (785-823-5125), the best place in town for pizza and sandwiches.

If the children have too much stored-up energy to be in the car one more minute, get off Interstate 135 at the Crawford exit and, just off Centennial Road at 1634 Sunflower Lane, find **Jumpin' Joe's Family Fun Center,** the place to let off some steam. There is a thirty-six-hole miniature golf course, go-carts zooming around a track, a laser-tag room, and a video-game area. There is even a soft play area with tubes and tunnels where preschoolers can take off their shoes and play. The outdoor things, of course, are seasonal, but the laser tag and video area are open year-round. Hours are Fri from 4 p.m. to 10 p.m., Sat 10 a.m. to 10 p.m., Sun 1 to 7 p.m. See www.jumpinjoes.com or call (785) 827-9090 for ticket information.

At **Rolling Hills Zoo** (625 Hedville Rd.), just outside Salina, there's a lot more here than buffalo. Thriving in this prairie landscape are a 7,000-pound Indian rhinoceros, some exotic snow leopards, a couple of orangutans, and white rhinos. More than sixty-one endangered species and about 200 animals call this place home. It is open to the public and features the Education/Discovery Center, a gift shop, and a restaurant. Hours are 8 a.m. to 5 p.m. daily in the summer, and the zoo opens at 9 a.m. in the winter. Admission is $10.95 for adults, $9.95 for seniors, and $5.95 for children ages three to twelve. All-day tram passes are available for $3. Call (785) 827-9488 for more information or see www.rollinghillswildlife.com.

Back in 1919, more than 250 acres of grapes were planted in the fields around Salina. Later, Kay Bloom and Steve Jennings converted an old riding

Buffalo Herd

Four miles south of Interstate 70, on the U.S. Highway 183 bypass, is a small herd of buffalo, a tiny remnant of the vast herds, numbering in the millions, that once roamed the North American plains. If you have never actually seen a buffalo, this is your chance. The herd was started in 1953 with a bull named Wild Bill and a cow named Calamity Jane (a cow is a girl buffalo, by the way). Now the herd has grown. The area once was home to the largest buffalo herd on the continent (which numbered in the millions). There is a life-size buffalo sculpture by local artist Pete "Fritz" Felton Jr., titled *Monarch of the Plains*, just outside historic Fort Hays. It reminds us that the Native Americans depended on the buffalo for everything—food, shelter, clothing, and tools—and felt they were worth fighting for when the railroad and white settlers began to slaughter them.

stable into a winery. ***The Smoky Hill Vineyards and Winery*** at 212 West Golf Link Rd. produces twenty-eight wines including dry chablis, clarets rich in oak and tannins, light, semi-dry blushes, and a dessert Icewein. Sunshine is essential for creating good wine, and Kansas has abundant sunshine as well as rich soil. The grapes are hand tended from spring pruning through fall harvest. Add to this the best equipment and the winemaking skills of Norm Jennings, and the results are wines that rank among the best in blind tastings of American and European wines. Wines are sold from the tasting room at the winery (as well as in Wilson and Wichita); tours and tastings are free. Check the Web site (www.kansaswine.com) for events such as the Orthodox church's annual "Blessing of the Grapes Festival" in Aug, gourmet winemaker dinners, and interactive Murder Mystery Dinners. Hours are Mon through Sat from 10 a.m. to 6 p.m. Call (785) 823-5231.

The town of ***Smolan*** is southwest of Salina on I-135. The old high-school building now houses ***The Hickory Tree Restaurant,*** at 304 East Walnut St. Some of the classrooms are used for private parties and the main restaurant is in the gym. Kathy and Lee Holzwarth "retired," he calls it, here from much more strenuous careers and now just cook for as many as 500 people. This is barbecue heaven with an extensive menu—all barbecued, smoked, seasoned, and glazed—and an all-you-can-eat philosophy that includes drink, dessert, and tax. This school is open only on weekends: Fri and Sat from 5 to 9 p.m. and Sun for lunch from 11 a.m. to 2 p.m. Lee is from St. Francis, up in the northwest corner of the state, and if you are headed west, he can tell you a lot about the history and landscape of that area, which they explore with horses and motorcycles. His parents own one of the last inhabitable sod houses in the state and love to show it off to visitors. Phone (785) 668-2164 or go to www.thehickorytree.com.

Too full to travel now? The ***C & W Ranch*** has a room waiting for you. This is a real working ranch headquarters with home-raised, homemade food. The quiet country atmosphere and pretty antique decor make it a perfect place to relax. If you are hauling horses, they have stalls as well. The ranch welcomes hunting groups and is fine for receptions, reunions, and all kinds of retreats. Look at the Web site at www.cwranch.com or call the Wimer family at (785) 668-2352. The ranch is at 4000 South Halstead Rd. just south of the I-70 and I-135 interchange at Salina. Rooms are $95 to $150 a night.

Southwest of Salina, ***Kanopolis Lake and State Park,*** off Highway 141, is perfect for fishing, boating, and camping. The park also contains ***Kanopolis Trails,*** a 26-mile hiking and horse trail, which is also open to mountain bikes. You can get a self-guided driving tour of the area on Legacy Trail, which focuses on the history of the valley. It will guide you to places such as pioneer cemeteries and old homesteads along the old Butterfield Stage Coach route. For trail information contact the Kanopolis State Park office at (785) 546-2565.

Two miles south and 2.5 miles west of Highways 140 and 141 near Ellsworth is **Mushroom Rocks State Park,** unique for its Dakota sandstone formations that mimic mushrooms. It's managed by the state park office at Kanopolis (785-546-2565).

Two miles north of New Cambria, **Iron Mound** passes (in Kansas) for a mountain, with an elevation of 1,497 feet. Visible from I-70, it is crowned with greenhorn limestone, the easternmost outcropping of Cretaceous limestone in Kansas.

trivia

If you are looking for a scenic drive, take Highway 14 from Ellsworth to Mankato. You can get that buffalo burger you have been wanting to try at **Buffalo Roam Steak House.** Call (785) 378-3971 for hours and directions.

Continuing southwest on Highway 140 brings you to the town of **Ellsworth. Drover's Mercantile** (119 North Douglas Ave.) is run by cowboy Jim Gray. He dresses the part and sells all manner of western goods—boots, chaps, gear, and reproduction 1870s shields, lances, and tomahawks made by the Lakota Sioux of South Dakota. Jim and his partner, Linda Kohls, also carry a large selection of books on the Old West. There is a real chuckwagon that was on Jim's family ranch, and the walls of the shop are covered with siding from a family barn. Get Jim started telling stories, and you can plan on spending the rest of the day in the shop if you want to. He loves talking about Ellsworth's cow-town history and literally wrote the book on Ellsworth history. In the 1870s, Ellsworth was the end of the trail for longhorns. The herds passed down the street right in front of where the Mercantile stands now. Call (785) 472-4703 to speak to Jim or visit www.droversmercantile.com. Hours are from 10 a.m. to 5 p.m. Mon through Sat.

The town also has **Ellsworth Antique Mall** at 210 North Douglas Ave. (785-472-4659). Hours are Mon through Sat 7:30 a.m. to 5 p.m.

When the sun sets, it is the perfect time to find the **Kanopolis Drive-In** at 804 North Kansas Ave., which has been in continuous operation since 1952. Any warm night 740 cars can pull in for the double feature Apr through Sept. Call (785) 472-4786 to see what the movie du jour is.

As you near Wilson Lake, past Salina on I-70, you will notice the dramatic silhouette of the two 80-foot-high wind generators built by the U.S. Army Corps of Engineers. This area has the most constant wind in the state. They generate 86,000 kilowatt-hours of power annually to the Smoky Hill Electric Cooperative. The object is to substitute clean power for fossil fuel, and it's about time. A scale model of a Wilson Lake wind generator is in the Aerospace Museum at the Smithsonian Institution in Washington, D.C.

For some breathtaking views, get off I-70 at exit 206 and turn north on Highway 232. You'll be on the **Post Rock Scenic Byway,** driving along **Wilson Lake.** The lake occupies 100 miles of shoreline and 9,000 acres of water. Highway 232 goes to Lucas, the Grassroots Art Capital of Kansas. Turn west on Highway 18. You can see Wolf Creek Valley, a part of the Smoky Hills greenhorn limestone escarpment. Notice the bluffs south of the valley and the level valley floor. At the roadside park in Luray is the first log cabin built in Russell County.

Continue on Highway 18 to Paradise to see the limestone water tower, or head south on U.S. Highway 281 at the

trivia

The COWBOY Society (Cock-eyed Old West Band of Yahoos) was created to preserve and encourage the cowboy stories of Kansas. You can visit their Web site at www .droversmercantile.com.

junction of Highway 18 and US 281. US 281 cuts though layers of limestone, revealing outcroppings of Dakota limestone, Grancros shale, and greenhorn limestone. The Saline River Valley provides some rugged landscape and dispels the notion that Kansas is flat.

From I-70, pull off at the **Wilson** exit and take something from Kansas home with you. Just about anything you want, as a matter of fact, can be found at the **Kansas Originals Market** at 233 Hwy. 232. It features fine folk art, crafts, and food. The huge steel building houses art and crafts from most of the artists mentioned in this book, so if you are having second thoughts about a piece you didn't buy somewhere else in the state, you might be able to find something like it here: stained glass, quilts, pottery, wood carvings, and jewelry. You can also take home apple cider, *kolaches*, jams, and wheat snacks. The market is open from 9 a.m. to 6 p.m. Mon through Sat and from 11 a.m. to 6 p.m. Sun. Call (785) 658-3372 or (877) 457-6233. The Web site is www.kansasoriginals.com, where you can order something you forgot to buy.

In the town of **Dorrance,** Tom and Janet Taggart have been turning out good food at the **Bunker Hill Cafe** at Sixth and Elm Streets in **Bunker Hill** for more than twenty years. Originally built as a drugstore in 1916, it is a unique nineteenth-century eating place. Fresh-baked raisin bread is a specialty of the house, along with catfish, Norwegian salmon, and steak.

All entrees are ordered by weight to satisfy appetites of all sizes. They serve homemade bread from the bakery they added to the back. They advertise the "best meal you'll ever have"; how's that for confidence? Hours are 5 to 10 p.m. Wed through Sat. Call (785) 483-6544.

Leave I-70 at exit 184 and enter the Saline River Valley and the town of **Russell.** You'll see a building that looks more like a miniature stone castle than a museum, complete with turreted towers and an arched stone entry of greenhorn limestone known here as post rock. The **Fossil Station Museum** (785-483-3637) at 331 Kansas St. was built in 1907, the original block-stone stage station on the Smoky Hill Trail and formerly the county jail. It captures the spirit of the history from the late 1800s to 1930 and is open from Memorial Day to Labor Day, Mon through Sat 11 a.m. to 4 p.m., Sun 1 to 4 p.m., and by appointment. Admission is free, but donations are welcome.

trivia

Russell is the hometown of former senator Bob Dole.

Hungry? Russell has a couple of good spots to eat. Stop at **Meridy's** at 1220 South Fossil St. for some down-home cooking. You can get breakfast, lunch, or dinner here. Hours are from 6 a.m., so you can get an early start, to around 9 p.m. seven days a week. Call (785) 483-4300. Maybe you don't think of Kansas as oil country—think again. The **Oil Patch Museum,** two blocks west of the Fossil Station (785-483-6640), contains the story of the history of black gold; walk through an actual oil storage tank and study the geology, drilling, and production of oil. Outdoors you can see the drilling rigs and steam engines. You will find it near the intersection of I-70 and South US 281. It's open daily from 4 to 8 p.m. The **Gernon House** at 818 Kansas St. is one of the oldest post-rock stone houses, built in 1872 by a blacksmith and one of the original settlers. It has been fully restored and furnished to the period.

The **Heym-Oliver House** at 503 North Kansas St. is another 1870s stone house, though this one is sawed stone, rather than faced or chipped. Ask your guide to explain the difference. It is also furnished. Hours are the same for both houses: 1 to 4 p.m. Sat and Sun; by appointment in the winter. Call (785) 483-3637. Admission to all four attractions in Russell is a suggested donation of $2.

Deines Cultural Center (785-483-3742) at 820 North Main was given to the city of Russell as the permanent home for the wood engravings of the nationally known artist E. Hubert Deines. The gallery also features the work of other artists, and exhibits change monthly. Admission is free; donations are welcome. Call for hours or visit www.deinesculturalcenter.org.

As you zip along I-70, a church spire will catch your eye. St. Fidelis Church, known as the **Cathedral of the Plains,** is 9 miles east of Hays in **Victoria** at 900 Cathedral Ave. This Romanesque limestone structure was finished in 1911 by German-Russian settlers. It is a remarkable feat of architectural

The Settlement of the Saline River Valley

The earliest people to inhabit the Great Plains region lived during the Paleo-Indian period, about 12,000 years ago. These people were hunters and gatherers who roamed widely in search of mammoths and large bison. Prehistoric carvings may still be found in the weathered sandstone outcroppings in the area. European explorers and traders entered the Saline River Valley in the 1500s. A Frenchman, Etienne Bourgmont, made contact with the Padouca Indians, who hunted buffalo on horseback. During the nineteenth century the Pawnee and Cheyenne lived here. In the late 1850s, white settlers began to establish homes here despite drought, invading hordes of grasshoppers, and prairie fires. In 1964 the dam built to make Wilson Lake was closed, and the waters inundated the Saline River Valley, changing it forever from open prairie to domestic farmland.

beauty named for Capuchin Friar St. Fidelis. The church and monastery form the shape of a cross. Romanesque in design, the immense sanctuary holds enough pews to seat more than 1,000 people. Eighteen 10-foot granite columns, each weighing fifteen tons and topped with hand-carved capitals, reach to the 44-foot-high, arched and ribbed ceiling. Each family in the parish hauled six loads of stone with horse and wagon from a nearby quarry and contributed $45 to help finance construction. They hand-cut the massive sandstone blocks and dressed them in their spare time. The rose petal–shaped stained-glass panels above the doors represent harmony. They were shipped from Germany in 1916. Be sure to notice the hand-carved Austrian stations of the cross purchased in 1919 and the Italian Carrara marble altar installed in 1986. The church was dubbed Cathedral of the Plains in 1912 by William Jennings Bryan. It is open daily during daylight hours. Donations are appreciated. Call (785) 735-2777 or log on to www.stfidelischuch.com.

There are a dozen Roman Catholic churches in the small towns off I-70 between Russell and Hays. All but two of them are constructed of post rock, the area's unique building stone characterized by its brown streaks. These are the churches of the Volga Germans, who settled here in the late nineteenth century, each group from a different German town. Since travel by horse and wagon was so difficult, the immigrants built a church in each of the new settlements. Some older residents of this part of Kansas still speak one of the German dialects of their forefathers. All of the churches have stained-glass windows and a tower with a cross on top. All are handcrafted. Carvers shaped capitals for huge granite columns, while carpenters sculpted ornate altars of intricate design.

One of the most beautiful of the group is the **_Holy Cross Shrine_** at **_Pfeifer_** (12 miles south of Victoria), finished in 1918. Red-and-blue

St. Fidelis's Feather Muffins

You can get some divine recipes from *Sharing Our Best*, a cookbook offered by St. Fidelis Church in Victoria. It contains 500 pages of 1,300 Volga-German, Russian, and other ethnic recipes along with proverbs, household hints, and German prayers from members of the parish. The proceeds are used to keep the Cathedral of the Plains in good repair. The book is $25, including postage. Make checks payable to St. Fidelis Church and mail to St. Fidelis Church, 601 Tenth St., Victoria 67671.

These feather muffins are a highlight. They truly are light as a feather!

2 cups flour
3 teaspoons baking powder
½ teaspoon salt
¼ cup sugar
¼ cup butter
1 egg
¾ cup milk

1. Preheat the oven to 350°.
2. Sift flour, baking powder, and salt.
3. In a large bowl, cream sugar and butter. Add egg and mix.
4. Add the dry ingredients alternately with milk to the creamed mixture.
5. Bake at 350° for 20 minutes.

Yield: 12 muffins

stained-glass windows are supported by delicate, vaulted arches and pillars. It has been called the two-cents church, because each family was asked to give two cents on each bushel of wheat they grew while it was being built. Many of these old churches have closed due to the area's dwindling population, but this one can be seen as part of Hays's summertime evening tours. Call the Convention and Visitors Bureau at (785) 628-8202 for more information.

The ***Sternberg Museum of Natural History*** is located just off I-70 at 3000 Sternberg Dr. in ***Hays.*** The museum has a huge four-story dome re-creating Earth eighty-eight million years ago. Visitors can walk from the ocean bottom to land among several animated, life-size replicas of dinosaurs and other animal life. Under the Kansas Seaway, you will see giant prehistoric marine lizards and fish that lived millions of years ago. The Discovery Room is a hands-on learning center for all ages. Touch models, use computers, and explore to your heart's content. Natural history, including recent vertebrates and invertebrates; geology; history, including objects dealing with the period of discovery, exploration, and settlement of the Great Plains; fossils—whatever your interest, you'll find it here. This is the home of the world-famous "fish within a fish" fossil. Its previous home was the Cretaceous period, some eighty-eight million years ago.

Traveling exhibits are also brought to the Sternberg Museum. One of the best known was a cast copy of "Sue," the *Tyrannosaurus rex* from Chicago's Field Museum of Natural History that toured only fifteen museums in the country.

Hours are 9 a.m. to 6 p.m. Tues through Sat and 1 to 6 p.m. Sun. Admission is $8 for adults, $6 for seniors, $4 for youth ages four to twelve. For more information, call (877) 332-1165.

The Hays Convention and Visitors Bureau sponsors Twilight Tours each summer. Every night from June through Aug, a bus stops at all of the motels on Vine Street to pick up anyone who wants to take one of the seventeen free tours of the area. Guests get to see some of the ranches, a limestone quarry with a post-rock demonstration, a horse farm, historic churches, and a beautiful Kansas sunset. Call the convention and visitor bureau at (785) 628-8202 for a schedule.

These local eateries come highly recommended by Hays residents. ***Al's Chickenette*** (700 Vine St.; 785-625-7414) specializes in fried chicken and chicken-fried steak cooked to order and served with mashed potatoes, gravy, and veggies. The decor is all "Early Chicken" (you will understand when you see it). Hours are Tues through Sat from 11 a.m. to 9:30 p.m., Sun from 11 a.m. to 8:30 p.m.

A Treasure of Fossils

On a knob in a Morland pasture, scientists have found prehistoric fossils of rhinoceroses and mastodons, as well as bamboo plants and bulrushes. The director of the Sternberg Museum of Natural History in Hays sees this Miocene period treasure chest as a major discovery.

How this knob was formed is still unknown. The plants and animals may have been in a riverbed, and somehow a cap of erosion-resistant rock covered the deposit. It went undiscovered until a young boy found a rhinoceros tooth and made it part of a 4-H project. The rest is history, or prehistory.

The Sternberg Museum now owns the site, called Minium Quarry, and plans to enclose it within a building. When it opens to the public, visitors will watch scientists at work in an active dig.

Rooftops at 1200 Main St., on the sixth floor of the Emprise Bank Building (785-628-8631), is not exactly off the beaten path, but for steaks, seafood, and a great view of the city, you can't beat it. It is an elegant place where the waiters wear tuxes and candles light the tables. Lunch is served 11 a.m. to 2 p.m. Mon through Fri. Dinner hours are Mon through Sat from 5 to 10 p.m. See www.rooftopshays.com.

Sculptor Pete "Fritz" Felten's *Stone Gallery* is at 107½ West Sixth. The Hays native uses native limestone to create works that can be seen all over the state. He carved the figures of the four famous Kansans that stand in the state capitol in Topeka; his works can also be seen in front of the Cathedral of the Plains in Victoria and the Lindsborg Museum. The statue of Wild Bill Hickok on Hays's Main Street is his work, too. Pieces ranging in size from tabletop to life-size are on display at the gallery and in the sculpture garden outside. Most pieces are for sale. Call (785) 625-7619 for hours and other information.

Visit the unique *Kansas Mercí Boxcar Museum* on the grounds of the Hays American Legion post at Thirteenth and Canterbury. It is made from a boxcar that has crossed the ocean. Filled with food and sent to war-torn France by the United States in the 1940s, the boxcar was returned by the grateful French, filled with gifts from every province. Open by appointment; call the Hays Convention and Visitors Bureau at (785) 628-8202.

Pheasant Run at 3201 Vine St. in Hays serves breakfast and lunch from 6 a.m. to 3 p.m. seven days a week, so if you are on the road early, this is the place to start. You can eat breakfast all day if your early start doesn't start as early as planned. Call (785) 628-1044.

trivia

If you're traveling along U.S. Highway 183, you will notice a lot of metal sculptures. These are the creation of Curly Leiker, who lives on the Sweetwater Ranch. You will see his work all over the area. He has made many life-size mailbox characters and Southwest coyotes. It is just a hobby, he says, that developed from a welding class he took at the local university back in 1970. Watch for his creations as you drive.

The century-old *Kansas State University Ag Research Center* is at 1232 240th Ave. in Hays, just off the US 183 bypass. The 3,600-acre farm has demonstration plots for nonirrigated wheat and sorghum and has 800 head of beef cattle. Call (785) 625-3425 to arrange a tour and learn about the research the university is doing.

The *Tea Rose Inn Bed and Breakfast,* at 117 West Thirteenth St., is a neatly restored 1909 Victorian with architectural features such as beveled art-glass windows and an open handcrafted staircase. But it also has all the modern amenities, including whirlpool baths and telephones in the rooms. You can stroll down the original brick-paved streets of Hays to shopping, art galleries, theaters, and church. Restaurants are nearby for lunch and dinner, but breakfast here is not just breakfast, it is a day-starting event, with freshly ground coffee or fine teas. Rooms are $79 to $129. Call (785) 623-4060 or (888) 623-1125. Visit the Web site at www.tearose.net.

Fort Hays State Historic Site is located on US 183 Alternate just south of Hays. An important U.S. Army post from 1865 to 1889, the fort was built to protect stage lines, workers on the Union Pacific Railroad, and settlers, and to serve as a supply base for other area forts. Wild Bill Hickok, Buffalo Bill Cody, and Lt. Col. George Armstrong Custer all have connections to the fort. Fort Hays was also home to the Tenth U.S. Cavalry, whose black troopers were also known as Buffalo Soldiers.

Four original buildings survive: the stone blockhouse (completed in 1868), a guardhouse, and two officers' quarter buildings. A modern visitor center displays furnishings, weapons, and other artifacts. Fort Hays is open from 9 a.m. to 5 p.m. Tues through Sat. Closed some holidays. Admission is $3 for adults, $1 for students (kindergarten through twelfth grade and college); KSHS members are free. Donations are welcome. For more information call (785) 625-6812 or check the Web site at www.kshs.org/places/forthays.

Between Hays and WaKeeney, *Ellis* calls itself the "Antique City of the High Plains." To back up that claim, you'll find *Wiesner Antiques Mall* at 819 Washington St. (785-726-4575) and a half dozen individual shops, one near the interstate and the others downtown on Washington Street.

The *Bukovina Society of America's Headquarters and Museum* is also in Ellis. It is a stately two-story limestone building at Eighth and Washington Streets. The Bukovina people came here in the 1880s from the Rhine-Palatinate and Württemberg in Germany and the Bohemian forest of Austria. Although a minority in their new country, they lived in ethnic German communities and neighborhoods, preserving their language and customs. The museum has artifacts, historic photographs, and genealogy materials. It is open by appointment only. Call (785) 726-3388 or visit www.bukovinasociety.org.

trivia

Hays was a wild town in the late 1860s, with plenty of saloons and dance halls. Wild Bill Hickok was sheriff for a few months, but he left town after a brawl with some troopers. While her husband, Lt. Col. George Custer, was encamped there, Elizabeth Custer said that "there was enough desperate country's history in that little town in one summer to make a whole library of dime novels."

The **Walter P. Chrysler Boyhood Home** at 102 West Tenth takes you back to the 1880s and lets you peek into the early life of the Chrysler Corporation's founder. Chrysler moved to Ellis with his family at the age of three, lived here until his teens when he went west to work, then returned to marry a local girl. The house is furnished in period style; an adjacent museum shows a short video and displays personal memorabilia.

Hours May through Sept are 10 a.m. to 4 p.m. Tues through Saturday, and 1 to 4 p.m. on Sun. The home and museum are open from Memorial Day weekend through Labor Day weekend 10 a.m. to 4 p.m. Tues to Sat; the rest of the year, hours are 11 a.m. to 3 p.m. Admission is $3 for adults, $2.50 for seniors, and $1 for children ages eight to fifteen. Call (785) 726-3636 or visit www.chryslerboyhoodhome.com for more information.

trivia

American automaker Walter P. Chrysler worked first on train locomotives, then for Buick, General Motors, Willys-Overland, and Maxwell Motor, before founding Chrysler Corporation in 1925.

The **Ellis Railroad and Doll Museum** is at 911 Washington St. (785-726-4493). There are working model trains, including one that pulls a bright yellow Union Pacific caboose. The kids can ride on a miniature General Motors Aero Streamliner on 2.5 miles of track outside the museum. On the third floor is a collection of more than 1,600 dolls dating from 1900. They include bridal dolls, Howdy Doody, and Barbie. Hours are seasonal. Call for hours and admission information.

High Plains

About halfway between Kansas City and Denver on I-70 is the town of **WaKeeney,** with a golf course, a swimming pool, antiques shops, a Christmas shop, and two drugstore soda fountains on Main Street (Cleland Drugs and Gibson Pharmacy). WaKeeney is known as the Christmas City of the High Plains. Every holiday season several tons of fresh greenery are made into a 40-foot tree and covered with more than 3,000 lights. Another 3,000 lights decorate the town.

Dave and Mary Hendricks offer accommodations at their **1906 Cottage Garden Guesthouse** at 510 Warren Ave. in WaKeeney. You'll love the front porch, cottage garden, and white picket fence. The two guest rooms are $85 per night. Mary will deliver a breakfast basket with homemade breads, fruit, juice, coffee, and tea.

Mary offers a country wildflower tour in the warmer months on their sixty-acre wildflower restoration and on the native western Kansas prairie. You can identify not just the several varieties of sunflowers, but purple poppy mallow, stemless hymenoxys, and two kinds of cactus that grow in western Kansas, the prickly pear and pincushion cactus. You can hear meadowlarks, finches, and red-winged blackbirds and stand in a buffalo wallow that was formed when the buffalo roamed free on the prairie. This is just a taste of what the pioneers in covered wagons saw. Reservations for the tours are requested. The wildflower tours are operated on a donation basis. Visit the Web site for more details, www.kbba.com/wakeeny.shtml, or call (785) 432-0032 and let Mary or Dave tell you about it.

In **Quinter,** off I-70 at exit 212, is **The Q Inn** (785-754-3820), where you can get buffalo steak or a buffalo burger. You must try this lean and tasty meat before you leave the state. Hours are 6:30 a.m. to 2:30 p.m. Tues to Sat and 7 a.m. to 2:30 p.m. Sun.

This is the crossroads of the High Plains, where shimmering golden fields of sunflowers dazzle your eye and ring-necked pheasant thrive. Twenty-two miles southeast of Quinter is a 70-foot-high chalk spire and natural landmark known as **Castle Rock.** It's formed from calcified deposits in an ancient sea and is extremely brittle and not safe for climbing.

Castle Rock is shown on Kansas highway maps, but getting there isn't easy. Coming from the west, it's not visible from the road. To see it, you'll have to cross a pasture that's private property and will probably need a four-wheel-drive vehicle to do so. You might do better to approach on a county road from the east and try to get a photo from the road.

Keep your eyes open. Hereabouts, in Gove, Scott, Logan, and Lane Counties, you will see great chalk monoliths rise from the earth, pale and eerie against the prairie sky. Remnants of the same inland seas that left the salt deposits near Hutchinson in southwest Kansas, these tall stone watchtowers were once the calcareous bodies of tiny sea creatures. Now they make a strange moonscape.

At the I-70 and US 83 interchange, you can head south 20 miles and east about 7 more to see **Monument Rocks.** These chalk bluffs and pyramids reveal a wealth of intriguing fossils to paleontologists and amateur fossil hunters alike—fish, pterosaurs, sharks, and oyster shells, to name a few. A mesosaur was found here. There is no fee to visit the landmark, but it is private property, and no fossils may be removed without the owner's permission. Do not climb the pyramids, as the chalk breaks easily. For more information call (800) 252-6727.

The history and development of **Oakley** (at US 83 and I-70, exits 70–76) are told here at the **Fick Fossil Museum** (785-672-4839, www.discoveroakley .com) at 700 West Third St., along with the prehistoric era (remember, you're in fossil country). There are railroad displays, cattlemen's brands, photographs, paintings, a general store, and a sod house that looks cozy enough to move into tomorrow. The museum contains more than 10,000 petrified shark teeth, crinoids, and an unusual collection of artwork made from fossils 100-million-plus years old and designed by Vi and Earnest Fick, including a wall of fossil folk art done by Vi, a bas-relief sculpture of a shark made of shark's teeth. Also on exhibit are a complete *Xiphactinus audax*, a large predatory fish, and some wing bones from a flying reptile known as a pteranadon (its wingspan is estimated to have been upward of 20 feet).

From Memorial Day to Labor Day, the museum is open Mon through Sat from 9 a.m. to 5 p.m. and Sun from 1 to 5 p.m. The rest of the year, it's 9 a.m. to noon and 1 to 5 p.m. Mon through Sat only. There is no admission charge, but donations are appreciated.

Continue west on US 40 from Oakley, then south on Highway 25 to **Russell Springs.** Founded in 1865, it was a water stop on the Butterfield Overland Dispatch stage line, which ran through rough Indian country to connect the goldmines of Colorado with Fort Riley. The railroad replaced the stagecoach in 1911, but the town suffered an economic double whammy when it lost the railroad line in 1917 and then the county seat in 1963. The Renaissance-style stone-and-brick courthouse today stands as a shrine to the pioneers who blazed the trail west.

Elkader is a ghost town now, with only a couple of deteriorating chalk buildings indicating where it was. In the 1870s this was the starting point for fossil-hunting expeditions into the chalks. But modern-day fossil hunters should remember that nearly all of this is private property and that they should get the owner's permission before entering a pasture. This area is also home to rattlesnakes in warm weather. Enough said.

If you stay on I-70 northwest to **Colby,** be sure to see the **Prairie Museum of Art and History,** at 1905 South Franklin. The "Little Smithsonian of the West" features the famous Kuska Collection, which includes dolls, glass, porcelains, textiles, furniture, and other antiques. The museum complex includes the largest barn in Kansas, a sod house, an old church, and a one-room school. The barn measures 114 by 66 by 48 feet. It was moved in one

ALSO WORTH SEEING

Sylvan Grove
Smoky Hills

White's Factory Outlet Center
Colby

piece into the museum complex and now houses an agricultural exhibit called *From Prairie Grasses to Golden Grain*. The exhibit chronicles the past century of agricultural history in northwest Kansas in more than 150 photographs, antique implements, and memorabilia.

The cavernous second level of the barn has been left empty and is used for dances and other activities and for all visitors to experience the immensity of this facility. Hours are Mon through Fri 9 a.m. to 5 p.m., Sat and Sun 1 to 5 p.m. (closed on Mon in winter). Call (785) 462-4590 or visit www.prairie museum.org. Admission is $5 for adults and $2 for children ages six to sixteen.

You can tour the **Kansas State University Northwest Research Extension Center** (785-462-6281) at Twenty-fourth Street and Experiment Farm Road, where beautifully landscaped trees, shrubs, flowers (including roses), and crops are labeled for easy identification and studied for hardiness and disease resistance. Oh yes, and Colby has a **White's Factory Outlet Center** too. You won't have any trouble finding that.

Goodland is the site of the **High Plains Museum** at 1717 Cherry St. Displaying the usual pioneer and Indian artifacts, the museum also has an automated replica of America's first patented helicopter, built in Goodland in 1910. You can push the buttons and watch the blades turn, and remember that people laughed at the idea of a flying machine like this when Leonardo da Vinci drew a helicopter in the 1490s. (They may have laughed at the Kansas inventor who designed this one, too, but it worked.) The museum is open 9 a.m. to 5 p.m. Mon to Fri and 9 a.m. to 4 p.m. Sat; during the summer, it's also open 1 to 4 p.m. Sun. All hours are mountain time. Call (785) 899-4595 or visit www.goodlandnet.com./museum. Admission is by donation.

Go south on Highway 27 to Sharon Springs, a well-shaded town bisected by the Smoky Hill River, then turn west to **Weskan** and **Mt. Sunflower.** Weskan gets its name from the first three letters of "west" and "Kansas." Ten miles north and 4 miles west of Weskan is, officially, the highest point in the state. Mt. Sunflower peaks at 4,039 feet above sea level. It is also the place, unofficially, to see the most beautiful sunsets in Kansas because of the soft pinks and vivid purples of the prairie here. Ed and Cindy Harold, who live near the pinnacle and own the property, enjoy sharing their mountain view with visitors. The property is part of the original homestead of the Harold family, and they have had a number of famous guests climb to the summit. Charles Kuralt called it "my kind of mountain." You won't need much in the way of gear to climb this peak—the most strenuous part of the ten-minute walk is avoiding gopher holes.

The windmills, wildflowers, and occasional coyote make this pure Kansas. Mt. Sunflower is located in a typical western pasture with cattle grazing, but you don't have to worry about any gate. Just drive over the cattle guard. To find Mt. Sunflower, take the Kanorado exit off I-70 and head south. You will come to the Harolds' ranch.

There is some very unusual scenery up here in northwest Kansas, and it is very much off the beaten path. In fact, this next trek should not be taken if there is any rain in the forecast because the dirt roads turn to mud and the canyons are steep. From **St. Francis** (on US 36 at Highway 27) go north on Highway 27. It will bend west, then turn back north again. From the area where it turns north again, the scenery becomes sagebrush and cactus with deep dirt canyons formed by the Arikaree River, which flows across the corner of the state from Nebraska to Colorado. The **Arikaree Breakers** are canyons so deep that people come here to hang glide, believe it or not. Marie Holzwarth has on her farm one of the last inhabitable whitewashed sod houses in the state. She and her husband live in town now, but they love to show off the house, where they sometimes spend weekends. Call (785) 332-3449 and ask for Marie.

Atwood, north and east of Goodland, is nestled amid beautiful trees in the Beaver Creek Valley at US 36 and Highway 25. Every morning at seven o'clock the old town whistle blows a wake-up call to late risers in this community of about 1,600 people. But nobody's sleeping in Atwood. The town is filled with people who care about the quality of life here on the High Plains.

A group of citizens bought the old 200-seat **Jayhawk Theater** (420 Main St.) when it was sold for back taxes, and they joined together to rejuvenate it. The woodwork was carved and cut, and a High Plains mural was painted around the ceiling. Large neon lights in blue, red, and yellow proclaim jayhawk on the marquee, and current movies are shown there. Call (785) 626-3372 to see what's playing.

trivia

Do you know what famous personage was born in Atwood? I'll give you a hint: He's very big, and very furry, and wears a ranger hat. Right! Smokey the Bear was given life here by artist Rudolph Wendelin, who is remembered in the Rawlins County Historical Society Museum, where he painted a 28-foot mural of the county's history.

The Ol' Depot (785-626-3114) at Highway 25 and Lake Road is a cooperative effort of thirty-nine artists and craftspeople. The depot was saved from destruction when the railroad began tearing stations down. It was moved to its present location and renovated with funds raised locally. Soon two rooms of arts and crafts were on display downstairs. Granny's Attic was opened upstairs, without much renovation, to display antiques and collectibles sold on consignment. Now both floors do an enormous business. Call for hours of operation.

The *Rawlins County Historical Museum* is at 308 State St. Inside is a 20-by-10-foot mural by Rudolph Wendelin, creator of Smokey the Bear, taking you back over the history of the county. You can listen to a tape of the artist explaining the mural's history. Then you can step into *Sts. Cyril & Methodius Catholic Church,* built in 1906 and moved into Atwood as part of the museum complex. Admission is by donation, and hours are 9 a.m. to noon and 1 to 4 p.m. Mon through Fri. Also open Sat 1 to 4 p.m. during the summer. Phone (785) 626-3885.

Spending the night? *Country Corner* (785-626-9516) on South Highway 25 is a large two-story home where town and country meet. Charles and Connie Peckham invite you to relax by the fireplace or watch TV in the common room. They will serve a continental-plus breakfast. The price is $50 for a double room with shared bath, $44 for a single.

Wander north on Highway 25 to the town of *Ludell* for a fine bed-and-breakfast that is part of the Atwood Association. At the *Kastens' Homestead* (785-626-3111 or 785-626-9223), Francis ("Ted") and Gertie Kastens share their large, old farm home and German heritage. They offer five guest rooms and one private bath. A full breakfast is served. Their home is 13 miles northeast of Atwood (or 5 miles north of Ludell) on US 36. The price is $40 per bed.

US 36 is an array of commercial sunflower fields: Acres of natural sunflowers color the side roads from *Oberlin.* As the day passes they turn their faces with the sun, giving you the real feel of Kansas. Oberlin, at the junction of US 36 and 83, was the site of the 1878 massacre of forty settlers by the North Cheyenne. *The Last Indian Raid Museum* at 258 South Penn Ave. (785-475-2712) focuses on the history of Decatur County, not only at the time of the raid, but through the 1930s and 1940s. A Native American room displays spears,

Free Land

Are you tired of life in the big city, tired of crime, high cost of living, bad schools? Well, then, three towns in Rawlins County have the answer for you: *free land!* You can build a house and spend your free time on one of the area lakes, hunting, golfing, trap shooting, hiking, camping, or just relaxing. Whether you have a family with children or are just ready to retire, the cities of Atwood, Herndon, and McDonald offer free land to anyone willing to move their family and become part of the community. There are incentives for people who want to start their own business in these towns, too. Call (785) 626-3640 to talk about the application process.

arrowheads, moccasins, and beadwork. A sod house is here, and an 1885 train depot, only 100 yards from its original site, as well as a 1922 one-room schoolhouse, complete with potbellied stove and many original textbooks. A country store, doctor's and dentist's offices, a blacksmith shop, a print shop, a millinery shop—there's a whole village here. Admission is $5 for adults, $3 for children ages six through twelve. It's open Tues through Thurs 9:30 a.m. to noon and 1 to 4:30 p.m. from Apr through Nov. Dec through Mar, the museum is open for research only.

sheepinkansas

Western Kansas has been cattle country for over a century. But during the late nineteenth century a vast number of sheep grazed here. Both local flocks and transient ones enjoyed the Kansas grasses. Livestock grazed on open public lands at no cost to the owner. A flock could easily be herded by one man and a dog, and the sheep produced a double crop—spring lambs and summer wool. Since a ewe often gives birth to twins, raising sheep proved to be very profitable, and the sheep industry boomed here.

The LandMark Inn (189 South Penn Ave.) is in the historic Bank of Oberlin building, a circa 1886 beauty downtown. Guest suites ($69 to $119) are decorated in high Victorian style. The Carriage House Loft features much simpler, but stunning Arts and Crafts–style furnishings in the living room and bedroom (complete with a Murphy bed—remember those?). In the upstairs parlor you can socialize and enjoy the fireplace. All rooms in both buildings have private baths. Call (785) 475-2340 or toll free (888) 639-0003.

Teller Room restaurant, on the first floor of the LandMark Inn, has been restored to its nineteenth-century splendor with cherry woodwork and reproduction gas lights. You can almost imagine the Victorian elegance of this place in a bustling frontier town. The menu changes daily and features fantastic desserts. Lunch is served Mon through Sat from 11:30 a.m. to 1:30 p.m. Dinner is served Thurs through Sat evenings from 6 to 8 p.m. There's also a gift shop, the *Oberlin Mercantile Company,* inside the inn.

Farther east on US 36 at US 283, the First State Bank of *Norton,* at 105 West Main St., is the home of the *"They Also Ran" Gallery,* featuring photos and biographies of those presidential candidates (including Horace Greeley) who were unsuccessful in their bid for the nation's highest office. It is open "bankers' hours," Mon through Fri from 9 a.m. to 3 p.m. year-round, except on legal holidays. There is no charge. Call (785) 877-3341 for information.

Norton calls itself the Pheasant Capital of the World, attracting hundreds of hunters during the pheasant season every year.

You are cordially invited to spend the night at the **Rose of Sharon Inn Bed and Bath,** at 603 East Main St. Gale and Sharon Shulze will make you comfortable in their 1880 Victorian home. Your choice of a three-room suite with whirlpool tub or two rooms with adjoining baths. Prices range from $60 to $70, and breakfast is not available on-site. Call (785) 877-3010 for reservations.

Near **Calvert,** east of Norton, there are deposits of volcanic ash 20 feet thick, consisting of tiny fragments of glass or congealed lava. Ash was deposited in this area during the past few million years from volcanoes in New Mexico, Wyoming, and California; prevailing winds carried it here. Pioneers used the ash in toothpaste and cleansing powder, and mining operations are still in business here.

Barbeau House is at 210 East Washington Ave. in **Lenora,** which is south of Norton on US 283. This bed-and-breakfast Queen Anne Victorian was built in 1889, and many of its features are original. Rooms with private baths are $90 on the main floor, and rooms with shared baths are $85 on the second floor. A full breakfast is served each morning. Call (785) 567-4886 for reservations.

Hill City is the location of the **Pheasant Inn Bed and Breakfast** at 609 North Fourth Ave. It's in the middle of great hunting country, with plenty of game birds and deer. This charming vintage home has stained- and beveled-glass windows and hardwood floors. The inn offers a full breakfast to guests, and rooms are $75. Call (785) 421-2955 for reservations.

Morland—population 200, located south of US 24 on Highway 85—has some lakes with excellent fishing. It is also in the heart of a splendid upland game-hunting region with 57,000 acres of public hunting areas. Quail and pheasant are especially abundant here.

trivia

You may have noticed a shortage of woodland out here, and so did the settlers. The adobe house at Prairie Dog State Park (on Prairie Dog Creek off US 383, near Norton at Sebelius Lake) was built in 1892 of mud and straw and still sits at its original location. Even the Kansas winds huffin' and puffin' couldn't blow it down! Today, you can picnic, fish, boat, and camp at the park. Call (785) 877-2953 for information.

trivia

Legend has it that Horace Greeley ("Go West, young man . . ."), Pat Garrett, Roy Bean, the parents of Billy the Kid, and other notable historical figures spent a stopover together at **Stage Station 15** in Norton. The current station is a replica of that building, and you can look through glass at papier-mâché figures of the famous folks and push a button to hear the station's history. It is on US 36 beside the water tower.

A few miles farther west on US 24 and just north of the town of **Studly** is an English settlement dating from the time after the American Civil War, when leaflets promoting land in the western United States, especially Kansas, were distributed throughout Great Britain. The lure of 160 acres of prairie just for homesteading drew many Europeans to the vast plains. One settler, John Fenton Pratt, who arrived in 1880, built a native stone house and raised sheep. Now the state-owned **Cottonwood Ranch** is open to the public. A complex of stone outbuildings at the ranch was constructed in a pattern similar to farms in the Yorkshire, England, area, where the southern faces of the buildings were aligned and then connected with a stone wall, creating an accessible corral for livestock. The ranch grounds are open daily for self-guited tours from dawn to dusk. Call (785) 627-5866.

notasignof studly

You'll find the town of Studly, Kansas, marked on state highway maps, and indeed, the little burg is right where it's supposed to be. So why no sign on the highway marking it? So many have been stolen as souvenirs that the state highway department has stopped replacing them.

Smoky Hills

The **Dane G. Hansen Memorial Museum and Plaza,** on Main Street in **Logan,** on Highway 9 (northeast of Hill City), is a 1-block monument to the man who left much of his estate to the town he loved when he died in 1965. The museum features traveling exhibitions from the Smithsonian Institution and other museums, as well as permanent exhibits of Oriental art, guns, and coins. It would be considered a fine museum in a big city, and it's a surprising attraction in this small town. It is open Mon through Fri from 9 a.m. to noon and 1 to 4 p.m., Sat from 9 a.m. to noon and 1 to 5 p.m., and Sun from 1 to 5 p.m. Admission is free. Call (785) 689-4846 or log on to www.hansen museum.org.

The Church of the Transfiguration at 210 Washington St. is an Episcopal Church constructed in 1890 of native limestone and surrounded by buffalo grass. This lovely church is worth a rest stop. You can get the key at the Hansen Museum and just enjoy a quiet moment there alone.

The Kirwin National Wildlife Refuge attracts birders from all over. Here 10,800 acres of grassland, shelterbelts, croplands, and open water provide roads and trails with excellent opportunities for birding. Species include pelicans, herons, owls, goatsuckers (whippoorwills), and snowy egrets. Hunting

Nicodemus: A National Treasure

The eastern portion of Graham County on present-day U.S. Highway 24 was the first black settlement in Kansas. Nicodemus was established in 1877 by "exodusters," former slaves freed after the Civil War, who had been offered land in Kansas. The town is the last survivor of the dozen all-black Kansas settlements and was declared a National Historic Landmark in 1976. Now Nicodemus has fewer than sixty residents, and it struggles to hold on to its rich past. Since 1878, the town has pulled together for its annual Emancipation Celebration in July.

of pheasant, quail, geese, and ducks is allowed in season. The entrance is off scenic Highway 9. Call (785) 543-6673 for information.

Kirwin Lake is a reservoir off Highway 9. Here, too, you may find a variety of shore- and waterbirds, especially during migratory seasons.

On the banks of Beaver Creek is the log cabin where pioneer Kansas doctor Brewster M. Higley wrote "My Western Home" in the late 1870s. "So what?" you say. "Never heard of it," you say. Well, somewhere along the line, the name was changed to "Home on the Range," and it is now the Kansas state song. *Home on the Range Cabin,* restored in recent years, is 1 mile west and 8 miles north of Athol, on Highway 8. Call (785) 695 2251 to arrange a visit.

The *Old Dutch Mill* in Wagner Park is the most picturesque attraction in *Smith Center,* on US 36 at US 281. It was built in the 1870s of native logs; its burrs were made from native stones.

The *Ingleboro Mansion* (785-282-3798) at 319 North Main St. in Smith Center is a carefully restored 1879 Victorian house-turned-bed-and-breakfast. Owners Bruce and Bobbi Miles are proud of the home's stained glass, cherry, oak, and maple woodwork, as well as the impressive stairway and fireplaces. Modern conveniences are here, too: air-conditioning, cable TV, a microwave, and a refrigerator stocked with soda, juice, and microwave popcorn. There are three suites, all with private baths. Rates are $60 to $90, including continental breakfast. Call for a reservation, or visit the Web site at www.ingleboro mansion.com.

Osborne has a neat little bed-and-breakfast, aptly named *Riverbend,* with wall-to-wall windows overlooking the Solomon River from its upper level. The room on that level includes a private bath and deck; two more bedrooms can be found downstairs, each with a private bath. The library has a fireplace and DVD player at your disposal, and the inn is located near golf courses, a lake and a ghost town; tours are available. Wireless Internet is available throughout the house, and a full breakfast is served. Rates are $80. Call

A Moose Named Kirwin

There's a sign at the edge of Kirwin, east of Logan on Highway 9, that says WELCOME TO KIRWIN, THE GOOSE CAPITAL OF THE WORLD. Well, that's what it used to say. Then the G was crossed out and an M added. Thousands of years ago, moose roamed over Kansas, but there haven't been any in modern times until a few years ago, when a moose named for the town showed up near herds of cattle, looking lonely and flirting with the local cows. Soon people started coming to see this unusual apparition. Now Kirwin, it seems, has moved on to greener pastures. No one is sure where the moose is these days, and the cows he mo-o-o-oned over aren't talking.

(785) 346-5217 or visit www.riverbend-retreat.com. In 1918 the Rock Island railroad station burned at *Courtland,* and a temporary depot was made from a boxcar. Later it was cut in half and moved, and 20 feet were added to the center. When the railroads disappeared, the abandoned station stood empty until Dan Kuhn and his wife, Carla, began to raise apples and pumpkins and looked for a market. They purchased the building and moved it again to the intersection of US 36 and Highway 199, a mile north of Courtland, where it has been restored and has become the *Depot Market and Cider Mill,* 1103 30 Rd. (785-374-4255). You can tour the apple orchard and pumpkin patch in season and buy apples, jellies, homemade fudge, and gift basket assortments from July through Christmas.

trivia

Russell Stover was born at a spot halfway between Alton and Natoma. He's the man who gave us two American institutions—the Eskimo Pie and Russell Stover candies. To reach the candy-box marker commemorating him, go 1 mile south from Alton's Main Street; turn right at the river; 1 mile west, 8 miles south. At the Pleasant Plains Methodist Church turn left, then go 1 mile on a dirt road.

A famine in Scandinavia during the 1860s forced many Swedes, Danes, and Norwegians to move to the United States and added new flavors to the Kansas melting pot. A group of Swedes moved here in 1868 and formed the town of New Scandinavia, later renamed *Scandia.* The *Scandia Museum* on Main Street off US 36 tells the story. Call (785) 335-2266 for hours.

The *Pawnee Indian Village Museum,* 3 miles southwest of *Republic,* is a modern museum constructed around the floor of a Pawnee earth lodge occupied in the early 1800s. This valuable archaeological site contains artifacts found there. It is a walk through history, showing evidence of the way the Pawnee lived more than 150 years ago.

The entrance, the only opening in the structure except for the hole in the roof, leads visitors back in time. You still may see the fire pit, the buffalo skull, which was the chief item of worship, the cistern-like hole where meat was stored, and iron pots that were left behind.

The Kansas State Historical Society uncovered items left by the Kitkehahki or Republican band of the Pawnee tribe and left them just as they were found. The museum is open Wed through Sat from 9 a.m. to 5 p.m., Sun from 1 to 5 p.m Call (785) 361-2255 for information, or visit the Web site at www.kshs .org/places/pawneeindian.

In a small shop called **BEKAN** (785-527-2427), in a small town called *Belleville,* on US 81 slightly north of US 36, Bud Hanzlick creates hand-carved furniture using the most unlikely native wood—Osage orange, commonly referred to as hedgeapple. Bud creates tables, chairs, bowls, and cutting boards that accent the natural contours and unusual beauty of this rock-hard wood.

He calls the furniture "refined rustic," and it is special indeed. He is the only person using this wood, also called *bois d'arc* or bow wood, because it fights being cut every inch of the way. It dulls saws, it's too tough to nail, and it has thorns that attack any craftsman who is foolish enough to like it. "It's as tough as the pioneers who planted it," says Bud. They used it for wheel hubs, and the Indians used it for bows because it bends without breaking.

A Sacred Heirloom

Around 1873 in the southwest corner of Nebraska, 1,000 Sioux warriors swarmed around a band of 400 Pawnee men, women, and children in what is now known as Massacre Canyon. The Pawnee were returning from a buffalo hunt. As the battle raged, a Pawnee father tied his five-year-old daughter to the back of a horse and lashed a sacred bundle to her back. "Take care of the bundle and it will take care of you," he told her. The girl made it safely back, and she lived on the Pawnee's reservation. Sacred bundles were always passed from mother to firstborn daughter to care for, although only the men of the family could open it or perform any of the ceremonies associated with it. In 1987 this girl's granddaughter, Elizabeth Horsechief, donated the bundle to the Pawnee Indian Village Museum with the understanding that it would not be opened and would be displayed with respect. It is one of the few in the nation on display.

Tied on the outside of the bundle are a long pipe, arrow fragments, a meat fork tipped with a raccoon bone, and small American flags.

Careful not to open the bundle, the museum X-rayed and CAT-scanned it, revealing stuffed bird bundles, hawk bells, counting sticks, and glass beads sewn on a leather strip. It hangs today as it would have a century ago—above a buffalo skull altar.

But Bud likes the grotesque shapes it gets into, and he can guarantee it to last a lifetime outdoors on your patio. It won't rot, bugs hate it, rain and snow only make it tougher, and it is one of the hardest woods in the world. Its tight grain and color make each piece unlike any other. BEKAN (for Belleville, Kansas) is at 901 N St.; Bud's workshop is in the backyard, and his wife, Pat, has a shop in the house, where items are displayed. *Rustic Remembrances Bed and Breakfast* is in *Glasco* 2 miles off US 24 and 6 miles from the junction of US 81 and 24. In this century-old home, all the rooms are furnished with antiques, and the large deck and patio give you a quiet spot to relax. This is a working farm. Owners Madonna and Larry Sorell raise Belgian draft horses, mini donkeys, Jacob sheep, turkeys, seven breeds of chickens, and llamas. Madonna is a spinner and weaver; she offers classes for these forgotten arts. Larry collects antique machinery. There are four rooms with a shared bath. Rates are $45 to $85. Call (785) 568-2777.

On Glasco's main street is *Hodge Podge* (113 East Main) with a good old-fashioned soda fountain with six cast-iron stools and a brass rail footrest. The dark oak back bar is more than one hundred years old. You can get a chocolate soda, milk shake, malt, or Green Dragon here. Call (785) 568-2542 for hours.

If you want to miss the interstate altogether, take US 24, the scenic route west. If you have the time, it's more interesting to travel on than the interstate.

St. John's Catholic Church at 701 East Court St. in *Beloit* was completed in 1904 and is believed to be the first church in the United States featuring flying buttresses, the same architectural feature that makes the cathedral of Notre Dame in Paris so impressive.

The completely restored *Little Red Schoolhouse* on US 24 in Beloit is original, built in 1871. It is affiliated with the National Library of Congress and contains the Living Library Museum, with Old State Printer books, Lorraine

The World's Largest Ball of Twine

Lately there have been disturbing rumors on the Internet that there is a bigger ball of twine than the one in Cawker City. They say it's someplace in Texas or Minnesota. The local people are not worried, though. They say it's no contest because the Texas ball has string and plastic stuff in it. Not pure twine from hay bales like Cawker City's. And the one from Minnesota? Well, it might have a big snowball inside. Who knows. Meanwhile, Cawker City keeps adding hay bale–twine to its ball every year. The city has its own Web site if you want to know more about this fascinating race for fame. Look it up at www.skyways.lib.ks.us/towns/cawker/twine.html.

The Stained-Glass Capital of Kansas

Cloud County was designated the Stained-Glass Capital of Kansas by the Kansas legislature in 1994. There is magnificent stained glass in churches in Concordia, Clyde, Glasco, Jamestown, St. Joseph, Aurora, Miltonvale, and Huscher. The rose window at the Nazareth Convent in Concordia, at Thirteenth and Washington, is in the *Motherhouse of the Sisters of St. Joseph,* built in 1903. The Motherhouse (but not the convent) (785-243-2149) can be toured. You'll also find stained glass in businesses, houses, and stained-glass studios in Glasco, Concordia, and Miltonvale. For details contact the Cloud County Convention and Visitors Bureau at (785) 243-4303.

Wooster editions, and other historic educational material. It is open by appointment. Call (785) 738-2717, the Beloit Chamber of Commerce.

Glen Elder has a unique castle-like structure on the National Register of Historic Places called (believe this?) the *Castle Filling Station,* which was built in 1912 on the northeast corner of the New England–style town square.

Want to try some buffalo meat? Slip into *Butterfield's Buffalo Ranch* 1 mile west and 0.5 mile south of the junction of US 24 and Highway 14. Larry Butterfield Sr. will wrap up a couple of steaks for your next dinner. The herd can be seen grazing 3 miles west and 2 miles north of Highway 24 and 14 Junction. They ask that you stay in your vehicle. Call (785) 738-2336.

The lovely oasis of *Glen Elder Reservoir/Waconda Lake* is 10 miles west of Beloit on US 24. It has fishing, hunting, a prairie dog area, and camping facilities.

In *Cawker City* on US 24, on the north side of the lake, the wide main street has been declared a State Historical District. Here you will see the old wooden storefronts of a frontier community, as well as evidence of a Jewish past.

Cawker City is also famous for having the world's largest ball of twine. (Yes, you read that right.) Twine parties on Labor Day weekend bring folks out to add inches to the over-40-foot ball of twine. The thing weighs almost nine tons. The sphere has been part of the town since 1960, when it was brought in by Frank Stoeber, who began it in 1953. The city fathers gave it a spot on Main Street, where it catches the eye of people passing through town.

The Carr Creek Valley on *Ringneck Ranch* is the setting for Keith and Deb Houghton's pheasant-hunting lodge near *Tipton* on Highway 181, south of Waconda Lake. Excellent hunting, complete with local guides, dogs, and comfortable accommodations, makes for an enjoyable experience.

The ranch has accommodations for fifty-four people. Arrive in time for a family-style dinner with homemade bread, fresh pies, and grilled steaks, and meet your hosts. Morning brings biscuits and gravy, and then it's off to the fields with your guide to hunt along creeks and through sorghum fields. The ranch has been featured on ESPN and PBS television networks.

Keith and Debra book hunters during the season, Oct through Mar. Their managed game-bird habitat is a "controlled shooting area," licensed by the Kansas Wildlife and Parks to harvest game birds in excess of the state limit of four birds because of the extensive habitat and breeding here. There are 10,000 acres of the best quail, pheasant, and prairie chicken habitat imagin-

trivia

The Republican River was named not after the GOP but after one of four bands of Pawnee that lived here. They were farmers and hunters who went west to the High Plains once a year for buffalo hunts. In 1875 white settlement forced their removal to Indian Territory in Oklahoma.

able. Four-wheel-drive field vehicles and good bird dogs are provided as part of the package. All you have to bring is your shotgun and some clothes.

The ranch has four new suites, each with private bath,. Please call for room prices. Hunting licenses can be obtained at the ranch. Hunters pay a daily fee. Nonhunters may use the ranch facilities and, if they like, the new "Crazy Quail" shooting game that throws clay targets in many directions

to keep the edge on your shooting, or just for fun. Guests are welcome to enjoy a stay at the working ranch in the off-season, too. Call (785) 373-4835 for more information and reservations. Check out the Web site at www.ring neckranch.net.

Blue Hill Gamebirds is also located in Tipton. They raise about 20,000 pheasants per year. They sell about that many chicks, too. So you can see that the hunting around here is very good. Summer is hatching season; call Don and Virginia Montgomery at (785) 373-4965 if you want a tour.

Tipton has many interesting things for a town of about 300. The **Tipton Grocery,** at 601 Main St., is famous in this part of the state for its old-fashioned German sausage, made fresh in the store by hand. The recipe is a closely guarded secret, handed down for several generations now. Fred and Vali Smith (Vali came here from Germany when she was eighteen) are the owners. Call (785) 373-4125 for hours.

The **Garden of Eden** (785-525-6395) in **Lucas** on Highway 18 is a most unusual place. Once the home of S. P. Dinsmoor, at Second and Kansas Streets, the house is made of post rock and resembles a log cabin. It is surrounded by scores of primitive concrete figures, all made by Dinsmoor after he reached the age of sixty-four.

Dinsmoor, a disabled Civil War veteran, spent twenty-two years constructing this amazing display (unique doesn't begin to cover it), using more than 113 tons of cement, native limestone, and various woods. At the front of the house stand Adam and Eve with outstretched arms, forming an arched entrance to the yard. A concrete serpent coils in a tree above them, a concrete devil watches from a nearby rooftop, and above all this is a red, white, and blue (concrete) American flag that actually turns with the prevailing winds. At age eighty-one, Dinsmoor married twenty-year-old Emily and had two children. He died when he was eighty-nine.

Dinsmoor's body lies in a concrete coffin (which he also made) with a glass top in a niche in the mausoleum wall. The body of his first wife lies below him in a steel vault entirely encased in concrete. The mausoleum is guarded by a concrete angel.

The monumental art forms are worth the drive. They have been featured on Ripley's Believe It or Not and in People magazine, as well as on every network morning show. You can take Highway 232 north from I-70, a pretty drive by Wilson Lake and fields of golden milo, surrounded by post-rock fences. Turn west on Highway 18; there are plenty of signs to guide you. The Garden of Eden is open May through Oct from 10 a.m. to 5 p.m. daily, Mar and Apr from 1 to 4 p.m., and in winter from 1 to 4 p.m. Sat and Sun. Admission is $6 ($1 for kids). Visit www.garden-of-eden-lucas-kansas.com.

Florence Deeble's Rock Garden at 213 South Main St. has been a Lucas landmark for more than fifty years, and it is no small feat. Mount Rushmore is a featured part of the display. Florence built it from rock she brought home from trips. Now the house has an interior garden as well, the first floor is the *Garden of Isis,* five rooms of art, made by Mri Pila of dolls, toys, kitchen gadgets, and recycled odds and ends. Admission is included as part of the Grassroots Art Center. Call (785) 525-6118.

Kansas's Prisoner of War Camps

During World War II, there were several POW camps located in Kansas. One was near Concordia. Two German prisoners escaped from the camp and were heading for Mexico, according to the video *Stalag Sunflower* (made at Emporia State University). The authorities knew of the escape but did not pursue the prisoners for a couple of days. Then they picked them up, took them back to the prison, and pulled down a wall map. They pointed out where they were and how far they had walked (they hadn't even crossed the county line yet). Then they pointed out how far it was to the Rio Grande. The Germans realized that America is a bit larger than Europe, and no further escape attempts were made from that camp.

The **Grassroots Art Center** displays the works of grassroots artists, who are self-taught and often use materials that they find around them. Some call it "recycled art." Many grassroots artists are retired and fill their yards with their works, much as the strange Mr. Dinsmoor did. Most are perceived as odd by their neighbors and most of their works are destroyed at their death.

The center is in three adjacent post-rock buildings on Main Street in Lucas. It is a community endeavor in this small town (population 475) to encourage self-taught artists.

The center has just completed a post-rock courtyard, which is filled with examples of how the native limestone was used for building homes and fences. Some of the stones that decorate the homes are very ornate.

The center was built to show the works of Inez Marshall of Portis, who carves and paints native limestone. She says she feels an inner voice when she touches a piece of stone. Her works are often whimsical and humorous (her Model T Ford has working headlights).

A striking display of Ed Root's glass-encrusted concrete creations fills the lobby of the center. His crushed-glass yard ornaments—a mailbox and a weather vane, for example—are made from available materials such as crushed Milk of Magnesia bottles or the family's dishes.

A farmer from Luray, Leroy Wilson, is another artist whose works are displayed there. He spent twelve years painting the walls and fixtures in his basement in colorful mosaic patterns. On display are the vanity and walls retrieved from the basement before his house was sold after his death.

The center is open May through Sept from 10 a.m. to 5 p.m. Mon through Sat and from 1 to 5 p.m. Sun. From Oct through Apr, the hours are 10 a.m. to noon and 1 p.m. to 4 p.m. Mon and Thurs through Sat and 1 to 4 p.m. Sun, or by appointment. Admission is $6, or $2 for kids age six to twelve. Call (785) 525-6118 or visit www.grassrootsart.net.

There is also a bed-and-breakfast in Lucas. The **Stone Cottage Farm Bed and Breakfast and Antiques Shop** is at 5010 Hwy. 232. Jonathan and Becky Pancost have furnished this beautifully restored house with antiques. The home was built in 1895 out of native limestone. In fact, this is what Jon does for a living—he creates custom stonework, everything from crafting garden benches by hand to rebuilding stone walls. The main house has three bedrooms, one with private bath, and all on the second floor. The old granary has also been made into a cabin with kitchenette, shower, sitting area, and a loft that sleeps four. There's an outdoor fireplace on one of the patios for cool Kansas evenings, and a garden to provide fresh vegetables and flowers in the summertime. The old barn even has an antiques shop in it. The entire farm is yours to wander. Rooms are $70 and $80 with a shared bath and $90 with private bath. Call (866) 567-3110 or visit www.stonecottagefarm.com.

The almost lost art of making sausage and bologna is still alive and well in Lucas. Doug and Linda Brant, of **Brant's Meat Market** at 125 South Main St., will give you samples of their specialty meats fresh from the smokehouse. These are family recipes passed down for three generations. This is a perfect spot to stop for picnic supplies. For more information call (785) 525-6464.

Yesterday House Museum on Main Street in **Sylvan Grove** features the largest barbed-wire collection in the region as well as the history of post-rock country. It is open May through Oct on Sat and Sun from 1 to 5 p.m. Admission is free. Call Vera Meyer for information at (785) 526-7270.

The Nielsen family has lived and farmed this land in **Denmark,** near Sylvan Grove and west of Lincoln, since 1870; their children are the fifth generation to live at the historic farm home built of native limestone. It is now the **Spillman Creek Farm and Lodge,** and Merrill and Kathy Nielsen welcome hunters to the farm, which is walking distance from a 120-year-old Lutheran church that still maintains an active congregation. Nielsen's great-grandfather homesteaded this land in 1871, and it has been a working grain farm ever since. Each lodge includes private bedrooms, two private baths, kitchen, a private phone line, satellite TV, and VCR. The lodge can comfortably accommodate up to fifteen. You'll receive three home-cooked meals every day, and the Nielsens will treat you like part of the family. The traditional pheasant hunt is rooster only. They also offer fine quail hunting and waterfowl hunting. Prices include a guide, dogs, lunch, field transportation, and birds cleaned and packaged. Combination hunts are available. A day hunt for pheasant (arrive in the morning, leave in the afternoon) is $280 and you can bag up to six roosters, but prices vary with the hunt. Visit the Web site at www.spillmancreek.com for more details. Call (785) 277-3424 after 6 p.m. for information on upland game and pheasant hunts.

Leo "Duane" Vonada and his son, Damon, own the **Vonada Stone Quarry,** at 532 East Quail Lane (785-526-7391) near town. As part of the Post Rock Tour mentioned at the beginning of this chapter, they will demonstrate the way early settlers found, quarried, and cut post rock using old-time tools in the original quarry on their farm north of Sylvan Grove. Signs, corner-post art, and engraving are also available there. A post rock with your name on it is about $100. They also make sundials, beginning at $210, and limestone benches for $225 and up. There is an interesting display of milling equipment on the farm, with a vertical mill and drill press used in making tools in the early 1900s.

Like the posts that line the fields, thick-walled post-rock homes and buildings predominate in this part of the mostly treeless prairie. In frontier days, trappers and buffalo hunters improvised dugouts built into the hillsides; railroaders utilized similar shelters. Later, the homesteaders found them still inhabitable when they came through in covered wagons.

A stone post weighs nearly 400 pounds; it takes two men to load one into a wagon. Even with modern equipment, post-rock buildings like the Lincoln County Courthouse in Lincoln would be a wonder. A self-guided tour available at the courthouse leads you through interesting places nearby. See www .vonadastone.com.

Get off I-70 at the Lincoln exit 221. Go 14 miles to where Highways 14 and 18 cross. The restoration of the stately 1906 **Woody House Bed and Breakfast,** in **Lincoln** at 629 East North St. (Highway 18 and North Street), preserved the authenticity of this historic Queen Anne home and retained its original charm in a peaceful farm setting. The elegant interior has curved glass windows, a decorative staircase, and a bathroom with its original fixtures. The rooms are furnished with antiques.

The place comes with an old-fashioned porch, where one can enjoy a lazy swing in a hammock. Three guest rooms, one with a summer terrace, await guests within. Ceiling fans and gentle breezes cool the rooms, and central air-conditioning helps on hot days. A generous continental breakfast is included in the $40 to $50 price. Each room has a wash basin and the full bath is shared. Ivona and Michael Pickering are the innkeepers; call them at (785) 524-4744. **Beverly** is the home of **Soaring Heart Gallery,** where J. R. Dickerman makes his "Creature Creations" that appear along the highways of Lincoln County. The studio is filled with more of the creatures, many made from bone, animal skulls, and feathers. Masks and costumes are also a part of this crazy but wonderful display. His Open Range Zoo appears along Highway 18, the best along the first few miles from the eastern county line.

Just 2.5 miles southwest of **Minneapolis** is a National Natural Landmark made up of more than 200 Dakota sandstone concretions known as **Rock City.** Nowhere in the world are there similar rock formations as large or as numerous. Some are almost perfect spheres; others have elliptical forms, with names like Kissing Rocks and the Widow's Tunnel. There are balanced rocks, pyramids, and palaces with diameters of more than 27 feet. Once called dinosaur marbles and jayhawk eggs, the rocks have appeared in geology textbooks from as far back as the 1870s. Be sure to take your camera because now there is a walking trail. Call the Minneapolis chamber of commerce at (785) 392-3068 for more information.

Minneapolis, by the way, has been designated the Official Boyhood Home of George Washington Carver. You can find the details of the town's contribution to Carver's career at the Making of the Man display at the Ottawa County

Historical Museum (785-392-3621) at 110 South Concord. A local dinosaur is also in residence, along with other fossils, meteorites, and Native American and pioneer artifacts. There's even a 1917 Ford tractor. Call for hours.

The town was built in the late 1800s, and each of the homes and buildings that line Main Street has a story to be told: bad stories of bankers running off with money and good stories of lining the street with hay to quiet the town so the buggy traffic wouldn't bother a sick woman's rest.

You will want to take the self-guided **Red Post Tour.** With a red post at every turn, you will be drawn through the area's picturesque scenery, unique landmarks, and rural heritage. Stop by the Minneapolis Chamber of Commerce at 213 West Second St. to pick up the map, or call (785) 392-3068 for more details.

A local rancher constructed a huge buffalo statue from fifty tons of concrete and rebar. It stands on the rolling hills of eastern Ottawa County. Watch for it in your travels.

There's a bed-and-breakfast 2 miles north of **Wells** (11 miles east of Minneapolis) on a blacktop road. **Trader's Lodge Bed and Breakfast and Fine Dining** is at 1392 210th Rd. Hosts Neal and Kay Kindall welcome you to their lodge of fir and native stone decorated with furs and Native American art, some of it handcrafted by Neal and offered for sale. The lodge is set in the rolling hills, only 4 miles from Ottawa State Fishing Lake on a wheat and cattle farm.

Guests are invited to enjoy the massive native stone fireplace in the large family room. You can bike or hike the hills on the blacktop road and enjoy the brilliant sunset from the large wooden porch. Rooms are $70 to $90. Call (785) 488-3930 for directions and reservations. Visit at the Web site at www .traderslodgebandb.com.

Places to Stay in Northwest Kansas

ATWOOD

Crest Motel
601 Grant St.
(785) 626-3213

BELOIT

Super 8 Motel
205 West Hwy. 24
(785) 738-4300

COLBY

Comfort Inn
2225 South Range Ave.
(913) 462-3833

Country Club Drive Motel
460 South Country Club Dr.
(785) 462-7568

Holiday Inn Express
645 West Willow
(785) 462-8787

GOODLAND

Best Western Buffalo Inn
830 West Hwy. 24
(785) 899-3621

HAYS

Fairfield Inn Marriott
377 Mopar Dr.
(785) 625-3344

Hampton Inn
4002 General Hays Rd.
(785) 621-4444

Super 8 Motel
3730 Vine St.
(785) 625-8048

Vagabond Motel
2524 Vine St.
(785) 625-2511

OAKLEY

Golden Plains Motel
3506 Hwy. 40
(785) 672-3254

OBERLIN

Frontier Motel
207 East Frontier Parkway
(785) 475-2203

RUSSELL

AmericInn Lodge & Suites
1430 South Fossil St.
(800) 634-3444

SALINA

Baymont Inn & Suites
745 West Schilling
(877) 229-6668

Country Inn & Suites
2760 South Ninth St.
(785) 827-1271

Days Inn
407 West Diamond Dr.
(785) 823-9791

WAKEENEY

Super 8 Motel
709 South Thirteenth St.
(785) 743-6442

Places to Eat in Northwest Kansas

COLBY

Montana Mike's
1855 South Range Ave.
(785) 462-7178

SELECTED CHAMBERS OF COMMERCE AND VISITOR BUREAUS

Atwood Chamber of Commerce
303 Main St.
(785) 626-9630
www.atwoodkansas.com

Colby Convention and Visitors Bureau
350 South Range Ave.
Suite 10
(785) 462-7643
www.oasisontheplains.com

Hays Convention and Visitors Bureaus
2700 Vine St.
(785) 628-8202
www.haysusa.net

Oakley Area Chamber of Commerce
216 Center Ave.
(785) 672-4862
www.discoveroakley.com

Oberlin Convention and Visitors Bureau
132 South Penn Ave.
(785) 475-3441
www.oberlinkansas.org

Salina Area Chamber of Commerce
120 West Ash St.
Box 586
(785) 827-9301
www.salinakansas.org

Marysville Chamber of Commerce
101 North Tenth St.
(785) 562-3101 or (800) 752-396

CONCORDIA

Kristy's Family
Restaurant
101 East Sixth St.
(785) 243-4653

HAYS

Gutierres Mexican
Restaurant
1106 East Twenty-seventh
St.
(I-70 exit 159)
(785) 625-4402

Rooftops Restaurant
and Lounge
(785) 628-8786

OAKLEY

Colonial Steak House
(I-70 and US 83)
(785) 672-4720

Mitten Truck Stop
(US 40 and I-70)
(785) 672-3062

OBERLIN

Landmark Inn
189 South Penn Ave.
(785) 475-2340

RUSSELL

Log Cabin Inn
1205 West Wichita Ave.
(785) 483-5538

SALINA

Bistro Café
1200 East Crawford St.
(785) 827-2728

The Cozy Inn
108 North Seventh
(785) 825-2699

Grandma Max's
1944 North Ninth St.
(785) 825-5023

SCANDIA

The Kaffe Haus
886 US 36
(785) 335-2251

WAKEENEY

Real Country café
(I-70 and US 283, exit 127)
(785) 743-5473

Index

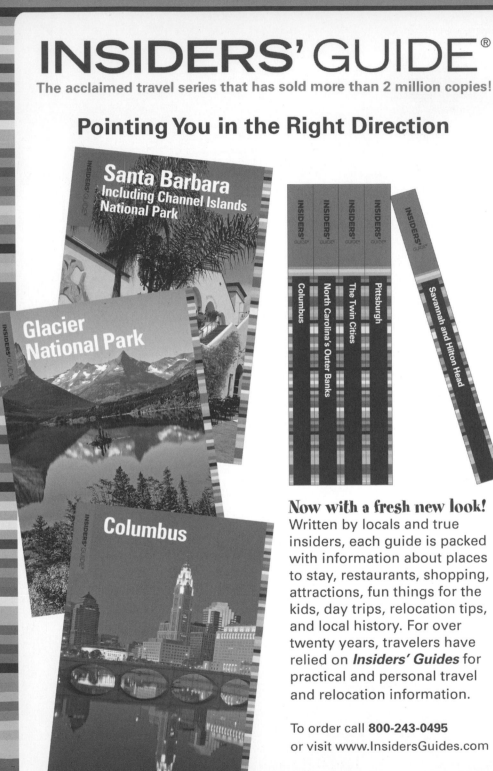